PROFESSIONALS OUT OF WORK

High technology firms in the Route 128 region, Greater Boston area

PROFESSIONALS OUT OF WORK

Paula Goldman Leventman

THE FREE PRESS
A Division of Macmillan Publishing Co., Inc.
NEW YORK

Collier Macmillan Publishers
LONDON

Copyright © 1981 by The Free Press
A Division of Macmillan Publishing Co., Inc.

The Free Press
A Division of Macmillan Publishing Co., Inc.
866 Third Avenue, New York, N.Y. 10022

Collier Macmillan Canada, Ltd.

Library of Congress Catalog Card Number: 80-1645

Printed in the United States of America

printing number
1 2 3 4 5 6 7 8 9 10

Library of Congress Cataloging in Publication Data

Leventman, Paula Goldman.
  Professionals out of work.

  Bibliography: p.
  Includes index.
  1. Professional employees—Massachusetts—Boston
—Case studies.   2. Unemployed—Massachusetts—
Boston—Case studies.   3. Industrial sociology—
Case studies.   4. Scientists—Massachusetts—
Boston—Case studies.   5. Engineers—Massachusetts
—Boston—Case studies.   I. Title.
HD8038.U5L48   331.13'781'000974461   80-1645
ISBN 0-02-918800-8

To my parents,
Ann and David Goldman

Contents

Preface

This book is mostly about people born in the 1930s, who depended heavily on educational opportunities provided in the 1950s and by the 1960s were launched, sometimes entrenched, in "important" careers. America's ambitious generation worked hard, studied, and planned. They deferred gratification to "make it" in bureaucratized, highly technological society. But mid-career frequently brought dissatisfaction and disillusionment—and, by the 1970s, decreased job opportunities. Abruptly work worlds shifted. Talented, qualified professionals were hit by structural employment instability. Many lost their jobs and had difficulty finding others. Some began to doubt their own abilities. Most questioned the cultural values of a society that had reneged on its promise of the good life.

Professionals Out of Work is the product of a decade's research involvement with selected populations of professionals. Social stratification was always one of my major fields of academic specialization and the rapidly growing, "new" middle classes were of particular interest. Salaried professionals were then the fastest growing social stratum in the United States: 5 percent in 1940, 6 percent in 1950, 10 percent in 1960, 15 percent in 1970. I wrote my first paper on the subject, "The Salaried Professionals," as a doctoral student at Bryn Mawr College in 1967. One year later I moved to the greater Boston area, where I was overwhelmed by the range of professionals positioned in service hierarchies, educational institutions, and private industry. My interest was galvanized by Route 128. Here, in one relatively enclosed geographical setting, were hundreds of advanced systems research and development firms. Scientists, engineers, and data analysts pushed the outer limits of discovery. In an era of missiles, moon landings, and computers, jobs for scientists and technologists seemed secure. These "men of tomorrow," prototypical of knowledge workers in postindustrializing society, represented an advanced guard. I planned a study of their career patterns, their values, and their lifestyles.

By the time my interview schedule was drafted, massive layoffs suddenly struck Route 128. New dimensions were added to the research problem. Unemployment among this group had never before been studied. I spent my first year in the field as a participant-observer among various employment crisis groups. From fall 1971 through spring 1972, when unemployment rates were highest, I conducted random sample in-depth interviews among the employed and the unemployed. These provided the initial data base and the case studies for the chapters that follow. Route 128 people were revisited in 1975. By then, their problems had intensified. In addition, insecurity spread to other types of professionals. "Mid-life crisis" and "disillusionment" were code words in the late 1970s. In 1977 I interviewed other types of professionals in varied contexts.

Professionals Out of Work is a book about people in my own age cohort. I've shared their aspirations, their opportunities, and their disappointments. I intruded on their lives, sometimes several times, and suprisingly encountered little resistance. They wanted me to "tell their story." It is a generational tale about those of us, hampered by organizational restrictions, who mourn a lost potential.

Specifically, *Professionals Out of Work* traces the careers of engineers and scientists through success and crisis. It encompasses the traditional sociological focuses of occupations and professions, industrial settings, stratification, and life crises. Students and researchers interested in examining the process of status fluctuation and downward mobility will find new material. This book reaches back to the 1930s to provide a historical perspective on and substance to a sociology of unemployment. Works by Karl Mannheim, Max Weber, and Thorstein Veblen constitute its theoretical core. My sociological framework centers on job related tensions in the lives of a special group of people in a particular setting. I analyze these tensions by relating them to fundamental structural arrangements and institutional patterns. In this way, I seek to explain the connection between subjective human experience and the complexities of objective social events.

There are data in this book for social workers and psychiatrists who help troubled middle-years clients and their families adjust to altered economic circumstances. It is also for people who hope to cope better with their own situations through sharing the experiences of others.

In an important way, Route 128 people are themselves responsible for this volume. I am indebted to Robert Fraser, Arthur Obermayer, Ephriam Weiss and Robert Salow, my key informants from the beginning and over the years. I am grateful to all members of the Lincoln Job Opportunities Group, the Economic Action Group, and the Association of Technical Professionals for welcoming the participation of a sociologist. It is to the randomly sampled professionals who opened their doors and shared their lives that I owe the most. I hope that my efforts in writing this book repay their trust.

I am grateful to my mentors and colleagues Reinhard Bendix, Harold Bershady, Zena Blau, Seymour Martin Lipset, Ritchie P. Lowry, and Eugene V. Schneider, who read parts of my manuscript at an early stage and offered suggestions and encouragement. Eugene V. Schneider helped me formulate my research problem and crystallize my thinking in relation to the sociology of work. My husband and closest colleague, Seymour Leventman, patiently read every version of each chapter. He provided continuing support and substantive suggestions, which sustained me through the many years of this endeavor.

The ultimate organization of this book owes much to Ivar Berg's incisive evaluation of the original manuscript submitted to The Free Press. His comments penetrated the core of my materials and sharpened my analytical focus. Kitty Moore, associate editor of The Free Press, provided stimulating criticism at several junctures along the revision road. Gladys Topkis of The Free Press, a savvy senior editor with intellectual sensitivity, was always a vital source of help and encouragement.

Special gratitude is reserved for my children, Rachel and Aaron Leventman, who provided strong moral support and who are in their own right astute critics and social observers.

Introduction

Unemployment, not tolerated in other Western democracies, is a constant of American economic life. The Swedish secretary of labor would be forced to resign if unemployment reached 2.5 percent (Rodgers, 1975:21). The French government, in its efforts to forestall labor unrest in October 1974, increased unemployment benefits to 90 percent of prelayoff salary (Levison, 1976:18). In contrast, American officials and government economists target an unemployment rate of 5 percent as a goal to be approached.

Now, as in the past, millions of Americans search for work but cannot find the jobs for which they qualify or frequently any job at all. Even during the best of times, the booming 1920s, 2 million were jobless. On the eve of the 1929 stock market crash, 2.3 percent of the active labor force was unemployed (Levison, 1976:9). Joblessness plagued one-third of the nation during the Great Depression; World War II eased the problem but only temporarily. Unemployment rates had risen to 5.9 percent by 1949 (U.S. Department of Labor, 1976a:146). Joblessness fell below 5 percent only during the Korean War (2.9 percent was the low in 1953) and later during the Vietnam war (3.8 percent was the low in 1966). But when the boys came home in the early 1970s, the economy slumped. By June 1975, 9.1 percent of the workforce (8,569,000 people) was officially listed as unemployed (U.S. Department of Labor, 1978a:108). Of course, figures from the Bureau of Labor Statistics do not reflect hidden unemployment: workers who have given up the job search in hopelessness, the long-term unemployed whose benefits have expired, and those who either work only part-time or are marginally employed.

Millions of Americans stand in lines at state department of employment security offices awaiting weekly checks in compensation for their unemployment. The lines were long in the 1970s, especially in the mid-seventies—they wound around corners in some places, down city blocks in others. The mixtures of jobless people differed with the type of community and part of the country. But increasing numbers of middle-aged, middle-class, well-dressed, white-collar workers and professionals were visible among the black faces, the blue-collar workers, the graying heads, and the youngsters just entering the labor force. People in unemployment lines don't say much to each other. An observer sees expressionless faces, hears few jokes, and senses an engulfing depression.

At one suburban Massachusetts Department of Employment Security office in June 1975, the machine that punched out the checks broke down. The staff went into a frenzy. A scruffy-looking, middle-aged man in work clothes stepped out of line and asked whether he could help. He politely identified himself as a mechanical engineer (apparently unemployed long enough to have given up the suit and tie). As if by instinct he moved to use his know-how in solving what for him appeared to be a simple problem. "The machine," he said, "probably just blew a fuse." He ran to his car and returned. In a few minutes he replaced the old fuse and the machine began printing again. The clerk then curtly told the engineer to go to the end of the line because he had moved out of place. "Okay," said the engineer, "but give me back my fuse." The clerk then allowed the engineer his former place. The incident was not even shocking to others in line—numb, atomized, sometimes desperate people without work.

The pain of unemployment goes beyond anxiety about physical survival for work itself is central to human existence. Great social thinkers of the nineteenth century—Karl Marx, Max Weber, Emile Durkheim, Sigmund Freud—all recognized the significance of work as a human activity that gives dignity and integrity to the experiences of everyday life. Society communicates individual worth through remuneration for doing a job. Paychecks enable people to fill their bellies. But employment also provides a broader sense of purpose and direction and the basis for feelings of accomplishment. Work is the foundation for the development of self-esteem, apart from what is possible within nuclear family relationships alone. Work binds people into the institutional networks of the larger community. It is through their occupational roles that individuals most directly encounter society's economic and political realities. And increasingly in industrial society, work provides the pivot for notions of the better life, for chances to move up the all-important ladder of achievement and social recognition.

Modern sociology has recognized the importance of work in the understanding of personality and society. The sociology of occupations and professions, a field pioneered by Everett C. Hughes, has emerged as a well-researched field of inquiry. Occupation is widely used as a criterion by which people are placed in the economic and prestige hierarchies of society. But if the study of work and occupations is so central, surely so, too, should be the study of what happens to people without work—in their daily life experiences and in their relationships with the disjointed institutional structures of a highly technical society. Despite the persistence of unemployment, most contemporary sociologists have neither recognized its importance nor studied its implications.

It was easy for sociologists and others to ignore joblessness during the 1950s and the 1960s. A growing gross national product gave substance to a traditional achievement ideology. The widespread assumption of seemingly limitless economic expansion deterred sociologists from viewing unemployment as particularly important. Indeed, during these years of optimism, unemployment and the related problem of downward mobility seemed dwarfed by the American opportunity structure. Sometimes unemployment was subsumed under more general studies of poverty or ghetto life. More frequently, statistical studies of unemployment sought to correlate such variables as age, sex, race, and occupational category, but without explaining how unemployment affects and is experienced by Americans in different life situations.

Expanding economic horizons in the sixties were eclipsed in the leaner seventies. Nine million people were officially listed as jobless in the summer of 1975—the highest number out of work in thirty-four years. An additional million or more were estimated to have given up the job search in despair. All areas of the economy, all types of industry, and all levels of the occupational hierarchy were affected. The National Urban League estimated that black unemployment approached 25 percent. The Bureau of Labor Statistics estimated that blue-collar unemployment hit 13 percent. For the first time, unemployment cut across occupational prestige hierarchies. Seven percent of white-collar workers and professionals were listed as out of work. Recent college graduates, state and municipal employees, engineers and scientists, teachers and academics, librarians and psychologists, even young lawyers and middle-aged business executives acutely felt the labor market squeeze. Similarly, among third-year law students concern with landing a first job replaced more traditional fears of failing the bar exam. And many college graduates from the class of '76 still "hung loose" a year later as they tried to stretch the part-time job that had helped them through school into full-time employment. Dimmed were expectations of a lucrative, respected career for which years of education had supposedly prepared them.

Employment insecurity extended well beyond those actually out of work. Individual initiative and deferred gratification no longer insured good jobs with economic security. The promise of a rosy future for one's educated children no longer mitigated the drudgery of the assembly line or pierced the boredom of the bureaucratic office routine. Employment insecurity, not so widespread since the thirties, brought fear and anxiety to many working middle- and upper middle-class Americans.

The drama and human tragedy of unemployment was last studied seriously in the Great Depression. In the 1930s the problem of joblessness forced itself into public consciousness. "Lazy" people could no longer be held the cause of unemployment, without jobs available for anyone and with one-third of the nation "ill-housed, ill-fed, and ill-clothed." Out of the depths of the thirties a few sociologists sought to examine and interpret the experiences of the unemployed. Their findings provide us with both the historical context and the important points of departure for further research.

The thirties Depression was an era of social change, a crisis in the transition from early to middle industrial society. The sociologists of the Depression viewed the effects of unemployment through the perceptions of people in trouble. At the same time, their studies involve us directly in personal reactions to the pivotal processes of this transition. Four decades later we witnessed another era of social change, now to a postindustrializing, highly technical society. Once again people caught in the transition experienced the crisis of job loss; some of these were the very scientific and technical elite whose knowledge had made the transition possible.

Professionals Out of Work examines the devastating effects of joblessness among scientists, engineers, and data analysts in the seventies. Career and lifestyle aspirations, psyche, family, social consciousness, and political awareness were all involved. Professionals unemployed in the seventies felt a particular sense of betrayal by a society that had allowed them success and esteem as the price of their faith in the system. They fell suddenly from high places. Although their subjective reactions to drastically altered circumstances varied, they coped with personal troubles in ways that were patterned. These patterns provide clues to understanding disillusionment, so apparent in contemporary American society.

Experiencing unemployment in the seventies differed in many respects from experiencing unemployment in the Depression decade. Even though thirties unemployment was massive, people out of work then usually did blame themselves for their circumstances since they saw others working. And while unemployed people felt isolated during the Depression, they pounded the pavements with multitudes of others. Politicians and the media were sympathetic to their plight. The thirties unemployed thought that government would help an honest guy. Perhaps most important, the Depression jobless had limited horizons. They sought steady work to feed their families. Few anticipated upward mobility.

The unemployment of the 1970s was substantial, as we shall see, but much of it was hidden. The tendency toward psychologically destructive self-blame was far greater than it was in decades past. Pessimism was pervasive since government institutions were no longer a repository of public trust. Worse still, the seventies labor force lived through a time of seemingly limitless expansion. Victory at the end of World War II ushered in an age of unparalleled industrial growth.

In response to the launching of the Sputnik spacecraft in 1957, President John F. Kennedy in 1961 got the United States "moving again" by vastly increasing aerospace and defense spending. In an important way the Apollo program symbolized the times by going beyond earthly parameters. But there was a dark side to this overexpansion of the American dream, called the "malady of infinite aspiration" by Emile Durkheim in a somewhat different context.

> What could be more disillusioning than to proceed toward a terminal point that is nonexistent? . . . It cannot fail to leave behind frustration and discouragement. This is why historical periods like ours, which have known the malady of infinite aspiration, are necessarily touched with pessimism. Pessimism always accompanies unlimited apsirations. (Durkheim, 1973:40)

Unlimited aspirations were encouraged and supported and seemingly realized by many in 1960s American society. The leaner 1970s brought a new kind of unemployment in which hope and achieved potential suddenly turned into deep despair.

Although national attention was drawn to the jobless in the 1970s, none of the ameliorative programs proposed were directed toward the needs of "superfluous" knowledge workers, a new class of forgotten Americans. It is for the purpose of calling attention to this group of Americans whose place in the national life remains important that this study was undertaken.

Experiencing Unemployment in the Great Depression

The Human Component

Qualitative factors are an integral part of the truth about social change and institutions. The discovery of such factors is often impossible by means of cold blooded research on the basis of carefully planned questionnaires or the tabulation of recorded statistics.

For these reasons I decided to work more intensively and humanly within a group small enough to enable me to lay the ground well, feeling that the advantage of freshness of outline and significance of the revelations from the witnesses would outweigh the disadvantage of relatively small distribution. (Bakke, 1934:298)

A sense of closeness to the real experiences of jobless people is the dominant characteristic of 1930s unemployment studies. These sociologists relied on the intimacy of involvement and participation; they compiled detailed case histories; they conducted lengthy personal interviews. They all used quantitative measures, where possible, as a basis for generalization. But always, they were unwilling to sacrifice depth for breadth and validity for statistical reliability. For this reason, their work has an enduring utility.

E. Wright Bakke's were the pioneering studies. He began in England, where the crisis of industrial capitalism, which resulted in widespread unemployment, predated the Depression in America by several years. Bakke immersed himself in the lives of the unemployed in the London borough of Greenwich in 1931 (*The Unemployed Man*). He chose, at that time, to penetrate the unemployment experience through a "descriptive," participant-observation, community study. Bakke boarded with a working-class family. He conducted both formal and informal interviews in various contexts—in the homes of the unemployed, in the queue at the Employment Exchange, during early morning lineups for temporary jobs, and among the men who idled in the streets when their daily search for work had ended in futility. He came to know many of the unemployed personally and several key informants kept diaries and daily time records that detailed their experiences and feelings. Upon returning to the United States in 1932, Bakke directed multifaceted longitudinal studies among the unemployed of New Haven, Connecticut, a project that extended through 1939 (*The Unemployed Worker* and *Citizens without Work*). During this eight-year period, Bakke and a research staff engaged in continuing participant-observation. In-depth case studies of 25 families, including detailed budgets, were obtained. Two hundred families, married and intact, who had experienced long term unemployment were randomly selected and interviewed. And in 1938, a 10 percent sample of households receiving the then newly established unemployment benefits were interviewed.

Marie Jahoda, Paul F. Lazarsfeld, and Hans Zeisel conducted an incisive community study, from the fall of 1931 through the spring of 1932, in an Austrian village whose entire population was unemployed following factory closings (*Marienthal: The Sociography of an Unemployed Community*). The Marienthal study used statistical data when available but, like Bakke's works, relied on a multidimensional "soft" methodology. A small research group lived and worked in this community for many months. They served on medical aid teams, participated in clothing distribution projects, and attended all organized public meetings. They maintained files on all 477 village families. Detailed life histories of 32 men and women were obtained. Eighty people kept time sheets, and 40 families kept intricate food records. The research even included content analyses of essays written by schoolchildren. Then in 1935, Paul Lazarsfeld, together with Bohan Zawadski, analyzed the memoirs of 57 individuals that had been published by the Institute for Social Economy in Warsaw, Poland, in 1933 ("The Psychological Consequences of Unemployment").

Mira Komarovsky studied the effects of unemployment on family life in New York City in 1936 (*The Unemployed Man and His Family*). She selected a stratified sample—57 families of white, Protestant, skilled and white-collar workers; in these families the father was the sole provider and had been unemployed for at least one year. Komarovsky interviewed all members of each family, separately and at length, and was therefore able to penetrate the dynamics of Depression unemployment among stable working-class families.

Collectively, these studies provide vivid documentation of the process of adjusting to the misery and demoralization that poverty and insecurity brought to industrial workers during the thirties crisis of modernizing capitalism. They reveal, among so many things, complex relationships between work (and its removal) and life goals, family aspirations, and social consciousness. Methodologically, the unemployment studies of the thirties underscore the utility of multidimensional qualitative research procedures for penetrating the core of the unemployment experience. Consequently, I adopted similar procedures to study unemployment among professional workers during the crisis of postindustrializing capitalism in the seventies. The legacy of the thirties sociology of unemployment is its disclosure of how the collapse of economic institutions, beyond the control or even the influence of ordinary citizens, destroys self-confidence, erodes individualism, disrupts family life, isolates people from community structures, and produces the kind of political atomization that undermines the potential for collective action.

The Many Meanings of Work

> Prestige and other indications of successfully playing a socially respected role, independence and self-determination, understanding; these are doled out to them in very scanty parcels, and for a large number not at all. Chiefly among the American-born skilled workers were those who had realized such noneconomic rewards. We know that the desire for these noneconomic rewards is strong—so strong that men in suggesting changes in their work environment stressed chiefly the factors that kept them from these rewards. (Bakke, 1940a:90)

The principal value of any kind of work in the thirties was that it enabled a man to support his family. The importance of a job, even a detested job, was disclosed by the dimensions of the void its absence created. The loss of weekly wages brought almost certain economic hardship. A steady job meant a modicum of security. The unemployed wanted jobs that would enable them to live in relative comfort—not in luxury, but beyond mere subsistence. The Depression ended dreams of upward mobility. Such aspirations were, at best, projected onto children. Economic survival, then, was surely the first among the many meanings of work.

But prolonged idleness was as difficult for the unemployed to endure as was economic privation. When Komarovsky (1940:82) asked, "What is the most important thing in life?" most of her respondents answered, "Work." All of the biographies analyzed by Zawadski and Lazarsfeld (1935:232) emphasized the importance of being "occupied" and placed great "value on the dignity of work." Bakke (1934:62) found the unemployed man "lost without the work to which he had become accustomed"; many expressed a "sense of being 'out of stride.' " What is lost with the job?—the feeling of doing something useful, tha basis of self-respect, a sense of social purpose, a reason to begin the day. Days and weeks and months seem empty. The passage of time collapses. Unemployed Marienthal men kept daily time sheets. These were almost blank. Getting up each morning, the midday meal (for which they were frequently late), and sleep at night were their only reference points. Without work, men were unable to mark the otherwise meaningless hours (Jahoda et. al., 1971:66–69).

A job meant respect from family, friends, and the community. Its loss removed a man from social roles that loomed, in retrospect, increasingly significant—the role of "good provider" for his family, the role of "producer" of useful goods for the community, and the abilty to identify with a good company and its products (Bakke, 1940a:5–17). A feeling of uselessness accompanied the loss of these statuses and was among unemployment's most devastating effects.

Economic necessity and the desire for social respect led workers to crave the jobs they had lost. But Depression researchers were surprised by the salience of noneconomic goals for American workers in the midst of economic disaster. Unemployment brought a new awareness of what the lost job should have meant. The unemployed wanted the kinds of experiences and rewards—on-the-job satisfaction, recognition for their efforts, clean and safe working conditions, courteous and dignified treatment by superiors—that had typically been denied them. "Do men get what they deserve?" asked Bakke (1940a:84). "No," said the unskilled and semiskilled. "Sometimes," said the skilled. To deprecate their former jobs and in other ways to express job dissatisfaction was a strong tendency among the unemployed despite the fact that work was sorely missed.

> They almost universally stress obstructions to satisfactions. What loomed up prominently in the memories of workers were the ways in which their conditions of work had retarded, rather than the ways in which their conditions had advanced their attempts to realize the essential demands of human beings. . . . the tendency was remarkably uniform from all nationality and skill groups. . . .
> They were concerned with getting rid of conditions which kept them from functioning in a socially acceptable role, and that made them conscious of control by forces they could not master or understand. These were the primary concerns of seventy out of every hundred. (Bakke, 1940a:37–38)

American workers of the thirties prized independence, strength, and individual initiative. The job, they supposed, was the best place to demonstrate these values. They wanted on-the-job influence, the opportunity to make decisions that mattered, and personal recognition for their accomplishments. The absence of these conditions was the major source of widespread worker dissatisfaction. Yet, the illusion that independence and initiative were possible in the industrial process survived while people had jobs. Workers swallowed dissatisfactions and followed bosses' orders to keep their jobs; yet they also took pride in identifying with their employer, with the products they indirectly helped to produce, and with American industry. The loss of employment, through no personal failing, brought the latent resentment of their powerlessness to the surface.

The unemployed worker sought to exert some control over his life circumstances. And these desires increased almost in proportion as the chances for their realization disappeared. Unemployment further reduced what little control workers may have had over their lives. Unemployment introduced a new source of control in the form of the state. Establishing eligibility for unemployment insurance or general relief meant providing details on one's daily life. Yet the jobless fought to maintain the illusion that individual autonomy was possible, all the more as they felt it slip away.

> Goals which are surrounded by clouds cannot forever remain uncorroded. The survival in the minds of many workers of an urge to evolve some scheme for controlling the forces which determine their affairs, the desire to make decisions that count, and the tendency of those who had tried and failed to substitute boasting and cursing, . . . gave proof that in the case of a significant number this motive was strong enough so that it should be recorded as a factor in the reaction of workingmen and women to their problems.
> . . . Faced with a practical disappearance of economic independence, the desire for control was asserted even more strongly, a substitution made more likely by the awareness that impersonal and uncontrollable forces had played a significant part in making one dependent. (Bakke, 1940a:30)

Eventually, however, many of the unemployed came to lose faith in the time-honored American values of hard work and individual initiative.

> "Now me, I've never lost my ambition. I've held on to her like a sweetheart. But she hasn't been very faithful to me. And I'll tell you son, she's a pretty dried up old lady now." (Bakke, 1940a:91)

These values, once the core of the American dream, lost their substance in the disillusionment of Depression unemployment.

Looking for a Job

> The search for work is the worst and hardest kind of work, tiresome and unpaid. (Zawadski and Lazarsfeld, 1935:233)

Pounding the pavement in fatigue, anger, and despair was the lot of unemployed working people in the 1930s. Everyone knew how tough times were. The unemployed were highly visible at state employment offices, at factory gates, on soup lines. Each man knew he had to fight hordes of others for any sort of work. But each knew he had to keep trying—somehow he had to feed his children. Most had been proud of their ability to provide for themselves and their families. General relief, with its loss of dignity and privacy, was difficult to contemplate. (Unemployment compensation was not available in the United States until 1938, and then only for a 13-week period.)

In both Europe and the United States, the unemployed began the search for work by seeking help from the state. Discouragement was immediate. Direct contact with multitudes of other jobless people was frightening. As one worker described the feeling of signing on at the Employment Exchange to Bakke (1934:82), "Do you know what it makes you feel like when you see all those men out of work three times a week; well you say to yourself even if you try not to, 'What is the use of looking for work with all this crowd after jobs?' " The next encounter was with clerks who screened people for job placement and for benefits. The unemployed were grateful for what benefits they could obtain. But they complained of being treated impersonally, brusquely, even harshly by state personnel. Resentment of the superior attitudes displayed by clerks was widespread. "They treat you like a lump of dirt, they do. . . . the bloody blokes wouldn't have their jobs if it wasn't for us men out of a job either. That's what gets me about their holding their noses up" (p. 80). Many felt summarily excluded from the opportunity to be interviewed for jobs for which they qualified, by clerks who were unfamiliar with qualifications for particular jobs. The unemployed quickly lost faith in the ability of state agencies to help them locate even the temporary work that might have been available. Only 20 percent of those who found work did so with any help from the Employment Exchange. Only 14 out of 161 interviewed by Bakke expressed confidence in the ability of the Exchange to help them find work. In the lyrics of a popular East End London song, "The Labour Exchange is closing down today, And father's going to work in the morning" (p. 115).

At five or six o'clock each morning the unskilled and semiskilled began to congregate at factory gates in the hope that they would be chosen for a day or two of work. Skilled workers, white-collar workers, and professionals first tried to find jobs that utilized their abilities. But as the weeks turned into months and despondency increased, they joined the ranks of the unskilled and were ready to take anything. Most could not waste money on carfare, so they walked and walked and walked—combing industrial sections for any possible work. When the early morning hiring period ended in failure, they would walk to factories and shops. They would try to sneak in through side doors to approach foremen or managers during shift changes. Most began the long trek energetically. But energy and ambition were gradually drained as failure piled upon failure. Simply to be unemployed (even with the vast numbers out of work in the thirties) was itself, they found, a stigma. The longer they were out, the more of a handicap they found their unemployed status to be. The work managers assumed that they were out of condition, that their skills had eroded. "You're rusty," "You're out of shape," or "You can't pull your load," were the kinds of things they were told. But some got temporary jobs, here and there, just by being at the right place at the right time. It was primarily luck, pure chance, they soon came to feel, that made the difference.

Newspaper advertisements were a poor lead for jobs. With so many to answer any ad that appeared, how could an individual hope to have a chance? Yet there was no option but to try. Each time a job was listed in the newspapers, the responses were staggering.

> A storekeeper placed an offer of employment in the local paper for two men with their own cycles. Wages were to be two pounds a week. . . . 1000 had tried to get near the place. The crowd was large enough so that extra police had to be called out to deal with it and to keep traffic moving on the street in front of the store. (Bakke, 1934:137)

So employers hesitated advertising available jobs.

Impersonal methods were fraught with failure. All types of workers found that the surest way to obtain employment was to know somebody on the inside who could put in a good word. It was personal contact, a friend's recommendation, a talk with the foreman that made the difference, where a difference could be made.

Ironically, the best workers from the point of view of steady employment records often had the most difficult time finding jobs. The unemployed in the thirties were not the least able workers. They were not industrial deadwood. Many were among those who had taken the greatest pride in their skills and had found their previous work experience personally meaningful. These men found it difficult, until forced by economic hardship, to contemplate "lousy" jobs at low wages. Moreover, their years of regular employment, frequently for a single firm, had not acquainted them with the intricacies of selling themselves on the open market. "What truth there is in the statement, 'Anyone can get a job if he tries,' is likely to apply to the man who in the past has *frequently* tried" (Bakke, 1940a:234).

Older workers, especially in the United States, felt the hopelessness of the Depression job market most keenly. Larger firms with group insurance or pension plans were loath to hire experienced people. As one of Bakke's respondents said:

> I would not hesitate to lie about age—it's that or the job. I blame compensation and pensions that make the boss think about needing young blood. I quite agree with the man who said everyone should be shot on his forty-fifth birthday. This world is no place for men over forty-five. (Bakke, 1940a:70–71)

The hopelessness and desperation of the fruitless job search brought an increased realization, among many, of the pervasiveness of impersonal, external forces that determined occupational opportunity. The unemployed came to recognize the futility of initiative and the powerlessness of the individual in the industrial era.

Strategies of Economic Survival

> From our conversations with the women, from the way they could remember all the relevant figures, we could tell that they were constantly preoccupied with working out how to spend the little money they had. . . .
>
> But it is equally significant that amid this strict economy we often came across traces of quite irrational spending. Sometimes these "splurges" are probably the first signs of disintegration, but sometimes they simply form the last links with the richer experiences of the past; it is not always possible to decide which. . .
>
> Flowers are growing on many of the garden allotments, although potatoes and other vegetables are vital; beds that could yield some 160 pounds of potatoes are filled instead with carnations, tulips, roses, bell flowers, pansies, and dahlias. When we asked why this was so, we were told; "One can't just live on food, one needs also something for the soul. . . .
>
> A family whose claims to unemployment relief expired a year ago, who for lack of money had to give up, for instance, all sugar and only uses saccharine, whose children are totally neglected, one day bought a cardboard picture of Venice from a peddler, albeit for only 30 groschen.
>
> Such episodes are frequently bound up with frustrated love for the children. A twelve-year-old boy who, on the day before the biweekly payments appeared at school without even a bite of bread, was given on the following day a salami sandwich, two doughnuts, and a piece of chocolate. (Jahoda et al., 1971:54–55)

Masses of unemployed industrial workers suffered from dire hunger, bitter cold in winter, and sickness during the early years of the Depression in Europe. Minimal public assistance prevented widespread starvation. Thirty-two of the 57 biographies analyzed by Zawadski and Lazarsfeld (1935:228–229) detailed experiences of prolonged hunger and the all-consuming expenditure of energy in search of *anything* for one's children to eat. The dole that was available for 13 weeks in Warsaw was spent primarily on food and shelter. Once benefits ceased, the most prevalent means of subsistence were occasional odd jobs. Women took in washing and sewing. Family possessions were sold. Some mentioned begging, some stealing, some sang for coins in courtyards; a few women resorted to prostitution.

In London, where unemployment insurance was available, workers told Bakke (1934:51–53, 81, 122–124) that benefits were enough to keep them from being hungry—but that was all. He found evidence of physical deterioration with prolonged unemployment. Almost half of those who had been unemployed for 74 weeks were not in good health, as compared with one-fourth of those who had been out of work only a short time. But dependence on the dole to forestall hunger was so great that men refused odd jobs or the undertaking of risky business ventures from fear of jeopardizing their benefits.

Financial survival for the unemployed in American cities was complicated by the absence of any form of unemployment compensation until 1938. Bakke's New Haven study showed that the poorest families spent 50 percent of what little they had for food. Eggs replaced meat, drippings replaced butter, canned foods, when available at bargain prices, replaced fresh fruit and vegetables. Seventy-six percent of the unemployed economized on food, 86 percent cut back on entertainment, and 88 percent purchased little or no clothing (Bakke, 1940a:236).

Only as a last resort did unemployed workers, on either side of the Atlantic, sell household goods or cherished family possessions. Without jobs or money for entertainment, more time had to be spent in the home. Its piecemeal dismantling painfully concretized the loss of social and economic status. The sale of possesions, Zawadski and Lazarsfeld (1935:228–229) observed, was a "matter of special mental stress because it is striking evidence of social decline if household equipment which was built up for many years goes to the pawn shop or second hand dealer."

As an unemployed New Haven worker commented, "You didn't buy a piano and victrola just to have them. Now us—we bought them to keep the children happy and at home. When you sell—you sell those things that are a part of you" (Bakke, 1940a:259).

As joblessness continued, families were frequently forced to move to cheap rentals in low status neighborhoods. During the Depression decade, two-thirds of the New Haven unemployed had to move to survive: 49 percent to the least expensive rentals available; 11 percent had to live with relatives; and 8 percent were forced to relinquish equity in homes they had struggled to maintain (Bakke, 1940a:270). Such changes of residence were among the most bitter aspects of the unemployment experience: "Living quarters are more symbolic of the family's social status than any other single item save clothes. 'Folks don't see what you eat, but they know where you live' " (Bakke, 1940a:270).

For millions of unemployed Americans in the thirties, surviving the Depression was a harrowing experience. What economic resources they had were quickly depleted. Bakke (1940a:253–254) found that 78 percent had been able to obtain short-term credit from grocers and landlords, 64 percent had some rainy-day savings, 43 percent secured loans, 12 percent cashed in insurance policies, and 19 percent sold or pawned personal possessions. When these options were used up, as they soon were, nothing remained. Wives and older children sometimes found ways of earning a few dollars. Occasionally husbands found temporary work, which held things together for a while. The more fortunate obtained WPA (Works Project Administration) jobs. But many were forced onto public relief roles.

When unemployment insurance, long accepted in Europe, became available in the United States the majority of the jobless were ineligible because they had been out of work for over a year. Beginning in August 1938, approximately 25 percent of the unemployed received benefits for a maximum period of 13 weeks. These checks, immediately "became the first line of defense beyond their own resources." Bakke (1940a:295–314) argued that unemployment compensation, geared to number of dependents as well as previous wages, was necessary to prevent the demoralization of the work force and the "status destroying attributes of relief." Eventually more comprehensive forms of employment insurance were legislated. But these benefits came too late to soften the harsh realities of economic survival during the Depression.

Psychological Reactions

One can present quite schematically as follows the typical course of the moods of the unemployed: (1) As a reaction to dismissal there comes generally a feeling of injury; sometimes strong fear and distress; sometimes an impulse toward revenge; hatred; indignation; fury. (2) Thereafter comes a stage of numbness and apathy which is gradually (3) replaced by calming down and an increase in steadiness, bringing one again to a relative mental balance. This mental stage is characterized by a resumption of activity; the unemployed become calm as they see that things go along somehow, and adapt themselves to circumstances; they trust in God, fate, or their own ability, and try to believe that the situation will improve very soon. (4) But this hope becomes constantly weaker when they see the futility of the effort. (5) When the situation becomes harder, the old savings and new sources exhausted; then comes the hopelessness which expresses itself first in attacks of fear, for instance, fear of winter and of homelessness, which culminated in distress, the expression of which is the thought of and attempt at suicide. (6) After these outbreaks usually comes either sober acquiescence or dumb apathy, and then the alternation between hope and hopelessness, activity and passivity, according to the momentary changes in the material situation. (Zawadski and Lazarsfeld, 1935:235)

Various aspects of the psychological reactions described above were documented in all of the Depression unemployment studies. Self-confidence, regardless of psychic predisposition, declined with the loss of accustomed work routine, the loss of economic function upon which social status depends, the loss of ability to provide for one's family, and repeated experiences of rejection. All of the unemployed ultimately became extremely distressed. Initial anger, rallying of resources and energetic job search, engulfing hopelessness coupled with continued failure, fear, acute anxiety, gradual retreat to apathy broken by episodes of rage or of frenetic activity—these are the psychological effects of prolonged unemployment.

Bakke (1934:62–66) detailed case histories of several men as they experienced the increasing severity of unemployment. "The mental effects are very difficult to describe," he said. "One sensed them rather than observed them." Competent workers initially felt confident that they would find jobs. At first, they worked harder and longer trying to secure employment than they had at their old jobs. With continued failure, "You feel like you're no good." "Family beginning to think I'm not trying. Don't talk to them much. Leave early, come in late, grab a bite, go to sleep. Sometimes without even talking." As time passed and hope faded, they became "sullen" and "despondent." This, Bakke concluded, "is what lies at the root of the demoralization of such fine workers."

Complete passivity was the psychological attitude of men long idle in Marienthal. Feelings of resignation were apparent among some; feelings of desperation and anger, among others. But as Lazarsfeld wrote in his new introduction to the reedition of *Marienthal* (1971:vii), prolonged unemployment had led to a state of such deep apathy that the men would have been unable to take advantage of opportunities had they arisen.

> Now they are no longer under any pressure, they undertake nothing new and drift gradually out of an ordered existence into one that is undisciplined and empty. (Jahoda et al., 1971:66)

Komarovsky's New York study emphasized the paralyzing effect of unemployment on men who had been out of work for more than a year and whose families were on relief. The men, she claimed, could derive no enjoyment from *any* kind of activity.

> Apparently, the very formlessness of the day and the week, the absence of any required tasks, caused a letdown and weakened the drive for any activity. . . .
> Even those men who do have hobbies get no satisfaction from their pursuit of them. They feel hobbies are trivial and undignified when they form the main content of life. (Komarovsky, 1940:81)

The unemployed became increasingly isolated from their families, their friends, and each other. The long trek in search of work was solitary. White-collar workers were rarely seen in public places. The unskilled, however, frequently gathered in the streets after the day's job hunt had ended in failure or while waiting to register at employment offices. There was little communication even about jobs. Continual rejection formed deep scars. Feelings of futility and personal demoralization were difficult to discuss. The unemployed did not frequently play cards, read books, engage in sports, or involve themselves in other forms of entertainment. Most of them stopped going to bars or pubs because, they said, they needed what few coins they had for food.

> The effect of unemployment is to cause a man to feel more and more alone simply because it reduced the possibilities of his sharing in group activities. His income will not permit it. (Bakke, 1934:197)

The absence of funds, combined with the inability to communicate the pain of failure, created a strong sense of loneliness.

The only leisure activities that researchers noted among the unemployed were sporadic attempts at escape. Some went alone to an occasional movie matinee. The movies of the thirties had special appeal for the jobless. Two bits bought a few hours of Busby Berkeley's follies. He-man adventure films fed the machismo fantasies of men whose feelings of masculinity had been deeply threatened. Laurel and Hardy slapstick depicted initiative as bumbling that could result only in foolhardy enterprises. Gangster films showed the bad guys as victims of a cruel society whose prison wardens were bastards and whose politicians were either windbags or crooks. The antics of the Marx Brothers demolished the pretensions of the respectable rich. Bedroom comedy farces ridiculed the empty lives of upper-class fops. Warner Brothers' social message films glorified the truck driver or the telephone lineman who risked his own neck to do the real work of society. And all the films had happy endings—bad guys met with violent deaths; the old-fashioned virtues of family, friendship, and community prevailed.

Penny-ante, long-shot gambling was the other diversion for some of the unemployed. Human interest stories about unemployed people who suddenly hit it big filled the pages of local newspapers during those hard times. So occasionally some played the numbers or bought a sweepstakes ticket.

> Far more important to these men than the thrill of gambling is the chance of increasing their income far beyond the point they can ever hope to reach by ordinary means. (Bakke, 1934:200)

Regular poker games, for instance, were very infrequent because they necessitated some steady cash and more personal contact than was welcomed.

Unemployment studies of the past did not dwell, for the most part, on the psychopathologies of men who sought escape in heavy drinking or sexual adventures. They focused instead on the psychological problems of men who were living with their families. For instance, Komarovsky noted:

> A considerable proportion of the men exhibited a certain deterioration of personality; loss of emotional stability, breakdown of morale, irritability, new faults such as drinking, unfaithfulness to the wife, and so on. (Komarovsky, 1940:66).

She later observed: "Out of 57 cases which yielded information concerning the man's behavior, deterioration in the man's personality was observed in 22 cases" (p. 68). But the depths of the deterioration process were not explored: this kind of data would certainly have been very difficult to obtain. But if there was a bias underlying the studies of the thirties, it was their attempt to justify the need for greater government support for the unemployed and their families. The researchers would probably have been loath to depict men using relief checks to support the local bar. Some of the studies briefly discussed alcoholism and sexual promiscuity as mechanisms of tension release used by a small minority of the jobless. But those who sank into degeneracy, deserted their families, or suffered mental collapse generally were excluded from these early, family based sociological investigations.

Superficially, many of the unemployment depicted in the thirties studies responded to shame, bitterness, and fear with resignation, isolation, and apathetic withdrawal. But anger and bitterness lurked just beneath the surface. All of the thirties unemployment studies noted incidents of misdirected aggression—explosions of rage at wives and children. Zawadski and Lazarsfeld (1935:242–243) found an "inert aggressiveness": as revealed by statements such as, "I hate everything and everybody," in 20 percent of the biographies they analyzed. They also noted an "increased sensitivity" caused by repressed frustration and hostility among many of the unemployed, which in some cases approached neurosis. Temporary patterns of superficial adjustment brought some degree of continuity to the fabric of daily life. But resignation and apathy were accompanied by aggression, at first self-directed, then projected outward in both specific and generalized forms.

Family Dynamics

"When you are not working, you do not get so much attention"; "She gets mad at me when I tell her that I want more love"; "When money goes, love flies out of the window"; "How can you love a husband who causes you so much suffering? Certainly I lost my love for him"; "I think the children have lost respect for their father"; "I am afraid the children don't think as much of me now that I am unemployed"; "The children act cold toward me. They used to come and hug me, but now I seldom hear a pleasant word from them"; "If I only had money, I could make the girl do things for me. Now that I cannot offer her a nickel for helping her mother with the dishes, there is no way of getting her to do it." (Komarovsky, 1940:14)

Such comments, from both husbands and wives, illustrate the disintegrating effects of the breadwinner's loss of employment along every dimension of family interaction. The dynamics of family adjustment to crisis was of considerable interest to the sociologists who studied unemployment in the thirties. When unable to pay the bills, fathers frequently lost the repsect of their wives and children. Authority relationships within the family changed, as role expectations shifted. Fathers suffered keenly from the loss of respect, authority, and affection that accompanied their joblessness. Some families weathered the resulting tensions; others did not.

When fathers lost their jobs, family life was affected, to different degrees, depending on the quality of existing affectionate relationships, the strength of accepted role definitions, and the personalities of family members. In families previously plagued with serious conflict, the added tensions of unemployment frequently resulted in complete disintegration. Most of those families studied, however, eventually managed to adapt.

> The frustration involved in readjustment becomes less acute as the passage of time dulls the sharpness of the comparison of former and present possibilities, and as the need for an active attack on present problems centers the interest and attention on today's opportunities rather than on yesterday's achievements. (Bakke, 1940b:175)

The thirties unemployment studies collectively suggest a series of stages involved in family adjustment to prolonged economic crisis; even though, as Bakke (1940b:227–228) cautioned, no two families experienced unemployment in exactly the same way.

Initially most families maintained preexisting relationship patterns. But this became more difficult as resources were depleted and economic pressures increased. Wives and older children tried to find ways of earning money. If they succeeded, the father's status, already threatened by his joblessness, was apt to be further diminished.

Some women found work such as ironing and sewing that could be brought into the home, and some found outside employment. There was general agreement, among both men and women, that "a woman's place was in the home," except in cases of dire emergency. While we don't know exactly how much Depression wives contributed to household finances, estimates indicate that their meager earnings were an important factor in the econimic survival of many deprived families (Elder, 1974:51). Although dictated by necessity, this was nonetheless a circumstance deeply resented by unemployed husbands. They greatly exaggerated, for instance, the extent to which women held jobs that might have been theirs. Only 13 percent of the married women with children in New Haven were gainfully employed in the thirties (Bakke, 1940a:118). Yet a prevalent feeling among the unemployed men was that "the machines and the women have the jobs. As one mechanic put it, 'If you want to get a job around here, you either have to wear wheels or skirts' " (p. 70).

As the economic crisis continued, the woman's position in the family was apt to change. Whether she worked inside or outside the home, she had less time for chores and had to convince other family members to assume a greater share of the domestic responsibilities. Usually this brought increased conflict with both husband and children. And most men, whether moping around or actively seeking work, did not help with housework. Even in Marienthal, where idle men had long since given up the job search, only 12 to 15 percent worked in the home. They chopped wood or watched small children when wives were busy. And according to the researchers (Jahoda et al., 1971:73), these men always exaggerated the amount of time they actually spent helping their overburdened wives. Many women resented the husband's unwillingness to help. Others accepted the traditional division of household labor and sought to place increased domestic chores only on their daughters.

> One wife put the impression of several in these words: "You know, there is something in the fact that a busy man can always find time to do more. But a man who isn't doing anythying doesn't find time even to do that." Probably just as important, however, is the fact that in many cases the hold of custom is strong. Both husband and wife feel that any thoroughgoing redistribution of domestic duties somehow is not a proper procedure (Bakke, 1940b:183)

Life with unemployed father deteriorated. He clung as long as possible to his former position of authority within the family. He tended to become increasingly frustrated, depressed, egocentric, and aggressive toward wife and children. He was apt to be withdrawn and sometimes disoriented. Many were no longer able to direct the affairs of the family. At this point, the deepening anxiety and continuing tension resulted in constant fighting, mutual recriminations, and explosive emotional exchanges from which some families never completely recovered. In order for the family to reestablish some sort of equilibrium, the wife then had to assume a more dominant role, as the husband adjusted to diminished authority. But, "No one in this period has a status which is recognized and customary, and the conflict in claims is a serious handicap to any degree of harmony within the family circle" (Bakke, 1940b:202).

Authority relationships shifted in many subtle ways. Some husbands withdrew in certain areas in order to retain control in others. But the wife had to learn how to exercise authority commensurate with her increased responsibilities. She had to assume control over the family's meager finances. She had to gain the father's support in order to control and discipline the children. At the same time, she had to recognize the contributions of older children who earned money themselves and tried to assert their independence from both parents. In order for the family to move beyond the crisis stage and for processes of readjustment to begin

> the father must accept his loss of status and stop trying to assert dogmatically the authority he has lost. . . . Criticisms which are used must begin to wear thin and no longer have their effect either in stimulating the person criticized or in giving satisfaction to the critic. (Bakke, 1940b:215)

Prolonged unemployment resulted in an erosion of the husband's authority, even in many of the most stable families. Komarovsky sampled couples who had been married 15 to 20 years. These families were also on relief, which meant that wives were still financially dependent on husbands, to whom benefit checks were addressed. Nevertheless, Komarovsky

(1940:25–33) found that in one-fourth of these cases, unemployment either "crystallized the inferior status of the husband," who had been tolerated but not loved or respected in the past, "undermined a more or less coercive control exercised by the husband over the wife," permitting some degree of role reversal, or "lowered the status of a loved and respected husband," resulting in role equality or role reversal. None of the husbands willingly relinquished authority to wives. But many were able to control their feelings and go along with distasteful role modifications, at least superficially, in order to reestablish some semblance of family cohesion.

As families adapted to crisis through shifting dominance relationships, the frequency of sexual intercourse declined drastically. Sexual activity is an important variable in family dynamics, but people rarely discussed sex openly in the thirties and data were difficult for researchers to obtain. Documentation of sexual patterns was attempted by Komarovsky (alone among the Depression sociologists) during separate interviews with husbands and wives.

Komarovsky found that unemployment was for many men quite literally an emasculating experience.

> He intimates that they have fewer sex relations. "It's nothing that I do or don't do—no change in me—but when I tell her that I want more love, she just gets mad." It came about gradually, he said. He cannot point definitely to any time when he noticed the difference in her. But he knows that his advances are rebuffed now when they would not have been before the hard times.
>
> The wife gives the impression that there might have been some decrease in sex relations, but declines to discuss them. (Komarovsky, 1940:28)

Approximately 60 percent of those who were willing to talk about sex intimated, if they would not say directly, that frequency of sexual intercourse had decreased. For some it had disappeared (p. 131). Since Komarovsky sampled only the more stable families, her findings probably underestimated the decrease of sexual activity among the unemployed.

Depression parents could not prevent their children from experiencing the effects of family crisis, disorganization, and attempted readjustment: "The problem of disciplining the children, to say nothing of enjoying them is increased by the tiredness and the temper which is encouraged by the lack of rest and the constant pressure under which the parents live" (Bakke, 1940b:206). Children could adapt to changed dominance patterns and even to prolonged economic deprivation more easily than could their parents. Content analysis of Christmas essays written by Marienthal schoolchildren, for instance, showed they had wished for only one-third the presents requested by children from neighboring villages not hit by unemployment. But Marienthal parents could provide few, if any, presents. Children's essays showed disappointment but they also showed acceptance, resignation, and the ability to adjust to an altered economic reality.

An eleven-year-old schoolboy wrote: "If my parents had any money I would like to have gotten a violin, a suit, poster paints, a paintbrush, a book, a pair of skates, and a coat. I did get a winter coat." A girl of the same age: "I would have asked a lot of things from the *Christkind* if my parents were not out of work. I did not get anything—only a pair of glasses. I wanted an atlas and a compass." A nine-year-old elementary schoolboy: "I would have loved to get a picture album. I did not get anything because by parents are unemployed." (Jahoda et. al., 1971:58)

Parents' moodiness was perhaps the greatest difficulty to which children had to adjust. Parents felt guilty when children had scanty lunches to take to school, wore only ragged, secondhand clothes, and were deprived of simple pleasures. Relief allotments in American cities did not, for instance, cover such necessities as pencils and notebooks for schoolchildren. Their own feelings of anger and frustration made parents impatient, unreasonable, short-tempered, and explosive; then, as if to compensate, they became overindulgent. Many parents, completely preoccupied with survival, looked after their children but withdrew from active involvement in their lives. Others used their children, whether intentionally or not, as objects upon which to vent their own frustrations. During period of intense family crisis, relationships between parents and children were apt to be erratic and unpredictable. This lack of consistency was most difficult for Depression children to handle. Many parents tried to protect their children from the depths of their own despair: sometimes they were successful, more frequently they were not.

It was the mother in most working-class families in the thirties who had major responsibility for care of the children and with whom they had close relationships. While employed, fathers had worked long hours and were apt to be remote figures dispensing severe discipline, as well as treats and extra money on payday. When there were no more paydays, many fathers lost the sole basis of their authority. As economic crisis continued, approximately three-fourths of working-class depression children came to view their mothers as the dominant family figure (Elder, 1974:161). Dominant mothers were frequently perceived with ambivalence as martyrs by their children (p. 112). Nonetheless, they often succeeded in instilling in children the adult responsibilities that economic survival dictated "domesticity among the girls, and social independence among the boys" (p. 82).

Komarovsky (1940:86–91) found that fathers had most difficulty dealing with older children, especially those who were contributing financially to the support of the family. They had least difficulty relating to young children, who did not yet understand the meaning of unemployment. Jobless fathers were most apt to lose the respect of their children if previously they had been coercive, uninterested, or unreasonably intrusive. In any case, the unemployed father tended to be a distant, often absent, reference point for his children.

Throughout the Depression, families remained relatively isolated social units. As it became increasingly difficult to keep up a front, even contacts with the extended family, except among certain ethnic groups, decreased. Questions, however well-meaning, from family and friends, were hard to answer. Bakke (1940b:14) compared the social activities of 200 families before and during unemployment. After job loss, the percentage of families frequently visiting friends and relatives, going to movies, and taking excursions dropped from 66 to 29, from 56 to 16, from 24 to 2, respectively. The nuclear family was thrown back on itself.

> The unemployed man, and his wife have no social life outside the family. The extent of the social isolation of the family is truly striking. This refers not only to formal club affiliation but also to informal social life. The typical family in our group does not attend church, does not belong to clubs, and for months at a time, does not have social contacts with anyone outside the family. Furthermore, the families do not give the impression of maintaining any ties with the community as a whole. (Komarovsky, 1940:122)

Perhaps it was this very isolation that helped facilitate the adjustments that reduced social status necessitated. Only when contacts with significant others from the past were decreased did it become possible to forget the once cherished dreams for a better future. And yet, the very isolation of the unemployed, both as individuals and in nuclear family units, mitigated against the development of a collective response from the unemployed masses that might have resulted in more basic political and economic changes than those eventually emerging from the Great Depression.

Blurred Class Consciousness

The simple word "employer" raised no consistent picture in the minds of the workers. One man phrased his response this way, "Do you mean the company, or do you mean my boss?"

In this response is a warning that workers' attitudes toward their "employers" are subject to no clear-cut definition. . . .

The "labor struggles" in the larger factories of New Haven were not a battle between labor and capital. There were conflicts between workers and their immediate bosses. The picture of the worker as a "have-not" reaching for the holdings of capitalists or the "haves" is a dramatic but untrue representation on the printed page of a real struggle in the shop. The real struggle is between two groups of workers for hire who are trying to establish conditions in which they can do a job required of them with minimum trouble and maximum satisfaction to themselves. (Bakke, 1940a:48–49)

Workers in the thirties displayed a diffuse awareness of their class interests but never developed militant class consciousness. The Depression unemployment studies show that workers wanted steady jobs, which would bring economic security to their families. They wanted the ability to buy some of the products created by their labor in the industrial process. And for the most part, they did not perceive of movement upward, out of the working class, as necessary for the attainment of these goals. Many, while employed, had been dissatisfied with their low wages, dangerous or unpleasant working conditions, and lack of on-the-job recognition. And they knew their feelings were widely shared by fellow workers. But dissatisfactions were muted by unemployment. Frustration and anger had to be repressed if one wanted to get or hold a job. And these reactions, too, they knew were prevalent among the jobless multitudes. The unemployed were certainly aware that their economic interests and fundamental needs were not being met. They understood that powerful societal forces were blind to their plight and blocked the enactment of ameliorative proposals.

> We have found . . . a common theme of dissatisfaction running through conversations which was monotonously similar for all workers. Workers cannot be unaware that the essential frustrations of each are the problems of all.
>
> Furthermore, many of these problems are primarily characteristic of the working group. The growing recognition of control by impersonal forces and by nonworking class individuals is one such problem. The obvious fact that these latter individuals are frequently opponents of adjustments, legislation, and regulation which to any worker seems a sensible attempt to improve his status, emphasized a difference in point of view which encouraged a recognition that there are at least two classes in society, workers and others. (Bakke, 1940b:87)

Workers in the thirties were aware of belonging to an amorphous although distinct social class, but the requisite of personal economic survival impeded the growth of collective consciousness.

Pervasive unemployment raised new tensions and brought new divisions within the working class. Workers were pitted against each other in fierce competition for scarce jobs. Zawadski and Lazarsfeld (1935:244) noted a shifting class consciousness. Widespread unemployment did not intensify conflict between workers and owners. Instead, it increased conflict between employed workers, anxious about possible layoffs, on the one hand, and the jobless, on the other. The total picture, however, was murky. Workers curried the favor of bosses and in other ways vied with each other to keep their jobs. They felt pressed by circumstances to behave in unnatural ways.

> They gave notice of impending dismissals. The workers are sad, resigned, gloomy; they look at each other with hostility. Who will be first? The worst is the uncertainty. . . . We suspect each other of spying and obsequiousness. Whisperings, guessing, bowing and scraping to the foremen to the loss of one's own dignity. All this for work, for a piece of bread. Down with fellowship and friendship. I am better than you. Humiliating, feigned, flattering smiling. . . . Handshaking, and in the heart the poison of hatred. In the mind, the thought, damn, let them fire me. (Zawadski and Lazarsfeld, 1935:244–245)

Working-class solidarity was undercut still further by the failure of the unemployed to identify clearly a single source of blame for their situation, as well as by some residue of sympathy for the company's position in the larger economy. The worker referred to the employer differently as the owner, the manager, or the foreman. And frequently he could not say *who*, specifically, had fired *him*. Furthermore, many workers believed that firms had been forced into layoffs because they were losing money. Some saw their former employers trapped by the same larger, ambiguous, uncontrollable forces that were plaguing them. This inability to designate a corporate enemy impeded the development of working-class solidarity.

Even those American workers who recognized an enemy in corporate interests had difficulty viewing *all* members of the middle classes as economic opponents. Unemployed Americans did not perceive all sectors of the middle class as milking the laboring class. Schoolteachers, for instance, sometimes showed special kindness to the children of the unemployed. Clergymen may not have helped in material terms but certainly they were not viewed as economic adversaries. And unemployed workers knew that many middle-class people were themselves unemployed. And so, as Bakke (1940b:97) commented, "Another barrier to class consciousness is the lack of an easily recognized opponent in other social groups in American society."

The absence of militant class consciousness among the unemployed was further revealed in their attitudes toward unionization. The organizational success of the labor movement during the thirties led many to overlook the fact that, as a group, unemployed workers did not participate in the labor movement. Legalization of the right of workers to organize and to bargain collectively came, in the United States, with the passage of the Norris-LaGuardia Act of 1936. The physical presence of millions of unemployed people in long soup lines created an atmosphere that made possible the official recognition that individuals could not bargain independently and expect a fair return for their labor. But the fight for labor unions, as Depression studies of the unemployed document, was waged largely without the help of the jobless. For instance, Bakke (1940b:14) found that although 32 percent of 200 randomly selected workers in his New Haven sample had attended union meetings while they had been employed, only 15 percent did so after they were laid off. Most American workers did not view labor organizations as a means of unifying working classes against oppressor classes. Rather, the worker was apt to perceive the union as a way of protecting his job. And since unions had not helped the unemployed retain their jobs, organizational activity became, for many, increasingly pointless.

To sum up, despite the depths of the economic crisis in the thirties and despite a general awareness of their class interests relative to those of more powerful forces in society, the jobless did not develop group cohesion, either as unemployed workers or as an employee class.

This fact of dissociation of feelings of solidarity among the proletarians, the shift in class consciousness, the split in the masses *explains the weakness of the unemployed as a mass; the masses cease to exist as such when social bond—the consciousness of belonging together—does not bind any longer. There remain only scattered, loose, perplexed, and hopeless individuals. The unemployed are a mass only numerically, not socially.* (Zawadski and Lazarsfeld, 1935:245)

Political Powerlessness

True, the noise in the audience came from a boisterous Communist group intent on breaking up the meeting. But lack of confidence was also displayed in a more quiet way by many of the staunch Labour men with whom I spoke. After all, what did their vote mean? It did not mean that they had any voice in shaping the policies by which they were governed. It simply meant that they put their confidence in a certain individual. Having done that by casting their vote, there was nothing more that could be done. If their representative acted in a way which they considered to be detrimental to their interest, there was a day of reckoning coming at the next election. Until that time they were powerless.

Having delegated their votes to one man, they rapidly shift their interest in politics from a consideration of what their representative is doing to a consideration of what the "Government" is doing. . . . Many were the cynical remarks, such as, "I see X has condescended to come around at last. Well, we'll perhaps not see him until another election." (Bakke, 1934:224)

Leftist political movements that developed in Western democracies during the thirties were not directly supported by unemployed workers. The atomized jobless who had themselves developed neither group cohesion nor class consciousness were isolated from active involvement in political organizations, much as they had become removed from active participation in other areas of community life.

Communists and Socialists made special appeals to the unemployed. Sometimes jobless men went to political meetings or listened to speeches at public rallies. But very few joined even liberal educational groups. And those who did were apt to be young bachelors. The unemployed distrusted political rhetoric and especially the exhortations of radicals. Those who listened, heard much in May Day speeches with which they could agree but the appeals always went beyond what was believable.

No one can deny the cases cited by radical agitators in their appeals to the workers and the unemployed. They are as vivid as the sight of a mother evicted from a dilapidated tenement house sitting in the street on a broken chair, trying to shelter her baby from the icy winds with a ragged blanket. . . . such pictures shouted from the soapbox were not sufficiently verified by experience to arouse confidence in their universality. Experience with "the government," with supervisors, with landlords, and bosses just didn't universally fit the agitator's picture. Even if some verification existed in his own case, the worker had enough associates who had contrary experiences so that the changes were too watered down to stimulate action. (Bakke, 1940b:57)

American workers, Bakke found, not only distrusted Communist activists but despised them. In order to test the extent of this antipathy,
Bakke assumed the role of a Communist supporter, in much the manner of
a modern ethnomethodologist.

> I joined a group outside a cigar store. . . . I asked where the Communist office
> was. The antagonistic reaction was instantaneous. A Greek (thirty years in the
> United States) said, "Take my advice and stay away from there. It's dangerous."
> When I questioned him as to what he meant by dangerous, he replied:
> "Somebody will hit you over the head, them foreigners will. This is what hap-
> pens. If you are working in a restaurant, dishwashing, and somebody sees you,
> they will go and say to your boss, 'He's a Communist.' " A very effective gesture
> indicated that you would be let go immediately.
>
> In order to draw them out I took up and defended the Communist
> cause—not one of the men would give ground on the subject. Two reactions to
> Communism were constantly reiterated:
>
> 1. Anyone who thought that slavery in Russia was desirable, not only was
> crazy but ought to be shipped back immediately. . . .
>
> 2. To be a Communist is similar to being a representative of a foreign power
> attacking our shores. Regardless of how badly one is treated, how much he
> despises his own work and employers, when a Communist is around, it is the
> American worker's duty to uphold America and American conditions. For ex-
> ample, two of the fellows said with pride that they were working for anywhere
> from twelve to eighteen hours a day at wages of ten-fifteen-twenty dollars a
> week. Their point was that there was work for any decent American who had
> energy enough to work or get out and look for a job. In the face of Communism
> the most insecure American workman becomes a hero by defending American
> conditions. (Bakke, 1940b:60–61)

The social insecurities of unemployment and marginally employed
Americans tended to intensify their prejudices toward racial and ethnic
minorities. When confronted by a challenge to capitalist institutions, they
became superpatriots. And all forms of radicalism were seen as foreign imports: "The 'un-American' judgment is emphasized by the fact that many of
the radical speakers are members of race and nationality groups which are
not trusted and frequently despised" (Bakke, 1940b:61). Even the few who
entertained Socialist ideas were put off by the "un-American" character of
the leadership. And combined with the need to feel 100 percent American
was the fear of violence—from "crazy" Communists, from police for participation in demonstrations, and from bosses as the workers searched for
jobs.

Consequently, unemployed Americans during the Depression were, by
and large, not among those who sought the destruction of the political-
economic order. Most had hoped that the existing system would become
more responsive to their needs. The New Haven Unemployed, Bakke
(1940a:98) found, expected the federal government to take increased
responsibility for their welfare: 88 percent wanted government to provide

social insurance benefits, to restrict the installation of new machinery, and to regulate rents and housing; 68 percent also thought that government should regulate wages and working hours. While most of the unemployed distrusted politicians, they retained enough faith in democratic capitalism to hope that things would get better without drastic measures.

Rarely did radicalism, in English or American cities, extend beyond a vague questioning about the possibility that an entirely different system might be an improvement. As long as a modicum of security is provided, or some faith in the potential responsiveness of the system exists, workers are loath to risk loss of what little they have. In England, Bakke found that unemployment insurance had undercut what revolutionary potential the Depression might have brought.

> The plain fact appears to be that there has been brought into the worker's life, even when he is unemployed, a sufficient degree of security, so that talk of undermining the social order which has given him even the small degree of security is an interesting debating opportunity rather than a vital discussion of actual possibilities. (Bakke, 1934:61)

And in the United States, the first 100 days of the Franklin Delano Roosevelt administration served a similar function.

The New Deal era gave American workers just enough hope to counter fear and frustration. They eagerly placed their faith in a president who sought to make the system, in which they desperately wanted to believe, responsive to their survival needs.

> The concern of Mr. Roosevelt for the "forgotten man" he interpreted as concern for his own welfare. He could use his only traditional political technique with more confidence. His increased confidence in traditional techniques reduced his inclination to try new and untried methods led by men whom he distrusted on other grounds. . . . It is evident that men turn slowly to new methods as long as there is a ray of hope that the old can be made to produce satisfactory results. For the time being at least, the new hope in what could be accomplished through the national government shone through the clouds of disillusionment with the politics of city and state with which he was more intimately acquainted. (Bakke, 1940b:55)

They hoped that this president, who seemed so different from most politicians, would initiate changes to help them share in the harvest of plenty that industrialization had promised.

The unemployed masses suffered acutely throughout the Great Depression. Yet, except for voting in national elections, they essentially remained politically impotent. Most were unable to translate their frustration into political action. And outbursts of political anger occasionally witnessed by researchers

> are only expressions of painful estrangement from the community, of the feeling of helplessness, of being forgotten, "locked out" or cast out. Such a feeling, it is true, is a condition for a revolutionary attitude, but it is not yet one by any

means. . . . The experiences of unemployment are a preliminary step for the revolutionary mood, but . . . they do not lead by themselves to a readiness for mass action. . . . They can easily lead to outbreaks of distress in the form of single acts, but they leave the mass inert, since they lead to ever-increasing mutual estrangement, isolation, dispersion, destruction of solidarity, even to hostility among the laborers, and ir this way they deprive the mass of its power. (Zawadski and Lazarsfeld, 1935:249)

Illusions and Disillusions of the 1930s

This great nation will endure as it has endured, will revive and will prosper. So, first of all, let me assert my firm belief that the only thing we have to fear is fear itself—nameless, unreasoning unjustified terror which paralyzes needed efforts to convert retreat into advance. . . .

More important, a host of unemployed citizens face the grim problem of existence, and an equally great number toil with little return. Only a foolish optimist can deny the dark realities of the moment. . . .

Our greatest primary task is to put people to work. This is no unsolvable problem if we face it wisely and courageously. It can be accomplished in part by direct recruiting by the Government itself, treating the task as we would treat the emergency of a war, but at the same time, through this employment, accomplishing greatly needed projects to stimulate and reorganize the use of our natural resources. . . .

We do not distrust the future of essential democracy. The people of the United States have not failed. In their need they have registered a mandate that they want direct, vigorous action. They have asked for discipline and direction under leadership. They have made me the present instrument of their wishes. In the spirit of the gift I take it. (Franklin Delano Roosevelt, First Inaugural Address, March, 4, 1933)

The Great Depression was the first massively experienced crisis of industrial society. It tore through all social sectors and ripped into the cultural fabric of American values and beliefs. When the rhythm of daily activity was disrupted by the crisis of unemployment, the illusions and disillusions of ordinary Americans—about life and work, about family and community, about business and government—were clearly disclosed. The cultural hangover of rural values had, by the thirties, merged with the realities of urban existence. The worker thought himself the backbone of the urban scene—hardworking, honest, independent. His sense of personal independence had, however, been diffused by his need to identify with a company and its products. It was not from his labor alone that a man's feeling of self-importance was derived. Instead, it came partly from the knowledge that his work contributed to the industrial progress of the larger society. His illusion that individual initiative made a difference was further eroded by the impersonality of the factory, where his efforts and accomplishments went unrecognized and unrewarded.

The family, therefore, had become the chief repository of idealized virtues from the preindustrial past. Joe Worker's role as good provider became his most important self-designation. The cherished illusions of family togetherness, mutual support, everlasting love, and tender understanding had been sustained by the weekly wages of the breadwinner. The worker in the thirties had few illusions about mobility into the middle class but he had hoped that through his diligence a little home with a white picket fence, a welcoming wife in a starched apron, and a few kids doing their lessons would greet him at the end of a hard day. It was only for the children, if they were ambitious and educated, that wearing a white collar to work each morning was seen as a possibility.

Unemployment did not destroy the worker's basic faith either in the "American way of life" or in its economic and political institutions. Many held grudges against particular companies or specific bosses but few questioned the fundamental superiority of industrial capitalist economics. Many felt that local politicians, only out for themselves, spent too much time playing poker and making deals in smoke-filled rooms, but faith in the democratic process remained unchallenged. Cultural memories of the prosperous twenties lingered. And workers wanted the government in Washington to help them get a bigger and more secure piece of the action. But for many, unemployment eroded illusions about individual initiative and family solidarity. It ended culturally perpetuated psychological naiveté. The Depression, as seen through the experiences of the unemployed, buried the remnants of the picket fence value syndrome of the preindustrial past.

To summarize, the destruction of the cultural ideal that the worker, as an individual, was important was the major source of thirties disillusionment. Unemployment crystallized pervasive feelings of powerlessness. Illusions about the significance of individual effort and initiative dissipated, as people lost their jobs through no personal failings and when good work records were held against them in their search for reemployment. Forces beyond anyone's control or understanding determined whether or not people were permitted to earn a living. Workers learned that nothing they could do as individuals made any difference. And the dependence of many of the unemployed on government assistance for financial survival cemented that realization.

Disillusionment with the nuclear family as the citadel of support, love, and devotion was one of the most pervasive effects of the breadwinner's prolonged unemployment. When he proved unable to support the family, the breadwinner's dominance was questioned, frequently for the first time. Women were divested of formerly held notions of masculine prowess and emotional stability. Men resented their wives' lack of sympathy, affection, and respect. Most of these families endured periods of severe crisis, then came to accept some flexibility in authority relationships, and subsequently worked out various readjustment patterns. But residues of conflict and loss of trust challenged illusions of love and marriage and living happily ever after.

The profound psychological effects of unemployment on so many men shattered prevalent notions about the superior mental stability of males. A machismo of the assembly line had reigned unquestioned until the thirties. Illusions persisted that the worker, always physically and emotionally strong, could, if he tried, take care of himself and his family. People, it was recognized, sometimes had problems, but usually these were caused by the tensions of city life. Men, it was understood, might take to fighting or drinking; it was the women who were nervous. But the husband's disintegration, which so frequently accompanied his unemployment, was all too apparent to wives and children. Psychological deterioration was all the more devastating because it did not fit expected patterns and exceeded commonsense understanding. Yet with disillusionment in this area came a greater sophistication about psychological problems, which had been hidden or ignored by traditional values.

During the Depression, widespread recognition of the weakness and inability of individuals to control life circumstances in industrial society had taken root. People could no longer depend on themselves or their families to cope successfully with the problems they faced. It was the federal government, personified by FDR and symbolized by the New Deal, that became the new repository of a common trust. A new kind of central government, many believed, concerned with the so-called forgotten man, had the power to improve the conditions of life for ordinary people. Workers looked to Washington to establish economic controls, enact social welfare legislation, and expand the opportunity structure. And, as the federal government assumed increased responsibilities, the American dream took on a renewed significance.

2

The New Unemployment
of the 1970s

From the 1930s to the 1970s

The U.S. was built on the work ethic, and for all the evolution in life-styles, the
first identification for most Americans remains what they do, the job they hold.
There are many monetary cushions, from unemployment to food stamps, to aid
the jobless in today's economy, but there is no balm for the sense of anomie and
loss felt by an able man or woman whose skills are no longer wanted anywhere.
The memory cells of the nation are still etched with the widespread corrosion of
self-confidence that occurred in the Great Depression, and last week's startling
disclosure that unemployment reached 8.2% of the American work force in
January stirred many memories uneasily. Some 7,529,000 Americans who
wanted to work were jobless last month, the highest percentage of the work
force since 1941. Tens of thousands more will surely be joining them in the
months ahead.

No segment of the nation was immune. ("Growing Specter of Unemployment," 1975:9)

Many of the changes hoped for in the thirties did occur during the
40-year interim between national bouts with massive unemployment. New
Deal reforms restored the illusions of Americans about the viability of their

27

system. Historian Arthur Schlesinger, Jr. (1959), among others, has maintained that New Deal legislation saved the American private enterprise system and restored faith in democratic political institutions. The New Deal was a two-pronged attack to control big business and to protect ordinary citizens. Through the establishment of review and control boards with unprecedented powers, the activities of big business, especially banking and finance, came under official scrutiny. But most of all, in the popular view, a level was established beneath which people could not fall during downward swings in economic cycles. This was accomplished by measures such as creation of public service jobs, insurance of savings accounts, provision of unemployment compensation, provision of labor unions with the right to bargain collectively and to strike for wages and conditions, and the establishment of a national social security system. The Works Projects Administration created jobs that were financially and psychologically necessary for those who obtained them. These jobs were also socially important—from the Tri-Borough Bridge in New York City, which facilitated urban and suburban auto transit, to the Tennessee Valley Authority, which provided electricity to the rural South. But there was little debate that New Deal measures *alone* ended the Great Depression: they did *not*.

Preparation for World War II (beginning in 1939), followed by the industrial boom of the war years and the expanded demand for consumer goods after the war, ended the Depression. The growth of government supported munition industries revitalized the American economy. And since 1939 no other route to economic stability has been envisioned by either political and economic leaders or the experts who advise them.

In order to support economic stability and jobs the federal government continued to underwrite the defense industries, and a garrison state atmosphere was therefore preserved after World War II. But the advent of the atomic age and the knowledge explosion that accompanied it brought both continued life and new problems for the defense industries. The Soviet explosion of an atomic bomb in 1949 meant that national security could be protected only by the development of an American hydrogen bomb. Fear of the Communist enemy was projected and maintained through the House Un-American Activities Committee's persecution of supposed radicals, the execution of Julius and Ethel Rosenberg ostensibly for giving the secret of the atomic bomb to the Russians, the conventionally fought Korean War, and the brinkmanship quality of American foreign policy. Nuclear superiority became widely accepted as the only means of achieving national security. And for that end, no cost could be too great. As C. Wright Mills predicted:

It is a hard fact for capitalism that the new weaponry, the new kinds of war preparations, do not seem to be as economically relevant to subsidizing the defaults and irrationalities of the capitalist economy as the old armament and preparations. The amount of money spent is large enough, but it tends to go to a smaller proportion of employees, to the technical rather than to the semiskilled. The people who make missiles and bombs will probably not put into consumption as high a ratio of their incomes as would the more numerous makers of tanks and aircraft. Accordingly, the new type of military pump-priming will not prime as much; it will not carry as great a "multiplier effect"; it will not stimulate consumption or subsidize capitalism as well as the older type. It is a real capitalist difficulty, and the military expenditures may indeed have to be great to overcome it. (Mills, 1958:61)

When John F. Kennedy got the economy moving again in 1961 by vastly increasing aerospace as well as defense spending in order to further the already flourishing arms race, the federal government began funding advanced systems research and development laboratories involved in all areas of science and engineering. John Kenneth Galbraith, a top Kennedy economic advisor, later explained the process in *The New Industrial State* (1967). These contracts, he maintained, enabled the government to secure the planning cycles that were necessary to the functioning of high technology firms. The expenditure of knowledge and capital at each phase of an operation became so great and the time sequence from original proposal to final product so long that government contracts with built-in provisions for cost overruns were necessary to guarantee the tremendous risks involved. Technological advancement, to say nothing of national economic stability, was felt to be at stake. These developments culminated in the use of computers with memory banks to store vast quantities of data and to direct the complex and intricate defense and aerospace operations. The personnel for this new industrial system came from an expanded university system, which had made possible the upward mobility of many children of the Great Depression.

The costs of technological advance through federal defense and aerospace contracts continued to spiral. In 1961 Robert McNamara instituted a system designed to regulate the management of the 20,000 firms (and their 100,000 subcontractors) associated with the Defense Department. This system, labeled "Pentagon capitalism" by Seymour Melman (1974:21), "maximizes cost and maximizes subsidies" for the state management. The McNamara system was based on a "historical-projection" method. Engineers were not permitted to present proposals based on a calculation of minimal cost estimates but had to use, as a base figure, the cost of the closest previously comparable project. Melman (1974:31) concluded, "By such methods dramatic cost increases of one product become the baseline for estimating acceptable costs and prices of the next product." These procedures culminated in President Gerald Ford's fiscal year 1977 Defense budget request of $113 billion. And Congress, facing unemployment in an election year, willingly appropriated even more. By 1978 the Defense Department budget was $120 billion. And for fiscal year 1980, $129,964,000,000 was budgeted.

Continuing federal support of computerized technological development certainly facilitated the transition from industrial to postindustrializing society. Advocates of vast defense and aerospace expenditures claimed that new technologies would have a beneficial effect on the rest of the industrial system. The computer, instead of the worker, could control the machine. Automation and cybernation, it was maintained, would so increase industrial productivity that leisure and pleasure would enter the lives of common people. These claims occurred simultaneously with the expansion in the public sector of bureaucratic administrations established by New Deal legislation. New demands were created for professional services and supporting white-collar personnel in the areas of labor, health, housing, education, social security, and public welfare. The transition to postindustrializing society was accompanied by a growing dependence on knowledge workers in science, technology, and the bureaucratically administered welfare state. Daniel Bell (1973:14), for instance, described postindustrial society as one in which (1) there is a shift from a goods-producing to a service-producing economy; (2) the "pre-eminence of the professional and technical class" dominates the occupational structure; (3) "theoretical knowledge as the source of innovation" becomes the central source of policy formation; and (4) decisionmaking becomes increasingly future oriented and is characterized by the "control of technology and technological assessment." The changes Bell described were accompanied by a growth in the number of salaried professionals who were needed within the defense, social service, and educational bureaucracies. The scientists, engineers, and data systems analysts; doctors, lawyers, and social workers; and teachers and professors who serviced the bureaucracies of the postindustrial society constituted the fastest growing (largely upwardly mobile) post–World War II social strata. They increased from approximately 1 percent of the work force before 1940 to about 5 percent in 1950, to approximately 10 percent in 1960, to roughly 15 percent by the 1970s.

The seventies witnessed a crisis in the transition to postindustrial society. Automation eliminated approximately 10 million industrial jobs. Increasing blue-collar unemployment, rather than leisure and pleasure, were among the most immediate effects in the new society. While expanded social service programs meant increased security for some Americans, it was often difficult to obtain the benefits to which one was entitled. The red tape problem was compounded by the computerization of government social service operations. But benefits from social programs were decreasingly felt for a second reason: over the years, a relatively smaller proportion of the federal budget had been delegated to them. The increase in federal government expenditures, from about $9 billion in 1939 to approximately $100 billion in 1956, went very disproportionately to defense. Melman (1970:117) calculated that in 1939, 42.5 percent of all government expenditures went to human services as compared with 7 percent in 1965. In terms of the value of the 1963 dollar, "$83 per person was spent in 1939; $75 was spent in 1953; and only $56 in 1963."

In contrast to the careful planning that occurred within large corporations, the transition of governmental controls to a postindustrializing society was haphazard. Relative prosperity in the fifties and sixties was joined with a faith in science, knowledge, and progress. There was an expanding occupational structure as jobs in military and space related industry, government and business hierarchies, human service agencies, and schools and universities mushroomed. But federal funding went so disproportionately to defense that the domestic economy progressively deteriorated. Melman documented the illusory quality of post–World War II economic expansion. Defense spending did not increase the use-value of either consumer goods or civilian industrial capabilities.

> An outward appearance of economic health can belie an underlying reality of economic decay. In the experience of many people during the thirty years since World War II, especially in the upper middle class and in the technical and administrative occupations, the expectation that war spending brings prosperity was borne out. What went unrecognized was that the war economy produces other, unforeseen effects with long-term destructive consequences. These include the formation of a new state-managed economy, deterioration of the productive competence of many industries, and finally, inflation—the destruction of the dollar as a reliable store of value. . . .
>
> From the economic standpoint the main characteristic of war economy is that its products do not yield ordinary economic use-value: usefulness for the level of living (consumer goods and services); or usefulness for further production (as in machinery or tools used to make other articles). (Melman, 1974:18–19)

Advanced technological development was not directly applied to commercial industries. Consequently, Japan and West Germany have come to hold the major patents on technologically based consumer goods. From 1960 to 1970, U.S. imports of high technology goods have increased 694 percent in the electrical apparatus area and 681 percent in transportation equipment. At the same time, productivity in the machine tool industry decreased drastically as old equipment became too expensive for managers to replace (Melman, 1974:92, 81–82).

Responding to the decaying domestic economy and a system of tax shelters, American corporate interests increasingly invested directly in foreign countries. As Senator Frank Church, chairman of the congressional subcommittee investigating multinationals claimed: "We have been losing jobs at the rate of 120,000 to 180,000 a year. And the effect is cumulative." (Rodgers, 1976:14). According to Melman (1974:103), this trend has decreased by as many as 4 million the number of jobs in the American labor market.

By the mid-1970s a depleted civilian economy was beset by the combined problems of inflation and widespread unemployment—a condition
popularly called "stagflation." Unemployment rates averaged more than 5
percent from 1960 through 1975 (Ginsburg, 1976:91) but not until they
reached double digits in 1975 did newspapers chronicle the plight of the
jobless. Only then were studies undertaken and ameliorative policies proposed. At the same time, however, the Consumer Price Index increased at
an astounding rate: from 100 at base year 1967, it rose to 147 in 1974; 161
in 1975; 171 in 1976; 182 in 1977 (U.S. Department of Commerce,
1977:313); and 201 in October 1978 (Farnsworth, 1978b:11).

The public was angered by inflation but misled about its causes. Even
though the $100 billion plus Defense Department budget and large public
service bureaucracies kept aggregate spending high and encouraged inflation, the media pumped the message that reduced unemployment would increase inflation. Joblessness can cool the economy, it was argued, because
compensation payments put less money in people's pockets than do salary
checks. Meanwhile President Jimmy Carter fed popular notions that
defense spending produces jobs. Carter promised to increase the defense
budget 3 percent beyond the annual rate of inflation.

> That would amount to $123.8 billion in outlays next year or roughtly 25 percent
> of all federal expenditures. At the same time, the Administration has decreed a
> cut of about $15 billion in a broad range of social programs, including Social
> Security disability insurance, Medicare and Medicaid, the water and sewer pro-
> grams of the Environmental Protection Agency and the Labor Department's
> public-service jobs program.
>
> This clear shift in federal priorities cannot fail to have a significant impact
> on the national economy. And the consensus among economists is that although
> the shift toward military spending will benefit some communities and workers,
> the impact on the nation as a whole will add up to more inflation and fewer jobs
> in the coming year. (Crittenden, 1978:F1)

Unemployment affected over 6 percent of the labor force during the late
seventies; it was higher among some groups than others, as we shall see.
Vast numbers of state supported jobs were threatened as the public outcry
for reduced taxation was heard across the nation. The problems faced by
jobless Americans were buried by statistical projections as an unemployment versus inflation debate seeded ideological controversy among policymakers and academics.

Ideological Perspectives

> The price we have to pay for lower unemployment is more inflation. With prices
> already increasing at record rates, the cost of lowering the unemployment rate
> may be too high. ("What the Unemployment Figures Really Mean," 1974:15)

The economic cost of unemployment is prohibitive. It is estimated that, since 1947, excessive unemployment above a 3 percent minimum level has cost this society some $593 billion in goods and services foregone—a loss equivalent to $8,500 in 1975 dollars, for every American family. (Humphrey, 1976:7)

Contemporary conservative opinion focused on inflation as well as on liberal programs as *causes* of the economic ills of the seventies. Unemployment was minimized as a problem. High rates were deemphasized or rationalized. The reason that unemployment continued to be high, editorialized *Forbes*, was that 2 million unskilled and therefore unemployable workers were entering an increasingly automated labor market each year.

To try to shoehorn them into the labor force through stimulating the economy would only produce inflation, since the stimulation would push the demand for skilled labor beyond the readily available supply. ("The truth about unemployment," February 1977:97)

National Review argued that we must expect 7 million to be jobless—namely, the frictionally unemployed (people between jobs, new entrants into the labor force, and people on temporary layoffs). They could be planned away only at the expense of the free enterprise system ("Planned Unemployment," 1976:55–56). *Fortune* advocated the curtailment of minimum wages and the reduction of unemployment benefits as the best ways to cut joblessness ("What It Takes to Create Jobs," 1977:133).

Liberals, for their part, tried to deny a correlation between unemployment and inflation. "Jobs could fight inflation" insisted economist Peter Barnes in the fall 1975 issue of *Working Papers*.

The case he [Barnes] states is that full employment would not necessarily cause inflation, and that it might even promote price stability. This is based on the idea that, contrary to the Phillips-curve proposition, "prices no longer fluctuate in accordance with supply and demand" in the American economy. Instead, as evidenced recently with automobiles, falling demand leads to higher prices, as the volume of production diminishes and per-unit costs rise. In economic areas where major industries "administer" prices, they raise them to compensate for lower volume and higher costs.

In this thesis, unemployment does not fight the resulting price inflation. It feeds it, since it reduces demand thereby encouraging a further round of administered price increases to compensate for lowered volume. It follows that putting the unemployed to work would fight administered price inflation, because the newly employed workers would not only increase aggregate demand but add to the supply of goods and services and thus tend to promote price stability. (Wicker, 1975:E15)

Sar Levitan, chairman of the National Manpower Council, called for programs to dent structural unemployment (the type of unemployment that affects special pockets of the population regardless of fluctuations in the business cycle). Such programs, Levitan argued, would be anti-inflationary. People in productive jobs do not need transfer payments (unemployment compensation, welfare, food stamps), and aggregate spending is thereby reduced (Shabecoff, 1978b:E4).

Liberal policies appealed to narrow constituencies only. Even organized labor was ambivalent about proposed full employment legislation. Publically, of course, unions supported jobs programs, but they feared loss of turf to government agencies. Unions, knowing they lacked the power to prevent layoffs, pushed instead for cost-of-living increases and supplementary benefits. Government job programs did not head labor's list of priorities. Unions mirrored public concern about rising inflation. The AFL-CIO Executive Council recommended the use of economic stimuli—looser monetary policies, low cost housing loans, lower interest rates, and government aid to cities—so that public service jobs would be less inflationary (Goldfinger, 1975:24).

Radical economists Gabriel Kolko, Robert Lekachman, and others expected high unemployment in the seventies. They anticipated deliberate establishment inaction. Marxists assumed that full employment is not possible in capitalist systems where an underclass is needed to keep wage scales low. Kolko (1962:78) examined Bureau of Labor Statistics figures to show that unemployment rates were two to three times higher among the unskilled than among the skilled in *every* decade (40 percent unskilled compared with 15 percent skilled in 1940; 12 percent compared with 6 percent in 1950; 20 percent compared with 10 percent in 1961). To reduce unemployment, Kolko contended, "require[s] the sweeping sort of political decisions concerning the economy which no administration has proposed or practiced except during World War II" (p. 131). Lekachman (1975:86) listed several social requisites for the elimination of unemployment: (1) there must be quaranteed federal government employment; (2) income maintenance programs must be established for those unable to work; (3) the prices charged by large corporations must be controlled; (4) the fees of professionals must be regulated; (5) taxation must be redistributive; and (6) eventually public ownership of utilities and major industries must be achieved. Only as society moves toward socialism do radicals envision decreased unemployment without increased inflation.

Inflation remained a major concern throughout the decade. The Consumer Price Index increased steadily (7.8 percent in 1973, 13.5 percent in 1975, 11 percent in 1977) (U.S. Department of Commerce, 1977:313). No social stratum was immune from the effects of inflation. The issue of job security, however, faded faster from the rhetoric of politicians and the calculations of academics than from the minds of the public. Yankelovich found that when a national sample was presented with a list of 12 problem areas, 79 percent identified inflation and 67 percent chose unemployment as serious or very serious problems (Ladd, 1978:32). "What do you think is the most important problem facing the country today?" asked a February

1978 Gallup poll. In what are high frequency responses to nondirective questions, 33 percent said inflation and 17 percent mentioned unemployment.

Liberals, radicals, and conservatives shared one assumption—progressive automation brings unemployment. Amitai Etzioni (1978:18) expressed a common view when he wrote that society chooses between industrial progress coupled with unemployment, on the one hand, and lack of such progress, on the other. Many thought joblessness the price of computerization of industrial and business procedures.

> The fundamental question is whether this social system can deal with the problems of the post-industrial world. The corporate leaders are skeptical about the future. The managers, agents and bureacrats of this "establishment" shortsighted as they are, encounter a tragic alternative: either to deal constructively with the problem of enduring mass unemployment, or, as they are doing today, just letting things drift. . . . That's a question no one wants to face. But it won't disappear by itself. (Kramer and Friedman, 1975:363)

Liberals and radicals faced the figures and sought ameliorative measures. A conservative establishment minimized the problem and chose to hold an unyielding course. High unemployment continued as ideological differences framed numerical analysis as well as causal explanation.

What Official Statistics Show

> In 1975 the United States was reeling under the impact of the highest unemployment level since the Great Depression. In May, 1975, statistics show, 8.9 percent of the labor force was looking for work and could not find it. When the discouraged workers—people who want jobs but have given up looking—are included in the statistics, it means that close to 10 million Americans were out of work. Not since 1941 had so many Americans been unable to find useful jobs and adequate income.
>
> The official unemployment rate (which excludes the discouraged) fell to 7.8 percent in February 1976 and fears of a general "crash" like that of 1929 largely passed. But unemployment remains America's most important social and economic problem. (Levison, 1976:1)

National unemployment rates are released monthly, quarterly, and annually by the Department of Labor's Bureau of Labor Statistics (BLS). These figures are accepted as the official tabulations of unemployment in America. They are categorized by sex, race, and occupation, as Table 2–1 shows. These figures, whatever their shortcomings, disclose aggregate annual rate variations. Even more, they reveal something of the differential impact of joblessness throughout the population.

Aggregate unemployment rose from 3.5 percent of the labor force in 1969 to 4.9 percent in 1970. It increased to almost 6 percent by 1971 and

Table 2-1

National Unemployment Rates (Percentages)

	1959	1965	1968	1969	1970	1971	1972	1973	1974	1975	1976	1977	1978
U.S. Total*	5.5	4.5	3.6	3.5	4.9	5.9	5.6	4.9	5.6	8.5	7.7	7.0	6.0
Women	5.9	4.9	4.8	4.7	5.9	6.3	5.9	5.3	6.1	8.6	7.9	7.0	5.2
Men	5.3	4.2	2.9	2.8	4.4	4.9	4.5	3.7	4.3	7.2	6.4	5.2	3.7
Black (all nonwhite)	10.7	8.1	6.7	6.4	8.2	9.9	10.0	8.9	9.9	13.9	13.1	13.1	11.9
White	4.8	4.1	3.2	3.1	4.5	5.4	5.0	4.3	5.0	7.8	7.0	6.2	5.4
Blue-collar	7.6	5.3	4.1	3.9	6.2	7.4	6.5	5.3	6.7	11.7	9.4	8.0	6.8
White-collar	2.6	2.3	2.0	2.1	2.8	3.5	3.4	2.9	3.3	4.7	4.6	4.3	3.5
Professional and technical	1.7	1.5	1.2	1.3	2.0	2.9	2.4	2.2	2.3	3.2	3.2	3.0	2.6

Source: U.S. Department of Labor, Bureau of Labor Statistics (1976a: 1978a, b, d).
*Men and women listed in this table are 20 years of age and older.

fluctuated between 5 and 6 percent for the next three years. The Council of Economic Advisors reported to President Richard M. Nixon that 1973 was a "full employment" year: "We believe that condition was approximately met in 1973, even though the average unemployment rate was 4.9 percent rather than 4.0 percent which conventionally defines full employment" (Ginsburg, 1975:115). By the first half of 1974 energy crisis related layoffs began to affect the employment security of adult males (Flaim, 1974:3–5). *U.S. News and World Report* headlined "Unemployment Spreads and the Worst Is Yet to Come" (1974:47); 1974 was then called a recession year—the jobless rate was 5.6 percent. Unemployment increased among blue-collar and white-collar workers, and there were numerous plant closings.

Joblessness jumped to depression levels in 1975. The national unemployment rate was 9.2 percent of the work force (Dale, 1975c:1, 24). This figure accounted for only the 8,538,000 actively seeking employment within a given four-week period. At least 1 million more were too discouraged to continue the job hunt, according to BLS estimates. In 1975 at least 10 million Americans who wanted to work could not find jobs. The Travelers Aid Society reported 1.3 million pleas for help from unemployed of all social classes who were desperately moving around the country in search of work. These latter-day Okies did not move to California as had dust bowl farmers 40 years before them. They moved from the South to northern cities with high jobless rates. Some moved to coal fields. People moved wherever they thought a friend or relative might help with a job. Many of the migrants were middle-aged people who took their families and belongings and left in the night with their bills unpaid, according to National Accounts Systems, a Chicago based collection agency (" 'Okies' of the 70s," 1975:17).

Unemployment in 1976 remained at recession levels—7.5 percent in April, 7.9 percent in September, 8.1 percent in November. Joblessness among heads of households was 2.9 percent in December 1973; 6.1 percent in July 1975; 5 percent in March 1976 (Dale, 1976:1). This critical indicator was up to 5.4 percent in November 1976 ("Joblessness over 8% and Prices Are Going up Again," 1976:1). The number of people out of work 27 weeks or longer rose by 130,000 in June 1976 to 1.3 million. The average duration of joblessness was 17 weeks (Cowan, 1976b:1).

Unemployment rates began to fluctuate downward, approximating 7 percent in 1977. The number of new layoffs decreased from 1 million in 1976 to 750,000 in the first half of 1977, and the average duration of unemployment declined from 17 weeks to 15 weeks (St. Marie, 1977:4, 5). Long-term joblessness remained problematic: over 1 million were out of work for six months or more; 35 percent of the jobless household heads had been out of work 15 weeks or more (Raskin, 1976a:E4). The longer the spell of unemployment, the less likely the prospect for reemployment, according to Department of Labor studies conducted in 1969 and in 1975. These studies found also that half of the men and 70 percent of the women who had left the unemployment status after 27 weeks had still not found jobs. They were no longer counted as unemployed because they had stopped looking (Garfinkle, 1977: 55–56).

Unemployment rates declined to 6 percent in 1978, but experts saw the possibility of yet another recession before the end of the decade. The Department of Defense budget, considered by Melman and others to be a primary source of inflation, exceeded $110 billion. Brookings Institution economists Arthur Orkun and George Perry feared a restraint of economic growth. Inflation continued; unions demanded wage increases. Companies raised prices partly in response to increased labor costs. At the same time the Federal Reserve Board maintained a tight money policy. Thus the conditions that induce recession and new waves of unemployment were seemingly again established ("Recession," 1978:41). From Argus Research Corporation on Wall Street to Data Resources in Lexington, Massachusetts, there was a consensus among nongovernment economists that a 1979 recession could be expected (Farnsworth, 1978a:D1).

> The risks of recession have clearly been increased sharply by the runup of interest rates and the money crunch to which it may lead. At the same time, however, prices are still rising sharply. Food prices this year are estimated by the Government to be rising at a 10 percent rate. The turmoil in Iran, combined with signs of restiveness in the Organization of Petroleum Exporting Countries over prices, makes it seem all the more likely that oil prices will go up more sharply than for the last two years. . . .
>
> When money really tightens hard landings have always followed. (Silk, 1978:22)

The number of hardship cases not represented by official tabulations remained high. The Department of Labor tried to determine what happens to people when eligibility for unemployment compensation expires and found that 25 percent had found jobs four months after checks stopped, 36 percent by the end of the year, 25 percent stopped looking for work and 7 percent were on welfare rolls. Thirty-two percent of the long-term jobless were no longer counted among the unemployed. (Raskin, 1976a:E4)

Aggregate statistics are difficult to interpret. More is learned about the extent and meaning of unemployment in the seventies when we examine annual rate changes within BLS categories of occupation, race, and sex.

The occupational groups among which increased unemployment was first apparent in the early 1970s were ironically those thought to be the most employable in the nation—scientists, engineers, and data analysts. Technical professionals were regarded as heroes in a postindustrializing society. Their education and training had placed them in critical roles. They built sophisticated weapons systems, put men on the moon, and paved the way to the computerization of everything. Suddenly in the early seventies they filled unemployment lines and captured national attention.

A temporary downward fluctuation in federal spending for research and development and a two-thirds slash in the NASA budget from fiscal year 1967 to fiscal year 1971 accounted for the layoffs of an estimated 200,000 aerospace professionals (Muttur, 1971:1). In large part for this reason unemployment rates in the BLS professional and technical category increased from 1.3 percent in 1969 to 2.9 percent in 1971.

Regions rich in advanced systems laboratories were hit much harder than aggregate rates indicate. The Route 128 area around Boston was particularly affected. Fifty thousand scientists and engineers had worked in the Cambridge–Route 128 area of Massachusetts in 1970. Twenty percent of them, or 10,000, got laid off (Rice, 1970:29). These are the people whose careers and unemployment experiences constitute the data base for *Professionals Out of Work*. Analysis of how technical professionals have coped with employment insecurity, layoff, and its aftermath is singularly important because these people were first to encounter a newly recognized middle-class unemployment problem. I examined their lives at a time when they felt alone and in crisis.

The number of professionals out of work was small compared with the figure for blue-collar or other types of white-collar workers. But they heralded a trend. If the most necessary become superfluous, reverberations will be felt throughout the labor force. In 1975 unemployment in the BLS professional and technical category rose to 3 percent, a level maintained through the decade. Included was a growing number of unemployed Ph.D.'s: of all people who held doctorates in the physical, biological, and social sciences, 1.7 percent were unemployed and actively seeking employment in 1977; of all people who held doctorates in the humanities, 2.7 percent were unemployed and actively seeking employment in 1977 (U.S. National Research Council, 1978: 15,41). Nowhere is the waste of human resources better evidenced than when the most highly educated and specifically skilled cannot find work.

White-collar unemployment in general increased from 2 percent in 1968 to 5 percent in 1975. Accounts of the plight of the previously successful filled newspapers and periodicals.

Ten years ago, when Paul L. Jarvis was 27 and a rising auto-styling engineer, he never figured it could happen.

But there he was one day this week: a $19,000 a-year fashioner of automobile interiors with a wife, two children and a $40,000 house in this Detroit suburb, standing his full six-foot-two in the unemployment line with snow swirling about his hooded head. (Stevens, 1975:1)

A foundation hired Paul Ryan a year ago to run a five-year project to discourage consumption of alcoholic beverages and he went out and hired four other persons. But then the foundation ran short of funds, so six months ago it terminated the project, putting Mr. Ryan, who is 37, and his aides out of work. Mr. Ryan has been job hunting ever since. (Kilborn, 1975:1)

The *New York Times* described typical cases of middle-aged, middle-class unemployment. Harold Frankel, for instance, was a married household head, father of two; he was laid off in 1976. Frankel was forced to sell his securities and life insurance. All savings were depleted. He had to sell his Long Island home and move into a small apartment in New York City. Frankel sent out 400 resumes, without success.

> At the age of 55, Harold Frankel is suffering through his first period of extended unemployment. A veteran of 20 years in the toy industry, Mr Frankel worked up from salesman to product manager to marketing director. He had been earning $500 a week before he was forced to leave the My Toy Company last summer, and he expected to be employed again very shortly.
>
> "At the beginning, you think it will just be a couple of weeks," he said. "But with each month that goes by, you start dragging and you need more of a charge to go out and face the world."
>
> "I have too much pride to ask anyone else for money and I don't want to go on welfare," he commented. "So I have my ups and downs—ups when I go on interviews and downs when I call and call and never get an answer." (Sloane, 1976:40, 53)

The sight of well-dressed people in the compensation lineup raised national consciousness about unemployment in America—a problem neglected through years of much higher jobless rates among unskilled and semiskilled laborers.

Blue-collar workers in the 1970s, as before, were more severely affected by recessionary trends than were others. Rates for the "surplus army of the unemployed" averaged 2 percent higher than national figures; 3.9 percent in 1969; 6.2 percent in 1970; 11.7 percent in 1975; 8.1 percent in 1977. Automobile workers were laid off by the thousands. Return to so-called normal (5 percent) levels of joblessness was not predicted, especially as the trend toward smaller cars produced in automated plants continued (Rothschild, 1975:4). Official unemployment rates in Michigan metropolitan areas remained at 8.5 percent through 1978 (U.S. Department of Labor, BLS, 1978e). Plant closings in New England, Middle Atlantic, and Great Lakes states resulted in the loss of 1.4 million manufacturing jobs. Unemployment in Johnstown, Pennsylvania, for example, soared from 4.6 percent to 17 percent. Bethlehem Steel laid off 3,500. Older blue-collar workers posed a special problem: people with seniority in a company, little education, families to support, and mortgaged homes to pay off could not follow firms south to uncertain jobs. Dependence upon a support network of neighbors and friends insured their immobility. As a *Business Week* article noted in its title, they came to form "a new layer of structural unemployment" (1977:142). It was the judgment of Eli Ginsberg, chairman of the National Commission for Manpower Policy, that beyond age 45 "the chances of reemployment are minimal unless the worker's old job reopens" (Raskin, 1976a:E4).

Black workers consistently have sustained higher levels of unemploy-ment than any other labor force category. In any given year, recessionary or not, black joblessness is twice white joblessness; in 1959 unemployment was 10.7 percent among blacks compared to 4.8 percent among whites; in 1969 unemployment was 6.4 percent among blacks compared to 3.1 per-cent among whites; in 1972 unemployment was 10 percent among blacks compared to 5 percent among whites; in 1975 unemployment was 13.9 per-cent among blacks compared to 7.8 percent among whites. When national unemployment fell to 6 percent in 1978, "recovery" was reported. This did *not* mean blacks: joblessness among blacks decreased only *slightly* to 11.9 percent.

Racism and automation combined to keep black unemployment at dou-ble digits throughout the seventies. Blacks were not able to move directly from farms, factories, and domestic service to white-collar and professional jobs without special assistance. Historically, whites had more time and preparation to achieve such mobility. (Wilhelm, 1971:159–161).

As the gross national product soared from $502 billion in 1960 to $623 billion in 1964, approximately 10 percent of the Negroes, by official figures, remained out of work.

The Negro becomes a victim of neglect—as he becomes useless to an emerg-ing economy of automation. With the onset of automation the Negro moves out of his historical state of oppression into one of uselessness. Increasingly, he is not so much economically exploited as he is irrelevant. . . .

In short, White America, by a more perfect application of mechanization and a vigorous reliance upon automation, disposes of the Negro; consequently, the Negro transforms from an exploited labor force into an outcast. (Wilhelm, 1971:162)

The new technology informs the Negro of permanent, workless years even as the economy establishes new productive records and profits. The Negro's fate is no longer tied into an economy in high gear; displacement rather than unemployment spells the difference.(Wilhelm, 1971:166)

Unemployment among untrained black youths in urban ghettos re-mained at 40 percent throughout most of the seventies ("Young People without Jobs," 1977:56). Sar Levitan estimated youth unemployment at twice official figures because of the large number of kids who hang around street corners and are never counted (Raskin, 1976b:1). Token programs to employ black youths in the summer of 1978 brought the teenage black unemployment rate down to 37.1 percent (Shabecoff, 1978a:24). Only massive programs to educate and train young blacks and directly linked with jobs could alter Wilhelm's dire prognosis. But neither government nor business was committed to sweeping policy change. Indeed, the legality of affirmative action in education and occupation was questioned as whites leveled charges of reverse discrimination. The imposition of retroactive seniority, for instance, could help newly hired blacks hold their jobs, but this device was prohibited by appellate court decisions (Edwards, 1976:555).

Conservatives confounded statistics to deny the extent of black unemployment. *Fortune* noted that black unemployment increased to 14.5 percent in October 1977 but attributed this to optimism among blacks about their chances of finding work: blacks moved from the "discouraged" to the active work force and were then counted as "unemployed" ("Beginning of Wisdom about Black Unemployment," 1977:75). White workers, themselves victims of inflation and employment insecurity, saw blacks as threatening their educational and occupational opportunities and joined ranks against economic gains for minorities and women.

Each year, in every job category, more women than men are listed as jobless: in 1968 unemployment among women was 4.9 percent compared to 2.9 percent for men; in 1973 unemployment for women was 5.3 percent compared to 3.7 percent for men; in 1975 unemployment among women was 8.6 percent compared to 7.2 percent for men; in 1978 unemployment among women was 5.2 percent compared with 3.7 percent for men. Furthermore, Frank Furstenberg and Charles Thrall (1975:56) found that one-third of the women then listed as out of the work force wanted jobs: many were not seeking employment because they lacked the money to pay for childcare while they did so; others were discouraged. Studies showed, too, that men found new jobs more readily than did women who had been laid off. After an extended period of joblessness, 75 percent of the men but only 50 percent of the women between the ages of 25 and 59 secured reemployment (Garfinkle, 1977:54).

Sex discrimination in employment became more intense with economic recession and depression. Passage of the proposed Equal Rights Amendment to the Constitution seemed assured until the mid seventies recession. Opposition mounted as the job market tightened. At the same time participation of women in the labor force increased at the rate of 1 percent a year: 750,000 more women entered the job market than previously indicated by demographic trend data alone (Wildstrom, 1977:29). "Women wanting work" were frequently blamed for high unemployment rates. The Council of Economic Advisors cautioned that the discouraged category should not be allowed to inflate the interpretation of BLS unemployment statistics, since two-thirds of the discouraged were women (Furstenberg and Thrall, 1975:48). *Forbes* editoralized that the entry of women into the labor force made it *appear* that there was a continuing unemployment problem ("Is Unemployment on the Way Out?" 1978:221). There was even some controversy about the validity of an unemployment rate that included women.

> Some administrative officials are reconsidering the meaning of the unemployment rate. "This may sound like heresy, but if the unemployment figure includes

more and more people who were not looking for work a month earlier, it changes its meaning as an indicator of hardship," says Peter Henle, a deputy under secretary of Labor. "It is still a good measure of the utilization of human resource potential, but that cannot be equated with hardship." (Wildstrom, 1977:29)

The issue of equality notwithstanding, conservative opinion and economists' statistics failed to note that many women in the 1970s were forced to work. Sometimes husbands were unemployed. Frequently inflation necessitated a second breadwinner. Rising divorce increased the number of female headed households.

As we have seen, official figures underestimate the extent of continuing joblessness. In July 1978 the United Association of Journeymen and Apprentices of the Plumbing and Pipefitting Industry announced that 1,700 applications for apprenticeships would be distributed and that no more than 550 apprentices would be chosen. Lines formed days before applications were to be distributed.

Equipped with sleeping bags and tents, food and vitamin pills, transistor radios and chess boards, more than 1,000 prospective plumbers and electricians camped out for the weekend on sidewalks in Flushing, Queens and in Manhattan, waiting to receive apprenticeship applications that will be distributed early tomorrow morning.

Mr.Sugarman, a prelaw major at City College, also brought along a barbecue grill, and friends and relatives provided chicken, spareribs, turkey and ham.

"I figured my chances of having a future here are a lot better than in law school," he said. "You either have to be in the top 10 of your law class or go to Yale or Harvard to succeed."

Irene Brown, the mother of six children between the ages of 9 and 12 years, said that she had already done some small plumbing jobs at home, "because you've got to be able to fix things. . . and I really want to get off welfare." ("Hundreds Vie for Chance at 550 Apprenticeships," 1978:35)

Incidents such as this remind us how much people need to work at worthwhile jobs.

Undercounting Unemployment

"What's the use of looking for a job?" he asked. "It wastes my time, it wastes their time; it wastes gas. The best thing to do is to come to the park and drink away my problems."

As he spoke, Mr. Santos gently gripped a quart bottle of beer wrapped in a brown bag, and the face of his waiting 3-year old son glittered on the mirrored surfaces of his dark glasses.

Mr. Santos belongs to one of the fastest growing categories of workers in the nation: he is a dropout from the job market.

After hunting for a new job daily for more than a year, after he was laid off as a spray painter in April 1974, Mr. Santos has simply stopped looking. (Lindsey, 1975a:27)

Mr. Santos was not counted as unemployed by the Bureau of Labor Statistics because he was too discouraged to search for work. The discouraged constitute the most blatant category among the uncounted unemployed but there are others. Each month the BLS surveys 47,000 randomly selected adults. In order to become an official statistic, a person must be jobless at the time of the interview, say that he or she wants work now, and show proof of an active job search within the past 28 days. Not represented in government unemployment rates are people who want full-time jobs but are weary of the fruitless search, those who have been forced into part-time employment, the underemployed, the subemployed, those available for jobs but are unable to look, and people in federal manpower training programs. The total amounts to several million uncounted adults each month. *Actual* unemployment rates always break the double digit.

The number of discouraged workers reached 1.15 million in March 1975 (Dale, 1975b:1). It was still 1.1 million in the second quarter of 1977 (U.S. Department of Labor, BLS, 1977b). Disproportionately the discouraged included blacks (Shiskin and Stein, 1975:8), women (Furstenberg and Thrall, 1975:48), unskilled youths and older workers (Rosenblum, 1974:28–30), and highly skilled professionals (Lindsey, 1975b:27). In 1975 3.8 million people wanted full-time jobs but had to settle for part-time employment. There were 3.4 million such people in 1976 (Klein, 1976:10). In the same year 6 percent of the "employed" labor force worked less than 15 hours a week; 798,000 less than five hours a week (U.S. Department of Labor, BLS, 1977a). Nearly 3 million between the ages of 30 and 44 who wanted work were listed as "not in the labor force" (Furstenberg and Thrall, 1975:56). The jobless rate was deflated still further, another .4 to .6 percent, because people involved in training programs were no longer counted among the unemployed even though no promise of work existed (Spring, 1972:190).

Unemployment in the broadest sense means the inability to earn a life sustaining wage. If, in a calculation of unemployment, people who work full-time but earn poverty level wages or less are included, joblessness reaches astounding proportions. In 1967 Secretary of Labor Willard Wirtz authorized such a survey. The computed index of *subemployment* was based on the following factors: "Those working full time, but earning at the poverty level or below, those working only part time but seeking full time work, and those of working age who dropped out of the labor force through discouragement" (Spring, 1972:188). In the urban ghettos subemployment rates were many times official unemployment rates. Subemployment in the Roxbury section of Boston was 24.2 percent; unemployment was 6.5 percent. Subemployment in the east Harlem section of New York City was 33.1 percent; unemployment was 8.3 percent.

Subemployment in north Philadelphia was 34.2 percent; unemployment was 9.1 percent. Subemployment on the north side of St.Louis was 38.8 percent; unemployment was 12.5 percent. Subemployment in the slums of New Orleans was 45.3 percent; unemployment was 9.5 percent (Spring, 1972:189). Rates this high are difficult for public officials to explain. The Department of Labor never repeated the subemployment survey.

The AFL-CIO and the National Urban League calculated what they called a "true-rate" of unemployment. These groups added to official numbers all of the discouraged and half of those with part-time jobs but desiring full-time employment. The true rate was 11.6 percent of the labor force in 1975 (Shanahan, 1975:25), compared with 8.5 percent listed by the BLS. If the true rate is supplemented by some of the available unemployed and a fraction of the subemployed, unemployement rates exceeded 20 percent of the potential labor force during most of the 1970s.

Susan Gore has pointed to the importance of using longitudinal data rather than monthly reports of net change in order to assess more accurately the impact of employment on work and life experience. The Current Population Survey follows a sample of households over a 16-month period: "In 1976, for example, 19.1% of all persons in the labor force experienced some unemployment, a figure about two and one half times the monthly rates of unemployment with which we are more familiar" (Gore, 1978:7). Those few studies that examined unemployment in particular locales or among special occupational groups all found joblessness to be much higher than indicated by official figures.

John Leggett, Jerry Gioglio (1977) and some of their young colleagues at Rutgers University undertook an unemployment survey in the industrial city of New Brunswick, New Jersey. They selected a random sample in each of the six political wards, collecting information about age, education, sex, race, occupation, and employment status from each respondent. Included in their tabulations of the jobless were the discouraged and unemployed single women with children. Married housewives, students, and the permanently disabled, even when actively seeking work, were excluded from jobless tallies, though the BLS includes these groups. The Rutgers researchers found an unemployment rate of 43 percent in the winter of 1975–1976. Only 14 percent of the unemployment was frictional (28 days or less) whereas 67 percent lasted 13 weeks or more. Blacks were overrepresented among the New Brunswick jobless but rates among whites were also very high. White unemployment was 19 percent; 61 percent of which were cases of long-term joblessness. And 22 percent of the male, white, white-collar workers in the sample were among the unemployed. The authors concluded:

Of the 310 adults in our sample, only 130 were employed full-time throughout 1975. Fascinating. Especially when we realize, as indicated earlier, that the official, monthly unemployment rate for New Brunswick-Perth Amboy-Sayerville hovered between 9 and 10 percent. Look at the figures another way. Almost three-fifths of the adult population was without a full-time job. Meanwhile, less than ten percent of the official New Brunswick labor force was counted as unemployed by the B.L.S. Think about it. Our tax money is paying for the compilation and distribution of a highly incomplete portrait.

Incomplete and blatantly inaccurate. . . . The B.L.S., a sacrosanct arm of an omniscient federal government, claims that its mission is to "measure precisely and objectively the extent of unemployment in the United States." Our data, and an ever-increasing flood of information from independent researchers throughout the nation, demonstrate that the B.L.S. has failed to accomplish its mission; and, in so doing has duped the American public into believing that the unemployment scene is not all that bad. (Leggett and Gioglio, 1977:11)

My own research among technical professionals in the greater Boston area showed that unemployment was much higher than statistics revealed. National Science Foundation (NSF) estimates are the most widely quoted federal government figures for professionals. The NSF (1971c:3) reported 3.5 percent of all scientists and 4.5 percent of all engineers (1971b:3) in the Boston area out of work in the summer of 1971. According to my findings unemployment was 21 percent at that time. I spoke with 279 randomly selected technical professionals classified as scientists, engineers, or data systems analysts in the occupational census of their residential communities; 59 of them (or 21 percent) were unemployed for varying lengths of time during the 1970–1972 period.

These findings were verified by Paul H. Thompson in a Harvard Business School study for the Department of Labor. Thompson estimated a 1971 technical professional unemployment rate of well over 20 percent. Out of 1,603 engineers employed in three large Route 128 electronics firms prior to the 1970 cutbacks, 387 (or 26 percent) were laid off in 1971 (Thompson, 1972:II–2). In 1972 the U.S. Department of Labor's *Manpower Report of the President* quoted unemployment rates of 3.5 percent for scientists and 6.6 percent for engineers. The Boston area was mentioned as a more serious pocket of technological joblessness, but no specifics were given. The Department of Labor did not disclose the results of the Harvard Business School study, conducted under its auspices for use in the *Manpower Report of the President.*

The difference between official unemployment rates and percentages holding full-time jobs is considerable, even for those with doctorates. In 1977, 1.3 percent of the Ph.D. physicists were listed as unemployed, but only 87.7 percent were employed full-time; 1.6 percent of the chemists were listed as unemployed, but only 85.6 percent were employed full-time; 1.1 percent of the biologists were listed as unemployed, but only 82.9 percent were employed full-time (National Research Council, 1978:31). Among art historians 3.7 percent were listed as unemployed, but only 81.8 percent were employed full-time. Among philosophers 4.3 percent were listed as unemployed, but only 83 percent were employed full-time. Among social scientists 1.3 percent were listed as unemployed, but only 88.1 percent were employed full-time (p. 41). Full employment is a double digit problem for the nation's doctorates in every field, as well as for blacks and women, factory operatives, and office workers.

Clearly a significant discrepancy exists between what official statistics show and the pervasiveness of unemployment. One sociological explanation for this holds that a "job rationing ideology" about who has the *right* to a job in a tight labor market is widely shared (Furstenberg and Thrall, 1975:46–48). Married women with children, students, older people on social security, and the handicapped on pensions answer Current Population Surveys so as to be discounted and allow male heads of household first crack at available jobs. Differences between rates and reality, whatever the cause, are masked by those with vested interests in order and apathy. One result has been that few sociologists have tackled unemployment as the subject for inquiry and analysis.

3

Sociology of Unemployment

An Understudied Area

> Recession and rampant inflation have been the central domestic issues in our society since 1973, and given their persistence, it is important for policy makers to know how damaging these dire economic events have been to the social fabric of society.
>
> The previous calamity in the American economy, the Great Depression of the thirties, inspired a broad range of social research on the effects of the depression on society. The disastrous state of the economy in the mid-seventies, however, has failed to stimulate comparable interest in research. (Caplovitz, 1978:52)

Joblessness, a social problem of sociological significance, was ignored by a burgeoning field itself part of post–World War II prosperity. The 1970s recession-depression stimulated research—however scant compared with the sociology of unemployment begun in the Great Depression. The fruits of a careful literature review are fragmented articles and narrowly focused dissertations. Alfred Slote's (1969) *Termination* and M. Harvey Brenner's (1973) *Mental Illness and the Economy* are the two touted exceptions. Primary interest was with the psychological and physiological effects of job loss. A few studied the broader effects of plant closings, a few dealt with the hard-core unemployed, and a few others focused on unemployed aerospace professionals. Government sponsored research revealed a quantitative orientation, manifest in tallies of months out of work, calculations of financial loss, and enumeration of reemployment earnings. Cumulatively, findings are sometimes potentially important, but they lack societal elaboration.

Individual and Pathological Emphasis

Donald Tiffany and his co-workers (Tiffany, Cowan, and Tiffany, 1970:74) were concerned with psychological predispositions among the unemployed and with the relationship between self-direction and reemployment. They found that rehabilitation programs were unnecessary for people who had the capacity for self-directed behavior. Ralph Click (1973:2923) compared an unemployed sample with a bereaved group and found that "the unemployed were the least happy, least satisfied, had the lowest positive feeling scores, took significantly longer to begin the recovery process and fewer ever came to accept the change." In a poignant nonfictional tale, Thomas Cottle traced the destructive influences of a working-class father's joblessness through to his son's delinquencies. Prolonged unemployment ravaged the psyche of a steady family man. Fear, anger, and frustration drove him from wife and children; his son lit fires and stole money.

> At the sentencing, the judge apologized to Mrs. Harrington for the way the boy had been detained. Eddie stood motionless, looking tough, but beaten. When the judge asked him whether his father was in the courtroom Eddie shook his head. The judge then asked, "Is your father alive?"
>
> The boy thought for a conspicuously long time. Finally he looked down and mumbled, "I don't know. But if he is, he wouldn't be here. He'd be out looking for a job!" (Cottle, 1978:15)

Braginsky and Braginsky (1975:69-70) conducted 46 interviews with men who answered their advertisement in a metropolitan daily. They identified some psychological consequences of unemployment: confusion, disillusionment, and feelings of betrayal. Studies such as these disclose a profound psychological dimension to the sufferings of the jobless. They encourage empathy but provide little enlightenment. These articles do not identify patterns of reaction, adjustment, or recovery.

Psychological factors attracted the attention of sociologists studying unemployment among professionals. Richard Estes (1974:4403-4404) looked at the psychological and political effects of middle-class joblessness and found evidence of stress, self-blame, and passivity. Craig Little (1973:429) found high levels of emotional stress, self-blame, and depression—all related to career goal blockage but unrelated to the length of time without work. Douglass Powell and Paul Driscoll (1973:19–23) listed several stages of adjustment to unemployment: (1) relaxation and relief, (2) concerted effort, (3) vacillation and doubt, (4) malaise and cynicism. Powell and Driscoll conducted open-ended interviews with men who came to an experimental Professional Service Center. Their nonrandom data are glib and seem superficial. In a tight job market "relaxation and relief" do not usually accompany notice of termination. Richard Cobbs associated such behavior, in the few cases in which it occurred among factory workers, with the unsuccessful attempt to construct mechanisms of denial (Slote, 1969:327). Powell and Driscoll claimed to describe *the* stages through which unemployed professionals pass as they cope with prolonged joblessness, but there are probably several patterns of adjustment reflecting structural as well as psychological variables.

Other research has concentrated on individualized (psychological, physiological, or pathological) effects of job loss. It was found that unemployment increased the incidence of physical as well as mental illness. Susan Gore (1974:5330) checked health records of 100 men in their forties through a plant closing process. Blood and urine specimens were taken before the plant closed, 6 months, 12 months, and 24 months afterwards. Respondents also kept health diaries. Gore found clear relationships between length of unemployment, number of health complaints, and psychological depression.

Studies of the hard-core unemployed showed that these people were favorably motivated toward work. Roy Kaplan and Curt Tausky (1972), for instance, interviewed 275 chronically unemployed from a large New England city and found that their commitment to work was as strong as that among blue-collar and white-collar workers. "If by some chance you had enough money to live comfortably without working, do you think you would work anyway or would you not work?" Sixteen percent of the hard-core unemployed, compared with 18 percent of the blue-collar workers and 11 percent of the white-collar workers, said they would not work. Eighty-four percent of the hard-core unemployed, compared with 82 percent of the blue-collar workers and 89 percent of the white-collar workers said they would work anyway (p. 479). On the issue of training programs, it was argued that such programs are needed to join motivation and employability. One study found that successful training programs had to consider the depths of "ecosystem distrust" especially among hardcore unemployed blacks (Triandis, Feldman, Weldon, and Harvey, 1975:51–55).

Pathological correlates of unemployment interested a few social problems researchers. John Helmer and Thomas Vietorisz (1974) related increased drug use to labor market failure. Merton Hyman and Alice Herlice (1972:148–159) found that arrests for drunken driving increased with the percentage of unemployed in the work force. These studies implied that labor force trends cause increased rates of drug addiction and alcoholism. They stress pathologies rather than social conditions.

Two Exceptions

Only two unemployment studies were regarded as "important" by the sociological establishment. In different ways both Slote and Brenner related illness to job loss. Slote interviewed workers subsequent to a factory closing. The story of the shutdown was told through brief biographic sketches. Case histories incorporated employment, unemployment, and reemployment experiences with medical complaints. Among the 54 men in the original study group

> the Baker plant closing and its aftermath precipitated 3 cases of ulcers, 8 cases of arthritis, 5 cases of hypertension that required hospitalization, 2 cases of labile (fluctuating) high blood pressure, 6 cases of depression severe enough to require medical help, 1 case of alcoholism, and 3 industrial accidents suffered by men in new jobs they disliked. In addition there were 2 cases of alopecia (loss of hair). (Slote, 1969:322)

Perhaps the best sociological generalization from this research was made by physician Sidney Cobb in the foreword.

> The unemployed role is one that is looked on with such disfavor in our society, it isn't surprising that some people prefer to move into the sick role and accept the identity "sick" in preference to the identity "unemployed." (Slote, 1969:xviii)

Brenner (1973:ix) analyzed relationships between unemployment and stress related illnesses. He found significant correlations between the employment index and admissions to mental hospitals in New York state. The Congressional Research Service of the Library of Congress commissioned a subsequent Brenner study for the Joint Economic Committee of the House and Senate. This was a study of the effects of increased unemployment from 1970–1975 on the death rate. Brenner found "that at least 26,000 deaths from the stress-related diseases of stroke, kidney and heart ailments, at least 1,500 of the suicides and 1,700 of the homicides during that 5 year period were related to unemployment" (Hicks, 1976:1).

Brenner's data were limited to aggregate rate correlations. With "hard" numbers Brenner "proved" that joblessness adversely affects health. Sometimes his findings are suggestive.

> Since middle-aged groups earn the highest incomes, they have the most to lose as a result of unemployment.
>   The economic loss model suggests then that for both sexes the middle-aged groups ought to show the highest inverse correlations between the economic indicator and their mental hospitalizations.

The data of the present study strongly support this prediction. For both sexes the age-differential magnitudes of the correlation between mental hospitalization and the economic indicator jointly resemble a nearly perfect hyperbola. (Brenner, 1973:160)

Brenner's economic loss model implies that unemployment is more painful for middle-class people than for the poor. The pain revealed in each interview conducted for *Professionals Out of Work* shows Brenner correct about this group. But Slote and Cobb documented the incidence of pain among the blue-collar unemployed. It might also be true that years of marginal living produce forms of even deeper injury. Comparative data are needed for a definitive answer to this question. We do know that sociological analysis should be more than statistical description, as E. Wright Bakke understood so well. Brenner's work might convince legislators that unemployment costs more in benefits paid than its maintenance is worth to the economy, but it fails to explain how unemployment is experienced or to trace its institutional ramifications.

Sociological Dimensions

Although it remains important to study the effects of unemployment on self, psyche, and family, profound life crises provide the opportunity to do more than describe symptoms of distress. Sociologists should identify characteristic types of reaction to prolonged crisis and attempt to sequence the stages through which people pass as they adjust to altered life circumstances. As Louis Ferman (1964:511) reminded us, the emotional component of unemployment varies with historical context. To be unemployed may be worse in the seventies than it was in the thirties, as I suggested previously. Physical survival is not as much in question now but workers in the Great Depression thought that steady employment would return whereas those displaced by technology in the sixties and seventies had no such expectations. To live in hopelessness affects mental and physical health in still uncharted ways.

Unemployment is a family matter as well as a problem for individuals, as the literature suggests. Slote and Cobbs found that wives sometimes suffered greater physical and mental distress than did jobless husbands (Slote, 1969:322). We saw how the father's unemployment affected family functioning in the thirties: authority relationships changed; conflicts erupted; families adjusted or they split. Four decades later, the family was less cohesive, and the impact of unemployment on intimate relationships must be studied anew. High divorce rates, eased codes of premarital and extramarital sex, and women's growing demand for full equality have caused new concerns about the values of hearth and home. The strength of family ties, changing family functions, and the meaning of terms such as "love" and "affection" are never better tested than when male breadwinners are out of work. Unemployment, as few other experiences or events, bares the functioning of the basic institution.

Sociologists since the thirties Depression have chosen not to recognize the effects of unemployment on dimensions of the social order beyond the individual and the family. Official denial, academic as well as governmental, shrouds the subject of joblessness. There is no coherent body of work after the 1930s to stimulate research. Apart from federal government publications, which underestimate the problem, psychology and counseling journals have more to offer on this subject than do sociological periodicals. Yet the study of unemployment is as fertile a field of sociological inquiry as the problem itself is substantively important. The study of 1970s unemployment has much to tell us about (1) role termination and cultural values, (2) role formation and social supports, (3) worker satisfaction-dissatisfaction, (4) the parameters of class and status behavior, (5) downward mobility, and (6) the absence of meaningful political responses.

Occupational role termination has an impact on employers as well as on the workers they fire. Both groups affirm prevalent values in different ways in the need to justify events. Employers emphasize universalistic goals such as profit maximization. Workers stress particularistic norms of fairness and loyalty. When relationships as basic as work roles are severed, cultural values are exposed.

Sociology understands little about how people make new social connections. The job search vividly illustrates roles in the process of formation. Individuals must present themselves anew, time and again, to indifferent audiences. Threatening encounters always disclose vulnerabilities of participants, as individuals and as members of groups. A quasi-personal system, the grapevine, works best for professionals. Networks of contacts—the friend of a friend—are most helpful (Grannovetter, 1974:51–62). Blue-collar workers have fewer resources; they take either personal or entirely impersonal routes. Many wait for recall from former employers or try to get help from government bureaucracies. The job search reveals the strengths and weaknesses of both formal and informal support systems as people try to link up with new social contexts.

Work increasingly does not bring on-the-job satisfaction. Harry Braverman (1974) suggested why this is happening: management needs tighter controls as efficiency and profit goals dehumanize and automation marches on. Chances for satisfaction decrease even further when jobs become scarce. Ivar Berg (1970) and James O'Toole (1975:26–33) predicted that educational inflation of the labor market will increase work alienation at each level because overtrained peole are bored with preorganized tasks. Despite monotony and strict regimentation there is evidence that people fight to make sense out of work tasks. Barbara Garson (1977) described how workers in various blue-collar contexts play with the system in order to create for themselves in tiny ways a sense of personal accomplishment.

Dissatisfaction does not alter the importance of having a meaningful occupation. "Without work you are nothing" is a common refrain on the assembly line, in the office, and in the research laboratory. The realities of a shrinking opportunity structure enhance the value of any kind of job. Layoff reveals the depth of felt alienation. The data I later present show that feelings of on-the-job dissatisfaction were substantial before layoff, exaggerated during the unemployment period, and minimized with reemployment in the same kind of job. Unemployment studies are an integral part of understanding the shifting matrix of work satisfaction, dissatisfaction, and the labor market opportunity structure.

Unemployment, perhaps more clearly than any other social condition, discloses each rung in the stratification hierarchy, along both class and status dimensions. When paychecks stop and when unemployment compensation expires, people are pushed to the wall. Strategies for economic survival depend largely on remaining resources. How long a family can hold out before applying for welfare, for instance, is as good an indicator as any of "class" position per se. Middle-class families frequently manage longer than they originally thought they could. Some have savings and securities to fall back on, insurance policies to cash in, homes to re-mortgage, and educated spouses who can find jobs. Working classes sometimes have supplementary union benefits for a time. The poor have no cushion at all, although they may have informal support systems in neighbors and family, which help them rationalize their plight and teach them survival—exchange of food staples, food stamp information, tips about the welfare system. The poor lose little status among friends and relatives when unpredictable, alien forces impose termination from routine factory employment. Middle classes, on the other hand, must keep up appearances to maintain friendships or "status" associations. People with possessions sell them if they must: which things go first and which are retained indicates the salience of status, reference groups, and class linked values in general.

Widespread unemployment provides a special opportunity to study downward mobility, a subject almost absent from the sociological literature in an achievement oriented society. We know little about adaptation patterns, attitudes, and behavioral changes of people who are forced down the social scale. A critical related dimension is the degree to which people are conscious of class, which workers from which strata are likely to identify with comrades in difficulty. The absence of class consciousness is as telling as its presence.

Sociologists understand little about the political consequences of unemployment. Attitudes toward political and economic establishments are less than clear. Right-wing and left-wing extremist political movements appear to gain strength in times of depression. Unemployed Germans disproportionately followed Adolf Hitler: "jobs" was one of the major planks in Hitler's program. Depression studies in the United States and elsewhere, however, documented political apathy in the 1930s. What there was of working-class radicalism in the United States was destroyed by 1950s McCarthyism and the Cold War. There is evidence that class resentments are strong but without respectable channels for political expression resentment turns to disillusionment. There is further evidence, however, that other factors must be taken into consideration. The most militant protests of the 1960s were among black Americans who wanted social and economic equality. Ferman (1964:13–14) found it significant that this movement sprang from the group with the highest unemployment rates. It may also be significant that in 1978, a year in which liberalism seemed silenced on the political scene, organizations demanding jobs emerged.

> The poor people's organizing campaigns of the 1960s are being revived this summer in Boston and four other cities across the country, pitting welfare recipients, Comprehensive Training Act (CETA) workers, jobless youths and unemployed adults against government bureaucracies. (Kenny, 1978:1)

It could be that the sociological key to the meaning of future political protest (or the lack of it) is the sociologist's willingness and ability to deal with social and personal reactions to joblessness among the full spectrum of unemployed Americans.

Middle-class Unemployment

> In one life span, Americans had moved from scarcity to abundance, from sacrifice to the freedom made possible by prosperity. (Elder, 1974:296)

> I am male, white, 46. I have undergraduate and graduate degrees from two reasonably well-known Eastern institutions. My first job lasted for 4 years, my second for 10, my third for 7. I have a wife, three daughters, a mortgaged home and a 1972 "Beetle" for which I paid cash.
> Whereas I once earned over $400 a week, New York State now provides me with $95 a week in unemployment benefits. I am smoking almost two packs a day. I try not to drink before 5 o'clock. ("Fired at 46," 1977:33)

Factory workers and their families preoccupied sociologists who studied unemployment in the thirties. It was because they filled roles then critical to industrialization that analysis of their reactions to unemployment proved especially revealing of the changing character of society—the meaning of work, family dynamics, psychological tensions, cultural values, community ties, political behavior. In contrast, an important point of departure for the study of seventies unemployment is the experience of middle-class knowledge workers, especially those who fill the pivotal roles in highly technical society. The middle and upper middle classes together constituted 44.2 percent of the 1976 population. (Family income averaged $15,000 to $25,000 for 30.2 percent of the population; it averaged $25,000 to $49,999 for another 14.0 percent [U.S. Department of Commerce, Bureau of the Census, 1976:7–9].) Many of these people were the children of the Depression who had, by the fifties and sixties, become salaried professionals in the bureaucratic hierarchies of postindustrializing society.

Analysis of the experiences of the technical professionals who were victims of 1970 cutbacks in defense and aerospace contracts discloses and highlights the following structural shifts and resulting alterations in life situations: (1) the changing characteristics of technically based society, (2) the satisfactions and dissatisfactions of bureaucratic careers, (3) the relatedness of career to psychological stability, (4) the nature of family relationships in this "new middle class," (5) the quality of personal commitments and values, (6) the importance of the status quest in suburban communities, (7) the degree of felt relatedness to economic and political sources of power, and (8) the quality of their hopes, dreams, and expectations.

Scientists and engineers were the first among the knowledge workers to experience directly the effects of the irrationalities of a lack of overall societal planning for the utilization of trained manpower. Military spending was subsequently increased—to $90 billion by 1975, to $115 billion by 1976, to $130 billion by 1979—but this was not enough to stem a recessionary tide. It was impossible to keep overinflating the defense balloon without adversely affecting the rest of the economy. The overexpansion of the national educational apparatus, largely at federal expense, created an educated population that the labor market could not absorb. And, as we have seen, by the mid-seventies, employment insecurity had hit almost all types of professionals.

A Professional Service Center was established in the greater Boston area in 1971, supported by federal and state funds. Ninety percent of those seeking help from the center in the early seventies were technical professionals. By the mid-seventies, 30 percent were scientists, engineers, or data systems analysts; another 30 percent were teachers and academics; the remaining 40 percent included counselors, social workers, psychologists, sociologists, architects, urban planners, librarians, corporate executives and managers, pharmacists, interior decorators, accountants, financial analysts, commercial artists, illustrators, and photographers. New college graduates, people over 50 years of age, and men and women in their middle years with growing family expenses were sullenly, silently scanning computer printouts while waiting for interviews with Department of Employment Security personnel. Most appeared dazed, barely able to focus on what meager advice was offered. Even the better law schools had difficulty placing their graduates.

Official unemployment rates for middle-class occupations stood at less than 5 percent. Reality was harsher. Longitudinal data showed that 21 percent of middle-class families suffered the unemployment of at least one major breadwinner in 1978. These figures were reported in a national random sample *New York Times*–CBS poll (Roberts, 1978:1, 10).

To some extent, middle-class unemployment and downward mobility have always been part of the American scene. There were many unemployed professionals in the thirties, and numerous businessmen were forced into poverty. But studies made scant reference to their plight. Depression sociologists sometimes mentioned differences between the responses of the few professionals they talked with and the majority of unemployed laborers. Bakke (1940a:47, 71, 138; 1940b:232, 236, 264) found that professionals showed much greater "foresight," the ability to plan for the future, than did industrial workers. If they had savings, for example, they could forestall economic catastrophe for a time, whereas industrial workers could not. But the failure of foresight to help professionals find reemployment had devastating psychological effects not experienced by other workers. Families that had become accustomed to middle-class living went through longer periods of crisis before readjustments occurred. Professionals whose skills had been a meaningful part of their self-conception had more difficulty finding reemployment than did laborers. They resisted, as long as they could, the degradation involved in accepting the kind of temporary, unskilled work that was available. But findings such as these were obscured by the dramatic presence of masses of hungry workers.

Sociologists probed the experiences of the unemployed in the 1930s but they were not equally interested in the process of downward mobility. The agony suffered by people forced out of the middle and upper classes by a Depression economy was compelling, however, even then. In the decades of economic expansion that followed, it was the glorious path of upward mobility that attracted the attention of researchers. People who were not as well situated as their parents, and there were many, were largely ignored. By the seventies, economic belt tightening, once again, brought insecurity to middle-class professionals, who constituted a much larger group than they had in the thirties. And prospects for their college educated children look bleak. If expectations of upward mobility based on education and a successful career can no longer be sustained, the seventies may have witnessed the closing of a last American frontier. Middle-class unemployment and downward mobility are problems, new only in their extensiveness, that can no longer easily be dismissed. An achievement oriented society must come to terms with the anguish of people who play the game by the cultural rules only to find themselves dislodged in their prime.

There were no easy answers to the complex problems of the seventies. The dominant munitions industry, supported by taxpayer dollars, sold the products of American ingenuity, such as microelectronic devices or nuclear missiles with multiple-strike capacity, to any nation willing to buy, especially if the price was met in petrodollars. The public relations industry, developed along with technological advancements in the fifties and sixties, used the mass media to create false needs, supplied sublimated satisfactions, and projected the imagery necessary for public support of the post industrializing society. But the PR apparatus of the Pentagon had an increasingly difficult time selling the Vietnam war to the public as the years passed and no one could see the "light at the end of the tunnel." The war culminated, after 10 years, with what little honor imagery could muster. But its ending brought inflation, increased unemployment, and deepened disillusionment with government. Among political liberals cognizant of the wasteful overexpansion of the sixties, opposition to foreign involvement and expansion of the defense industries increased. But liberals were ill prepared either to counter the power of multinational corporations and the vested interests of the various military-industrial complexes or even to convince the unemployed that economic stability is possible.

Clear differences distinguished the economic recession-depression of the seventies from the Great Depression. Fewer people in the seventies were jobless. Many of those who were unemployed were protected from severe economic deprivation by weekly checks. Lines for compensation checks replaced the bread lines of the earlier depression. Yet unemployment in the seventies brought suffering, demoralization, and despair, just as it had four decades earlier. Moreover, the seventies lacked the aura of hope that prevailed throughout the darkest days of the thirties. Large administrative structures created to service human needs mushroomed in every institutional area, but people had difficulty fighting their way through layers of inane bureaucracy.

The pivotal role of workers in the functioning of the industrial system in the thirties gradually was taken over by technical experts and computer programmers. And by the seventies, many knowledge workers had themselves become superfluous. The powerlessness felt by individuals took on new dimensions. Once idealized American virtues were considered "supercamp." Urban and suburban lifestyles became dominant role models. Increasingly, socialization occurred through imagery projections of the mass media—from the "city slicker" to the "jet set" to the "radical chic" to the "hipswinger" on the make and on the move. Preoccupation with the pursuit of these elusive and ephemeral images uproots people from social anchorages on which power is based. Problems were not viewed in terms of people but in terms of statistical regression coefficients. The economic recession of the 1970s was a crisis for postindustrializing society, in much the same way as the Depression of the 1930s was a crisis for industrializ-

ing society. Unemployment—this time among middle-class professionals—became a prism through which to examine the problems and prospects of contemporary life. Now let us look at a specific sample of such a
group.

Unemployed Technical Professionals: A Case Study

> My first visit to the Lincoln Job Opportunities Group was on a cold night in the
> winter of 1971. I drove up a long private road to an elegant house on the top of a
> hill. It was the home of a retired company executive who, together with a local
> minister, organized the group to help their neighbors. A dignified elderly lady
> greeted me. She invited me to return in the spring so that I might see their lovely
> view. I was escorted to a velvet sofa before a marble fireplace. Freshly brewed
> English tea was served in delicate Bavarian china. I asked myself if this was an
> atmosphere where people could discuss unemployment. My notes for that even
> ing showed that only 3 of the 16 present mentioned their personal circumstances.
> Instead, they detailed problems and policies of various firms as though they
> were corporate executives in decision-making positions. (Leventman, 1971)

> The problem of the sociologist in this situation is to develop knowledge of the
> insiders, to learn to understand them—their structure, their philosophy, their
> problems, and their personalities—well enough to become acceptable to them as
> companion and as confidante and recipient of confidential knowledge, while
> also maintaining in its full strength and integrity the point of view and profes
> sional identity which led to his being asked to do the research in the first place.
> This means, of course, keeping clear to himself and to these others at all times
> his role and the essential nature of the bargain between him and them. If the
> relationship does not get so close that one is tempted to break the bargain, to
> step out of the role, it is probably not a success. The problems of the social role
> and the research bargain of the industrial and other special sociologists are subtle
> and difficult. (Hughes, 1971b:528)

From among the millions of jobless in the 1970s, middle-class professionals were the focus of my investigation. In particular, I placed singular
emphasis upon the consequences of unemployment for technical professionals. Because they are prototypical knowledge workers in a postindustrializing society, their demoralization serves as a benchmark against
which to gauge the experiences of other jobless workers later in the decade.
In my research I applied techniques from unemployment studies of the
1930s to the urban-suburban Route 128 region in the greater Boston area, a
relatively enclosed, cosmopolitan geographical setting that contains a wide
variety of high technology firms surrounded by a number of upper middle-
class bedroom communities.

When in early 1971 large numbers of resident scientists and technologists found themselves jobless, self-help groups began to emerge. My research began with eight months of participant-observation in three of these groups.

On January 11, 1971, an unemployed engineer and his Unitarian minister called a public meeting of the middle-class unemployed at their church in Needham for the purpose of "telling their story" and trying to figure out ways of helping themselves. They formed the Economic Action Group (EAG). I telephoned the organizer, explained that I was a sociologist, and requested entry. He was excited by my interest and solicited my participation and active assistance. We met on Monday evenings for a year and a half thereafter. On February 3, 1971, a group of seven employed as well as unemployed scientists and engineers called a large public meeting (about 200) at the Lexington town hall. Representatives of business, government agencies, and self-help groups (a few others had spontaneously emerged), as well as politicians, were each given five minutes to analyze the problem from their own perspective. Discussion around the fringes after the meeting made it clear that a significant organization was in the process of formation. Since I wanted to attend planning sessions, I called the president of the local chapter of the Institute of Electrical and Electronics Engineers, who appeared to be the principal organizer. "You can come," he said in effect, "but don't expect just to sit around and study us. We want your help." Easy access in exchange for active participation was the nature of the research bargain (Hughes, 1971b:524–529) I made with what soon became the Association of Technical Professionals (ATP).

Each night I attended formal or informal meetings. I maintained daily contact with the organizers and activists of EAG and ATP, many of whom continued to function as key informants during the subsequent four years of my study. We worked together, during those early days, in many ways—trying to make food stamps available for unemployed professionals, encouraging local banks temporarily to postpone mortgage payments, lobbying state and federal political representatives for special support programs, counseling and helping to secure psychiatric placement in certain severe cases, contacting potential employers, helping those so unaccustomed to the job hunt to prepare resumes, and seeking publicity from newspapers and local TV stations. These activities sharpened my research skills and techniques, and provided a sense of immediacy with the problems of my subjects, which influenced all phases of my subsequent research.

From the outset my basic intention was to focus on intensive interviews with randomly selected scientists and engineers. Many months of prior participation paved the way for this undertaking. The Economic Action Group and the Association of Technical Professionals were very different kinds of groups. ATP attempted to help established professionals cope on the institutional level. To accomplish this they applied for and received both state and federal government contracts. EAG meetings consisted more of gut level reactions from engineers to their daily experiences of "living it out." Together these groups helped me learn what questions to ask, showed me how to probe particular items when people were timid, and taught me what key words elicited sensitive information.

Participant-observation helped neutralize what personal preconceptions I may have had. Objectivity was fostered by dual sets of records—the group's formal transcriptions of their proceedings and my own field notes. We frequently focused on different aspects of the same subject. My perspectives were correspondingly enlarged. Furthermore, involvement in these group processes diluted the bias inherent in one-on-one interview situations, in which respondents tend to provide answers in tune with values imputed to the researcher (Becker, 1970:47). I was viewed as a marginal if interested and sometimes useful participant. Respondents were constrained more by self-help group norms than by my presence. By observing interaction patterns I learned how better to veil my own opinions in future encounters. Participant-observation acquainted me with the broader parameters of the problem I then wanted to examine more systematically and enhanced my confidence that subsequent research findings would be valid.

The sample was chosen to be representative of the estimated 50,000 technical professionals then living in the Route 128 area. Twelve percent of all physicists, chemists, engineers, and data analysts listed in the annual census of Weston, Lincoln, Lexington, Newton, and Needham were randomly selected as the base from which initial contacts were made.[1] Lincoln and Weston (combined population of 18,437) had a large proportion of well-placed technical professionals. Needham (population of 29,303) had more lower level technical professionals in terms of education and supervisory and technical job responsibilities. Lexington (population of 31,588) and Newton (population of 91,263) spanned the spectrum. My sample consisted of 50 men who had experienced unemployment between 1970 and 1972 and 50 who had not: 17 were from Weston-Lincoln, 41 were from Newton, 24 were from Lexington, and 18 were from Needham. These numbers were based on the relative number of technical professionals in each of these communities.[2] Moreover, this community based randomized selection procedure produced a sample that reflected the relative distribution of technical professionals in terms of field of specialization (59 engineers, 31 scientists, 10 data systems analysts), education (median level

[1] The annual census of each city and town in Massachusetts lists all residents by name, street address, date of birth, occupation, and, in some towns, by voter registration. The following sources were used to generate the sample: Town of Lincoln, *Street Listing*, 1971; Town of Weston, *Street List*, 1971; City of Newton, *List of Men and Women 17 Years of Age and Over*, 1971 (listed and purchasable by wards); Town of Lexington, *List of Persons 17 Years of Age and Over as of January 1, 1971*; and Town of Needham, *Street List*, 1971.

[2] The sample size of 100 constituted 2.8 percent of the 3,535 technical professionals living in these five middle-belt Route 128 communities.

was the master's degree), income (the range was from less than $15,000 to over $50,000), present or prelayoff job title (six divisional vice-presidents, 16 middle managers, 39 top level staff, 39 regular staff), predominant type of supporting contract (43 percent worked only for the Defense Department, 19 percent worked for Defense and NASA, 19 percent had mixed contract support backgrounds), and firm employed by or laid off from (major Route 128 companies were represented in rough proportion to the relative size and importance of the company).[3]

The sample was stratified by employment status so that I had a comparative basis from which to assess the effects of unemployment. In the atmosphere of crisis and uncertainty that gripped Route 128 in the early 1970s, the employed did not constitute a control group in the strictest use of the term. People still employed were not insulated from the general effects of insecurity. Unfortunately, their fears were justified in the years that followed. The defense contract flow did return to Route 128 by the mid-seventies, as I shall later show, but people in my sample were now a few years older. They represented greater financial liabilities to their companies and a restricted commercial economy did not offer them new opportunities. By 1975 only 57 percent of the employed sample were still working for former employers. As for the others, 15 percent were laid off; another 22 percent were no longer living in the greater Boston area (they had been laid off or transferred); and prodded by the prospect of unemployment, 6 percent ventured mid-life career changes.

Nonetheless, the experiences of the unemployed differed markedly from the imaginings of the anxious. Unemployed experts in metallurgy, aerospace engineering, crystallography, or electrophysics were dislodged from carefully planned, government supported, and publicly lauded positions. They lost the income that made newly cultivated and comfortable lifestyles possible. They fought with their wives and were short-tempered with their children. They suffered psychological anguish, physical deterioration, and confused social identity. The employed, however worried, were still working. They had not personally shared, at least not yet, the painful experiences of their jobless former colleagues. Managers pushed them harder in tight times, but careers were not disrupted. Income, prestige, and position continued. Some contamination between "experimental" and "control" groups does exist in this study, but concrete material circumstances nonetheless clearly distinguish the jobless from the fearful.

By fall 1971 I began to telephone randomly selected technical professionals. During the next nine months, while still maintaining contact with

---

[3] Ten worked for Raytheon. Ten worked for Sylvania. Avco, Itek, RCA, IBM, Polaroid, Honeywell, Digital Equipment, Microwave Associates, LFE, EG&G, MITRE, NASA, DOT, and Arthur D. Little were among the large firms well represented. Nine were from middle-sized diversified and commercial firms. Six were from smaller diversified companies.

the self-help groups, I spoke with almost 300 scientists, engineers, and data systems analysts in order to arrange for the desired number of personal interviews. The questionnaire, constructed after six months of participant-observation, combined forced-choice, open-ended, and what Robert K. Merton and Patricia L. Kendall called "focused" items.

> The interviewer who has previously analyzed the situation on which the interview focuses is in a peculiarly advantageous position to elicit details. In the usual depth interview, one can urge informants to reminisce on their experiences. In the focused interview, however, the interviewer can, when expedient, play a more active role; he can introduce more explicit verbal cues to the stimulus pattern or even *re-represent* it. . . . This usually activates a concrete report of responses by informants. (Merton and Kendall, 1957:476–477)

All interviews lasted at least two hours and frequently three. We spoke in the respondent's home. I took copious notes during each session and transcribed them immediately thereafter. I chose not to intrude electronic recording equipment into our sometimes sensitive discussions: a voice recording identifies as surely as a fingerprint; my respondents were concerned about anonymity. They were fearful of disclosing company secrets, worrying that future employment could be jeopardized. Ultimately they were protected only by my word and I would not risk the trust we shared. I told my respondents that the computer would insure their anonymity. Technical professionals, more than most others, know how impersonal an ID number on an IBM card really can be. For purposes of systematic analysis I carefully coded and then computerized much of the qualitative as well as all of the quantitative data obtained during these interviews[4].

The initial refusal rate was low[5] and later there was a surprisingly lack of resistence to my probing questions. Rapport was easily established. Equality, the basic rule in conducting successful interviews (Hughes, 1971a:511) was built into the situation since interviewer and respondent were both middle-class professionals. The sex difference between female

---

[4] Nie, Bent, and Hull's *Statistical Package for the Social Sciences* (1970) was the selected program. For the most part, data analysis was done through one-way frequency distributions and cross-tabulations of scale components. The full data labeling capacities of the SPSS system were utilized to minimize errors of identification in the analysis. The recoding and variable transformation facilities of the SPSS also proved helpful.

[5] The overall refusal rate was 10.6 percent. Of the 282 telephone contacts only 30 refused to be interviewed: 18 were employed, nine were or had been unemployed, and three refused to discuss their employment status.

Six of the nine unemployed refusers where in such a high state of nervous tension about their situation that they were unable to cope with the type of interview requested. Some were suspicious. "This must be for the press." "Leave me alone." "What do you want with me?" This study is slightly biased away from the most psychologically disturbed types. The other unemployed refusers were reemployed and did not want to review a painful past. "Those months are only for my memoirs" said one Lexington engineer.

Of the 15 identified as employed who refused to be interviewed, 12 said they lacked the time and three claimed the right to privacy. Analysis of employed refusers indicated that no systematic bias was introduced into the sample.

sociologist and male head of household facilitated communication. Unemployed men frequently had difficulty dealing with their wives (details are explored in Chapter 8) and welcomed a sympathetic woman who was not, because of her professional role, in a position to be anything but supportive. Above all my study was positively received by the community because these people felt they had a special story to tell and were eager for the opportunity to talk in confidence about their careers, their lives, and their reactions to unemployment.

Three years later, in 1975, after computer analysis of my data and while maintaining communication with many key informants, I once again contacted the entire sample. By this time, technical professionals were not alone among the middle-class unemployed population. A second series of interviews enabled me to assess the changes that had occurred in the lives of these people, and retest my initial observations and conclusions. Once again in 1975, I made the rounds of unemployment offices, interviewed Department of Employment Security personnel, talked with officials in several Route 128 companies, and interviewed organizers of AFL-CIO technical and professional unions and people working within the established scientific and technical professional associations. I also interviewed, for the first time, several newly unemployed professionals to insure the validity of my overall findings and impressions in yet another way.

The analysis that follows is the product of four years of varied and intensive research within the context of upper middle-class suburban life. The quality of the illusions and the depth of disillusionment among professionals were revealed in sharp contrast to the hope the future had once promised.

4

The Wonderful World
of Route 128

"Golden Horseshoe"

> Like a golden tiara, a band of technology-related businesses crowned Boston's head in a phenomenon known nationwide in the 1960's simply as "Route 128. . . .
>
> From 1955 to 1971 the number of firms operating along the Route 128 corridor blossomed from 39 to more than 1200. . . .
>
> Then came the blow. The American economy went into a slide and aerospace and defense contracts were cut back. By 1971 more than 12,000 scientists, engineers and technicians found themselves without work and struggling for survival in the suburbs of the "golden semi-circle."
>
> The tiara is still there, a bit stronger perhaps after the bankruptcies, layoffs and mergers that peaked in 1971. (Blake, 1975:49)

Eight-lane Route 128 was completed in the mid-1950s. Nowhere else was the optimism of the fifties and sixties more apparent than in the phenomenal growth of the area surrounding this highway. All over the country, businesses sought to expand beyond the urban core. But in a postindustrializing era, the semicircular Route 128 was special. About 10 miles from central Boston, it provided easy access to numerous suburban communities. Most of all, it was connected, via Route 2, with Cambridge and the intellectual resources of Harvard and MIT.

During the 15 years subsequent to Route 128's completion, multimillion dollar federal defense and aerospace contracts accounted for the growth of hundreds of elite, high technology firms. Tens of thousands of scientists and engineers got jobs at the forefront of research and development, designing and fabricating complex electronic systems, computerized systems of data analysis and evaluation, and intricate control and delivery networks—and all in the name of scientific progress, national defense, and a better future based upon technology and planning.

Large, modern, rectangular, antiseptic looking buildings, located for the most part in industrial parks, line the 65-mile Route 128. If you begin at Westwood, Massachusetts, and drive north, the following are some of the larger companies you would encounter. Signs to EPSCO come into view first. EPSCO develops and manufactures avionic and electronic equipment, including data converters, flight controls, and navigational systems. Next, outside the town of Needham, are Microwave Development Laboratory, GTE Sylvania, and Honeywell. Microwave developed, among other things, control system filters used on missile projects. The Sylvania division has designed and developed satellite antennas for NASA, sophisticated transferable electronic telephone switching systems used to speed military communications, command data buffer systems for Minuteman weapons systems, and numerous other kinds of microelectronic devices. Honeywell has designed and developed military computers in worldwide use and infrared reconnaissance systems for the U.S. Air Force and was heavily contracted for work on the NASA Skylab. Further north, in the Waltham area, are divisions of Raytheon, Polaroid, and EG&G. Raytheon, with eight divisions near Route 128, is reputedly the largest military electronics firm in the world. Raytheon designed, developed, and fabricated the SAM-D and Hawk surface-to-air missile defense systems, the Sidewinder air-to-air missiles, Sparrow missiles, MIRV warheads, and electronic assemblies in the guidance system for the Poseidon fleet ballistic missile. Polaroid, with divisions in both Cambridge and Waltham, is known for innovations in consumer photography but also has designed filters for low-flying radar used on Raytheon's Sparrow missile. EG&G designed and developed high intensity terrain illumination systems for night photo reconnaissance.

At this point one can pick up Route 2, drive east, and within 20 minutes reach such firms as Arthur D. Little, Bolt Beranek and Newman, Electronics Corporation of America, MIT's Draper Instrumentation Laboratory, and a NASA research and development facility. The Draper Lab was the principal national center for the Thor, Polaris, and Titan missile guidance systems. A little further on one comes to Avco Corporation in Everett, Massachusetts. Avco which has two other Boston area divisions, solved the major nosecone reentry problems for the Defense Department and NASA. Avco designed and built the command module heat shield for the Apollo program and designed, fabricated, and tested reentry systems for the Titan I and Minuteman I and II strategic missile programs.

Returning to Route 128 and driving north, one comes to the Lincoln-Lexington area and another division of Raytheon, another division of Honeywell, the U.S. Air Force Cambridge Research Laboratories at Hanscom Field, Lincoln Laboratory, and Itek Corporation. Lincoln Laboratory has done important work in computer development, radar systems, and data processing for ballistic missile tests; it developed the air defense warning systems known as DEW, SAGE, and BMEW. Itek is known for its participation in various Defense Department and NASA photography, optics, and electronics projects. It was the prime contractor for TRIM, used for night target surveillance.

Further north along the golden horseshoe, in the Bedford area, are the MITRE Corporation, Sanders Associates, and two more Raytheon divisions. MITRE's specialty is advanced information and communications systems. Sanders has designed, developed, and fabricated countermeasure equipment, such as widely used airborne receiver-transmitter sets and the FAAR, a mobile radar system that detects and traces aircraft. Then on to Burlington and RCA Corporation, which once built 50 percent of the memory cores for the entire national computer industry. RCA produces consumer goods, nuclear propulsion jet engines, and missile fire control and guidance systems. RCA also manufacturers laser target designators, which illuminate the target and direct bombs to it.

These firms, and numerous others, attracted professionals from all over the country and even the world. They offered high starting salaries, impressive titles, excellent laboratory equipment, and extraordinary support facilities for all kinds of scientific and technological work. The federal government readily supplied the funds and supported the seemingly limitless expansion. Many worked on Defense Department projects and others had to "dress" contract proposals in defense related terminology (to insure funding 75 percent of all those I randomly sampled did so at one time or another). But displayed on many of the automobiles that filled the parking lots of these firms, on my first trip through in 1968, were "McCarthy for President" bumper stickers and other signs of support for the peace movement. Scientists and engineers may have worked on missiles but they also, it appeared, reflected the values of the communities in which they lived.

Status Communities

Professionals were drawn to the greater Boston area as much, perhaps, by the kinds of residential communities in which to live and raise their families as by technology row itself. The communities that flank Route 128 are towns and small cities independent of Boston's political control. They

have their own mayors or boards of selectmen, and independent committees oversee schools nationally recognized for innovation and excellence.
Housing is expensive but highly varied. It was difficult to buy a house during the sixties for less than $30,000 in any of these communities, many of
which boast venerable historical traditions that merged with the status
culture of the decade in myriad ways. Amid trees and greenery one finds
spacious Victorian homes, Cape Cod colonials, opulent masterpieces of
modern architecture, and new developments of split-levels—all within a
short drive of the Route 128 job, the intellectual and hip Cambridge scene,
and the Boston urban core.

Cosmopolitanism and diversity of lifestyle characterize these communities—the perfect stage on which to pursue the status quest of emerging
middle classes in the sixties. An enlightened, with-it cultural atmosphere
prevailed in these communities, populated in large part by the faculties of
some 50 colleges and universities in the greater Boston area and professionals in expanding business and public service bureaucracies. Quaint
New England merged with modern suburban living.

The town meeting tradition is still taken seriously, at least in this part of
eastern Massachusetts. And the local political orbit absorbed many of the
professionals who moved here during the fifties and sixties. Most do not
participate actively; rather, local politics provides a topic for conversation
and speculation. The *New York Times* is read more frequently than are the
local weeklies. Most often it is the "big" issues that occupy cocktail party
conversants. Racism is apt to be stigmatized in these predominantly white
communities, safe from the turmoil of Boston. Opposition to the Vietnam
war was strong. For many years the national peace movement was organized largely from within these communities, which enthusiastically supported Eugene McCarthy in 1968 and George McGovern in 1972. It was
difficult to get elected to a local board of aldermen during this period
without taking a stand in opposition to the war. It was popular to register
as an Independent rather than as a Democrat or Republican. Above all, one
had to appear "in the know" on the issues. It was therefore important to
sound liberal, rational, and reformist.

Living in one of these towns provided such important anchorage for
many of the newly arrived that I chose in 1971, from among these communities, a random sample of technical professionals to interview intensely. Career was their path of rapid upward mobility and residence in
Lincoln or Newton, Lexington or Needham proclaimed their successful ascent. As Joseph Bensman and Arthur J. Vidich explained:

> Having rejected its own past, this generation was in a particularly impres-
> sionable position in regard to its college experience; so that what it saw and did
> in college provided it with its first alternative to the rejected ethnic and rural
> culture. Thus the culture of the American university and the bearers of this

culture, the university professors, are of critical importance as models for shaping the new middle-class lifestlyes. . . .

These patterns, once seen, became a reservoir of lifestyle models which the college graduate could take with him when he entered the occupational world, especially during the fifties when he moved to the suburbs and embraced a way of life for which he had no role models.

Under the stress of having to adopt new leisure models for which his family background left him unprepared, the new suburbanite . . . could revert to these college-diffused but skin deep patterns of cultivated, genteel leisure. Since most of the new suburbanites' neighbors were in the same position, each helped the other in affirming the new suburban patterns. (Bensman and Vidich, 1971:132–133)

Since I inteviewed the men and sometimes their families as well in their own homes, I was able to see how they lived and thereby gain some perspective on how occupational histories meshed with family pressures and community values in this new middle class during a time of increasing uncertainty. Some case histories illustrate the occupational base of this way of life.

Route 128 People

Principal engineer, age 36
Born in Brooklyn. Son of an immigrant who owned a candy store. Went to a major polytechnical institute in New York City. Earned a master's degree in electrical and electronic engineering in 1950. Came to Route 128 in 1961 as a design manager. Promoted to project manager. Designed circuits for missile systems. Salary $21,500.

Senior engineer, age 45
Born in Orlando, Florida. Son of a construction worker. Earned bachelor's and master's degrees at MIT. Took first job at an MIT laboratory. Subsequently worked for three large Route 128 firms. Had responsibility for overall project electronic performance. Special interests: spectrum analyzers, swept–receivers, slow noise–wide range amplifiers, and digital filters. Salary $17,900.

Principal research scientist, age 43
Born in New York City. Son of a garment worker. Received his Ph.D. in physics from the University of Pennsylvania in 1955. Took a job in Philadelphia for one year. Was attracted by the research facilities and opportunities at an MIT laboratory. Subsequently held jobs with two large Route 128 firms. Worked with semiconductor lasers and electrophotography projects. Became chief of a NASA electronics research facility. Salary $29,250.

Principal engineer, age 51
Born in Berlin. Son of an engineer. Came to the United States at the age of 18, in 1938. Earned a master's degree at Harvard in 1953. Took his first job at a

nearby electronics firm. In 1958 changed to a higher paying position with another firm, where he eventually moved from staff to management. Worked on projects connected with supervision and development of cameras for lunar and military reconnaissance. Salary $30,000.

Engineering specialist, age 42

Born in New Jersey. Father was a carpenter. Received his bachelor's degree in physics from Princeton. Came to Route 128 in 1962. Worked on design and development of hybrid microelectronic circuits. Salary $19,300.

Divisional vice-president, age 46

Born in Detroit. Son of an automobile salesman. Received a bachelor's degree in chemistry from the University of Delaware in 1951. Took his first job with a major Route 128 commercial firm. Been there ever since. Promoted up the management line. Salary over $35,000.

Senior scientist, age 41

Born in Evansville, Indiana. Son of a lawyer. Completed all his work for the doctorate but the dissertation at the University of Chicago. Came to Route 128 in 1965 for a job with a large electronics firm. Changed jobs three times. Worked on classified infrared radiation optical effects projects. Salary $18,500.

Principal engineer, age 45

Born in England. Son of a London factory worker. Came to the United States to study and work at MIT. Received his doctorate in 1965. Has been with a large Route 128 electronics firm ever since. Worked on mathematical models of instrumentation for defense use. Salary $23,800.

Senior reliability engineer, age 31

Born in Boston, Son of a policeman. Received his master's degree from Northeastern University. Took a job with a large defense contract firm. Worked on an infrared reconnaissance system for the Air Force. Salary $17,500.

Two-thirds of the scientists and engineers who lived in Boston suburbs in 1971 came from working-class or lower middle-class families. Their fathers typically had been blue-collar workers or had owned small stores. A few had been farmers. Some of their fathers had been salesmen or clerical workers. And about one-third had been professionals—doctors, lawyers, professors, engineers, or teachers. Most of the technical professionals I interviewed, born in the thirties, were sons of the Great Depression (the sample in 1971 ranged in age from 29 to 62; the median age was 43). As children, many saw their fathers experience unemployment and their families endure economic deprivation. The strong upward mobility orientation, so prevalent in Route 128 people, had commonly been nurtured by origins in hardship. Glen Elder, Jr., followed Oakland, California, children of the Depression through their careers in the sixties.

The sons and daughters of the deprived middle class rank well above the nondeprived of similar origin on ability to surmount difficulties and profit from experience, to postpone immediate gratification for the benefits of long-range accomplishment, and to use talents to their fullest advantage. . . .

Family conditions associated with economic loss served to liberate boys from parental controls; oriented them toward adults and adult concerns, including the problems of earning a living; and stressed responsibilities in life. Economic hardships emancipated boys through the autonomy and obligations of work roles, and a household arrangement in which father had less to say in family matters than mother. Work roles involved boys from deprived homes in the adult-like experiences beyond family boundaries, enlarged their sphere of know-how, and brought greater awareness to matters of economic independence and vocation. These experiences, and the realities of family hardship, accelerated movement toward the adult world. Interest in the company of adults, the desire to be an adult, vocational thinking, and crystallized goals were associated with economic deprivation. In adult life, vocational crystallization tended to minimize the educational disadvantage of family deprivation in work-life and achieved status, regardless of class of origin. (Elder, 1974:248, 279)

Futhermore, according to Elder, the World War II years, followed by expanding educational and occupational opportunities, diluted the memory of economic hardship. What remained was a set of social-psychological factors related to career mobility. By the mid sixties, both the men in Elder's sample and those in mine were not concerned primarily with job security. This they took for granted (pp. 190–191).

They came to technology row to find career and lifestyle fulfillment from Brooklyn, the Bronx, and Zanesville, Ohio; from Atlanta and Atlantic City; from rural Canada and Minneapolis; from Chicago, Cleveland, and Warsaw, Poland; from Philadelphia, Baltimore, and Hamburg, Germany; from Birmingham, Alabama, and Yorkshire, England. More precisely, 30 percent came from the New England states (24 percent were born in the greater Boston area and stayed there); 30 percent from the Middle Atlantic states (22 percent were from New York City); 15 percent from the Midwest and Far West; 8 percent from the South; and 17 percent from abroad (Canada, England, Germany, Poland, Italy, and Iran).

Route 128 people had worked hard to achieve advanced degrees, the prerequisite to upward mobility. The median level of education among the sample population was the master's degree: 24 percent held doctorates, 38 percent held master's degrees (many had completed most of the work toward the doctorate), 33 percent held bachelor's degrees, and 5 percent held associate degrees. Their degrees were in physics and chemistry (31 percent), engineering (59 percent, with 37 percent in electrical and electronic engineering), and applied mathematics (10 percent).

Most had completed their education in the fifties (36 percent) and sixties (30 percent). Many had come to the area initially to go to school; 30 percent earned degrees at MIT or Harvard. Others were educated elsewhere but moved here for their first job. Still others began their careers elsewhere but were lured to the area during the years of expansion. By the mid-sixties, Route 128 had become the place to take a job. There was a pattern of rapid movement both into the area and among Route 128 firms. It was important to be located here. If you did not like one job, you could always find another.

The money was good. The median annual salary of those I interviewed in 1971-1972 was $22,000; 10 percent earned $11,000 to $14,000; 35 percent earned $15,000 to $19,000; 10 percent earned $20,000 to $22,000; 35 percent earned $23,000 to $30,000; and 10 percent earned over $30,000. These salaries were much higher than those earned by scientists and engineers elsewhere. The average annual salary of technical professionals in 1970 was $15,000 (U.S. National Science Foundation, 1970:12), 50 percent higher than the national median income for a family of four. That $22,000 seems far from upper middle-class family income by 1980 standards testifies to the effect of inflation in the seventies. The median annual income of my sample in 1980 dollars was $42,096 (a 91.3 percent increase)[1].

Job descriptions sounded impressive. The sample consisted of divisional vice-presidents (6 percent), middle management personnel (16 percent, with such titles as manager of product research, data processing manager, systems manager, manager of advanced development, and project manager), top level staff (39 percent with such titles as, engineering section head, senior staff engineer, principal research scientist, and senior research group leader), and staff personnel (39 percent with such titles as research chemist, computer scientist, electronics engineer, and reliability engineer). Most of these people, at the turn of the seventies, thought they had arrived.

They were family men with an average of two to three children. They had anchorage points both in their Route 128 companies and in their suburban communities. They had skills and long years of experience in fields they thought were important and highly valued in society. Above all, they were rational men.

Their social origins and religious backgrounds predisposed them to qualities and attitudes such as calculability, sophistication, and skepticism, which are necessary in the performance of contemporary technical professional roles. A greater proportion of the Route 128 sample was recruited

---

[1] The comparative scale of the 1971 Route 128 sample in 1980 dollars, as computed from the Consumer Price Index, is as follows:

$15,000 = $28,702
 20,000 = 38,269
 25,000 = 47,835
 30,000 = 57,403
 35,000 = 66,970
 40,000 = 76,538

from urban cosmopolitan environments, and from the East than were scientists and engineers in generations past.[2] And, overwhelmingly, Route 128 people were secular. Ninety-five percent said that religious beliefs never influenced their on-the-job decisionmaking. Eighty-three percent claimed some degree of religious affiliation and/or identification (but only 27 percent attended church or synagogue regularly): 36 percent were Protestant, 13 percent were Catholic, and 34 percent cited Jewish roots (71 percent of these had fathers born in Russia or other eastern European countries). Catholics, most traditionalistic among major contemporary religions, were statistically underrepresented in a nation one-third catholic and in a state approximately 60 percent Catholic. Jews, on the other hand, were statistically overrepresented in a nation where less than 3 percent of the population is Jewish, and in a state where approximately 4.5 percent of the population is Jewish.

Long ago Thorstein Veblen (1934:229–230) predicted that Jews would be disproportionately represented among the technical elite of advanced industrial society. Jewish intellectuals were alienated from Christian culture, Veblen noted, and were removed from their own heritage as well. This double-binding marginality, he reasoned, liberated Jews from tradition and encouraged creativity. The qualities of secularism, skepticism, sophistication, and rationality, first apparent among Protestants in the United States (Knapp and Goodrich, 1952:284; Layton, 1971:10; Merton, 1957:357), were prominent among Jews who in the 1950s and 1960s became scientists and engineers in increasing numbers. Jews had been denied access to these kinds of careers in the 1930s. As barriers lifted after World War II, Jews, always urban and highly educated, quickly took advantage of new opportunities and entered the technical professions in disproportionate numbers. Thus, the ethnic factor cannot be overlooked in analyzing the world of Route 128.

Route 128 people had planned their lives and careers carefully. And for them planning and deferred gratification seemed to have paid off. As children, many had saved their pennies to go to college, long before they understood what going to college meant. They went to the right schools, took the right kinds of courses, earned marketable degrees, made useful contacts, and accepted each advantageous job offer as it had come along. They kept their networks of professional contacts flowing. Many continued to take technical courses and tried to keep up with developments in their fields. They regarded themselves as part of a scientific and technological elite that mattered.

[2] Pre–World War II scientists and engineers came predominantly from nonurban, midwestern, and Protestant backgrounds (Knapp and Goodrich, 1952:279–284; Layton, 1971:9–12; "The Scientists," 1948:106–111, 170–176).

Tough Times

128's Realistic View: Gloomy
  Boston Globe, January 3, 1971

Its Hard to Rebound from Layoff on Rte. 128
  Boston Globe, October 13, 1973

Route 128 "Golden Tiara" Tarnished, But Still There
  Boston Globe, October 13, 1975

Has Rte. 128 Met Its Match?
  Boston Globe, February 19, 1978

Pitfalls along Route 128
  Bay State Business World, March 22, 1978

By early 1971, funding for NASA had been cut two-thirds from its peak in 1967 and Defense Department contracts had slowed. Responding to cuts in funding for SAM-D, ABM, and Hawk missiles, Raytheon laid off 40 percent from its highpoint. EG&G cut its entire research department and laid off 90 percent from previous top employment levels. RCA laid off 50 percent. Avco's Everett Research Laboratory was cut 30 percent. Draper Laboratory laid off 300. NASA in Cambridge was cut in half, from 800 to 400, including most of the scientists working on theoretical projects.

As noted earlier, accurate official statistics were never available for Route 128 in general and for scientists and engineers in particular. Nonetheless, at least 20 percent of the technical professionals who had worked along Route 128 experienced unemployment in the 1971–1972 period. This figure was widely quoted by the media and acknowledged throughout the Route 128 community. My own survey disclosed an unemployment rate of 21 percent. These figures were confirmed by a Harvard Business School study conducted for the Department of Labor, which found unemployment among Route 128 engineers to be 20.2 percent (Thompson, 1972:11–12).

A renewed flow of military contracts came to Route 128 firms in the 1972–1973 period, albeit not with the abundance that marked the pre- 1969 years. These contracts resulted in some hiring, but other contracts were terminated and new layoffs resulted. Official statistics hid the depth of the problem. A self-help group of scientists and engineers that formed in Lincoln, Massachusetts, in August 1970 went out of existence in the fall of 1972. Of the 14 original founders (all over 45 years of age),

three are presently employed as professionals and two have started their own businesses (with varying degrees of success). Two are working as consultants an average of two days a week, and two are temporarily employed full time at their former salaries, but without fringe benefits. Four members who have now been out of work for two and one-half years have stopped looking for employment. The present status of the last member, a former Assistant Dean who had taken work at a town dump, in one of the Boston suburbs, is unknown.

None of the unemployed or underemployed mentioned above would be included in the data of the Bureau of Labor Statistics. If one has any income, one is "employed;" if one has given up looking for work, he no longer exists. Of 14 members of the Lincoln Job opportunities Group, the official statistics would be recorded as: 0 employed, 5 no longer in the job force—unemployment rate 0%." (Association of Technical Professionals, 1973:4)

By the second half of the 1970s, the flow of Defense contracts to such Route 128 firms as Raytheon, GTE Sylvania, Sanders, and General Electric had increased, as descriptions of contract awards published in the *Bay State Business World* indicate.

Raytheon received three Army contracts totalling $105.5 million for Improved Hawk anti-aircraft missiles and related ground support equipment. (January 14, 1976)

GTE Sylvania, Inc., Needham received a $5.1 million contract for the operation and maintenance of a missile-tracking radar system in the South Pacific, from the Army's Ballistic Missile Defense Systems Command. This brings the total contract award to Sylvania for this project to more than $60 million. (January 7, 1976)

Sanders Associates has received a $5 million multi-year U.S. Navy contract to provide automated four-color air traffic control (ATC) systems for the Navy's Fleet Area Control and Surveillance Facilities at various sites in the United States. (September 27, 1978)

The General Electric Company received assurance last week of a $100,000,000 federal contract for full-scale development of engines for the F-18 Navy fighter plane program. (October 19, 1977)

The Ford administration's 1976 $113 billion and the Carter administration's 1978 $123 billion Defense budget requests were even augmented by Congress. This promised continued prosperity to Route 128 electronics. An increased flow of petrodollars from Arab bloc nations was also encouraging. According to the *Bay State Business World*, GTE Sylvania, for instance, received a $2.3 million contract on March 3, 1976, to produce airborne transmitter-receivers for installation in helicopters purchased by the government of Iran. Kuwait paid $5.2 million for buildings and land in the Route 128 Westwood Industrial Park. In June 1976, Raytheon was in the final stages of negotiating a $1.14 billion contract for the Improved Hawk Missile System with Saudi Arabia, a project which the company claimed would insure 6,400 jobs at its Andover facility for five years. In October 1977 Raytheon received a $10 million contract from Egypt "to install a network of digital microwave telecommunications equipment." On October

19, 1977, Saudi Arabia awarded Sanders a $300 million contract to provide "facilities and services for a highway patrol system."

Nevertheless, the slackened American economy had affected the general employment picture for scientists and engineers. Many who were unemployed in 1971 were reemployed by 1975 but many others were unemployed for the first time. The Air Force's Cambridge Research Laboratories threatened massive relocations. Honeywell closed two Route 128 divisions. EPSCO laid off many engineers who had survided the 1971 cutbacks. Scientists mourned the elimination of all but directly mission or product oriented research. Companies could prosper for a decade by developing products based on research they had done in the past, scientists claimed. Company spokesmen, however, asserted that they had learned from previous mistakes and were running more efficient operations.

> Manufacturing employment along the "golden horseshoe"—state Route 128—has recovered, after a slump, to a point above its 1968 level. From 1969 to 1971, cutbacks in U.S. defense spending for electrical machinery, transmission equipment, instruments, and other hardward or services provided by Route 128 industries threw more than 10,000 people out of work. The annual average for manufacturing employment among the 20 cities and towns that border Route 128 was 90,255 in 1968; 83,518 in 1970; 80,437 in 1972; and 92,473 in 1974.
>
> This 1968–74 slump brought about an interesting change in the personnel policies of Route 128 firms. Now there are fewer public relations, quality control, and marketing people and more production workers, veteran observers say. ("Bright Side of Bay State Business," 1974:4)

Many looked optimistically to the Energy Research and Development Administration, established in 1974, as a new source of funding for Route 128 jobs. To a certain extent this hope was justified.

> The Department of Energy . . . has awarded a first phase contract, valued in excess of $3.6 million to Avco Systems Division to develop a process that will convert coal into acetylene and other chemicals through the use of an electric arc. (February 15, 1978)

The use of minicomputers, cited by some as evidence of positive defense spending fallout, expanded dramatically in every phase of business and industry, science and government, education and the mass media. This provided an important growth area for Route 128 firms, and data systems companies prospered. Digital Equipment Corporation was the giant, its sales growing from "$188 million in 1972 to $736 million in 1976, capturing 38% of the mini-computer market on the way" (Association of Technical Professionals, 1977:1).

Route 128 claims to dominance in defense electronics and minicomputers were challenged in the 1970s by the rise of California's Silicon Valley. Seeded by the intellectual stimulus of Stanford University, just as Route 128 originally sprang from people and ideas at MIT and Harvard, hundreds of high technology firms cluster south of San Francisco within a 25-mile reach of Palo Alto. Between San Francisco Bay and the Pacific Ocean, Route 128 western-style specializes in computers, semiconductors, and lasers. Hewlett-Packard is the largest of the companies. Others are IBM, Xerox, Lockheed, Varian Associates, and Advanced Micro Devices (Lenzner, 1978:73). Attracted by lower taxes, better weather, and easier access to venture capital, several Route 128 firms, such as Digital, sought western expansion (McElheny, 1976:D1).

> American industry is being increasingly influenced by new electronic capabilities for rapid calculation and communication. The Boston area once seemed to dominate these capabilities through its pioneering work in minicomputers. Now, there is a widespread belief in the electronics industry that the innovative and competitive advantage is shifting to the region south of San Francisco, This is largely because of that region's dominance in ultra-miniaturized semiconductor circuitry, such as the "computer on a chip," which crucially affects the price and features of such electronic machinery as minicomputers. For the Massachusetts area traversed by Route 128 and its concentration of high-technology companies, the forecast is cloudy. But for the California region known as Silicon Valley, named for the vital element in the micro-electronic chips, the climate is decidedly sunny. (McElheny, 1976:D1)

Nevertheless, Route 128 faced the competition and managed to survive the seventies.

Despite tough times and fluctuating fortunes, professionals stayed in the Boston area if they could. Salaries might now be lower than those offered elsewhere and taxes were usually higher but the lure of the cosmopolitan lifestyle continued.

> The greater the number of professionals who want to be near each other, the universities, the beaches and ski slopes, the greater the competition for available jobs and the greater the willingness to take less money in order to stay. (Foreman, 1978:21)

Schools continued to graduate trained professionals looking for work as the job market tightened. Many who were cut loose in the early seventies were still floundering several years later. The Massachusetts Association of Professional Engineers estimated 10,000 unemployed colleagues in 1976 (Foreman, 1978:23). But the number of unemployed technical professionals was dimmed by the increasing numbers of jobless teachers, academics, architects, psychologists, social scientists, and lawyers. A 1973 Massachusetts Bar Association study showed that there were "10 times more lawyers in Massachusetts than jobs for them." A 1976 Massachusetts Teachers Association survey found that there were "4.3 certified classroom teachers for every new job" (p. 21).

Technical professionals were caught in the web of tight company planning but found no overall planning in the larger economy. Eighty-seven men in my sample blamed the absence of federal planning for the utilization of scientific and technical personnel, more than any other single factor, for the pervasive employment instability. The situation was, in fact, so irrational that I found it impossible to predict who among those I interviewed in 1971 would be employed and in what capacity before I recontacted them in 1975. A major source of disillusionment among jobless professionals is loss of faith in rationality itself—a process begun by on-the-job experiences in bureaucratized research and development laboratories.

5

Careers in Bureaucratic Systems Labs

When we came out of school in the 1950's we were wined and dined. It was very schmaltzy. But it was not six months before they were treating you like a whore. Some questioned it: some didn't. But after 20 years of making transformers, what do you do? I had decided I was finished with the defense business. I found that being a professional engineer wasn't all that professional. I couldn't use many of the skills I had. I never saw the results of my work. I couldn't share my work with my family because it was classified. After 15 years I was frustrated and ready to leave. How many years can you put up with it? But a lot of them did and that's why they are having such a hard time now. (McLean, 1972:35)

The glamour of a career in science, the importance of technology to society—these were part of a culture that promised challenging careers to those with ability and education. The culture heroes of technological society—nuclear physicists, electronics engineers, and data analysts—all initially expected stimulating, gratifying jobs. For some these careers were the fulfillment of childhood dreams; for others, the culmination of the status quest of young adulthood. For all, interest in science and mathematics was deeply rooted. They assumed the work would be intriguing, the pay good, and the jobs plentiful. When they completed their degrees, positions with high salaries and impressive sounding titles were available. For those with talent, ambition, and credentials elaborate equipment was provided—all that government money could buy.

By the early 1970s my sample of Route 128 technical elite had worked at the forefront of science and technology an average of 15 years. Most had positive feelings of achievement: 57 percent felt highly successful; 30 percent felt at least moderately successful. And by commonly accepted standards of success they surely were. They lived in attractive homes in the suburbs and pursued fashionable lifestyles. They had the positions, to say nothing of the vocabulary, to sound *important* to family and colleagues, to friends and neighbors. Yet for many men at mid-career, the feelings that come from being productive and doing worthwhile things were far more elusive than the symbols of success they easily displayed. Many were satisfied with what they had accomplished. But just as many were dissatisfied; the dissatisfied included 30 percent of those who thought themselves very successful, 60 percent of the moderately successful, and 70 percent of the self-proclaimed unsuccessful. Obviously, success and satisfaction are not the *same* experience.

The reasons for their dissatisfaction were associated more directly with the functional requirements of large organizations than with either salary or position. Certainly, concern about employment security was part of the problem of the seventies. But the career alienation evidenced by so many of my interview subjects could be traced to operational procedures characteristic of the bureaucratized systems laboratories in which they worked.

Sources of Conflict and Tension

Microdivision of Labor, Underutilization, and Overspecialization

Boredom and monotony are part of the expected scene for factory workers. But professionals have been led to anticipate challenge and stimulation in their work. Instead, work alienation was rampant among the Route 128 technical elite.

Expensively equipped advanced systems aerospace and electronics laboratories were touted as the ideal environment for creative scientists and engineers. Organizational structures were geared to account for complex, interdependent, and highly varied functional operations, prototypical of postindustrializing society. But many professionals found themselves working under a microdivision of labor. Jobs were narrowly drawn. Tasks were so subdivided that the individual could rarely see his work through to an end product. As a result, skills were underutilized. Managerial controls were tight. Only minimal responsibility, initiative, and autonomy were allowed. Many were stuck for years on projects they disliked, but they lacked decisionmaking authority over work assignments so transfer was difficult.

A 10-year study of organizational requirements in R&D labs, such as those along Route 128, showed that scientists and engineers want to apply their training and skills and to understand the utility of their work. But management demands, above all, predictability and control. Organizational needs require "meeting the schedule within the budget, turning out a product that does the job to be done *only as well as it needs to be done*" (Ritti, 1971:27).

In order to accomplish these "goals of laboratory management" the "engineering work force is impersonally matched to specialized tasks that are produced by a management factoring of over-all organizational objectives" (p. 81). Technical professionals, especially development engineers, are apt to be relegated to highly *formatted* tasks, which "can be learned as a self-contained specialty, independent of background knowledge." [Such tasks are] governed by largely fixed procedures, standards, rules, which are relatively free of ambiguity and contingencies" (p. 20).

Management decisionmaking, largely a group process, is subject to carefully specified, highly impersonal controls. Needs of individuals are not part of the planning framework.

> Functions are established, projects formed, and bodies allocated on the anticipation, rather than the presence, of a work load. . . . the problem lies also in the interdependence of design functions and the division of labor among design specialities. If Stage 1 must be complete before Stage 2 and 3 can begin, there must be some reallocation of manpower after Stage 1. This is where the problems are generated. Add to this indecision, cancellation, and revision, and multiply a hundredfold in complexity; toss in some inevitable confusion and incompetence, and underutilization seems all but unavoidable.
>
> The laboratory work force is allocated to meet overall laboratory objectives rather than individual needs. Major development programs within the laboratory are factored down into smaller projects. Problems of coordination and articulation of the work in these various projects means that there will be times when individuals or entire groups will have little productive work to do—underutilization. (Ritti, 1971:106–107)

As these organizational processes become more complex and things go wrong, as they frequently do, the tendency is to remove what little autonomy laboratories might have retained. And top management shifts staff personnel, with little knowledge of immediate problems in particular situations (pp. 181–183).

Managers of bureaucratized systems laboratories increasingly come to rely on measurable mechanisms of coordination and control. Individuals can do little about influencing their own work situations unless they achieve, at the very least, the position of project manager or group leader.

This constraint partially explains (according to Ritti's data and my own) the push toward management among so many technical professionals. Career expectations are frequently thwarted by requirements that organizational operations impose. Individuals find themselves powerless to alter on-the-job realities, although some try. By their middle years, many scientists, engineers, and data analysts are frustrated and dissatisfied.

Organizational Constraints on Professional Autonomy

Sociologists have found that professionals in most types of organizations experience various constraints. Therefore, I asked my sample directly, "Do you think that tensions and frustrations caused by the structure or requirements of the organization are to be expected when professionals work in large organizations?" "Always," said 62 percent of the men I interviewed. Their reasons—impersonality, submergence of creativity, suppression of good ideas, imposed specialization, and inadequate communication. Twenty-three percent saw organizational constraints as inevitable but not necessarily troublesome. Individuals, they maintained, can make adjustments when required. Only a small minority (17 percent of the sample) did not view organizational hassles as part of the Route 128 scene. This group argued that constraints are part of any kind of work situation and provide the source of positive goals rather than generate conflicts and personal frustration.

Staff-Line Conflict

Many professionals could not describe their feelings of work alienation in abstract organizational terms. What they were apt to talk about was daily conflict with "interfering" managers. Sometimes managers were seen as technically incompetent; others were described as merely carrying out policies set from above. In any event, managers' authority to direct and evaluate subordinates' work was the greatest source of individual tension and frustration.

Conflicts between professional staff and management line personnel were described as constant by 45 percent of my sample.

Managers are interested in results, not problems.
Managers are only interested in profits, not science.
Managers often make the wrong decisions because they don't know enough.
Managers are only interested in pushing their own careers.
Managers are only interested in my ideas when they think they can get the credit.

Thirty-six percent said that they frequently, if not always, experienced staff-line conflicts.

It depended on the technical ability of the manager.

The personalities of the individuals involved made the difference.

How managers behave depends on the type of organization. No hassles for me at Lincoln Lab but always a problem before that.

Only 10 percent of the sample claimed never to have personally experienced such tensions. The level of frustration described by Route 128 people had little to do with educational achievement, expertise, or field of specialization. Position in the organizational hierarchy made the difference: 63 percent of the professionals as compared with 13 percent of the managers identified staff-line conflict as a constant factor in their careers.

Companies that depend on the expertise of professionals were certainly aware of these problems. "Enlightened management" sought ways to alleviate tension. Some experienced what were touted as dual organizational chains, that is, separate but equal promotional and salary scales for professionals and administrators. Some created manager-professional roles. Others tried "participative engineering" (O'Kelley, 1978:F14). Many firms claimed that scientists and engineers were rewarded for the pursuit of professional goals. But rarely did such experiments reduce conflict between managers and professionals along Route 128 or elsewhere. Robert Perrucci and Joel E. Gerstl (1969b:122) found that neither personnel nor engineers thought that companies either encouraged or rewarded professional activities. Fred H. Goldner and Richard R. Ritti (1967:488–491, 494–495) found that dual organizational chains functioned to keep scientists and engineers out of the promotional line. The dual ladder, they argued, removed scientists and engineers from the "decision-making and power process of the organization." Finally, they found that the proportion of professionals who saw the dual ladder as equal decreased with length of employment by the firm.

The Nagging Fear of Obsolescence

Mid-career anxiety for today's professionals, especially the technical elite, is fed by the feeling that their fields have moved beyond them. The knowledge explosion in all areas, but most markedly in science and engineering, has been staggering. For example, in electronics and electrical engineering, there are estimated to be approximately 100 journals and 30,000 to 71,000 papers written annually; in aerospace there are about 1,500 journals and 45,000 papers written annually; in metallurgy there are 600 to 900 journals and 35,000 papers written each year; and in chemistry there are approximately 7,500 journals and 150,000 papers yearly (Perrucci and Rothman, 1969:248).

Because organizations are structured so as to exacerbate the situation, individuals must cope on their own: some work hard at keeping up by reading journals and taking courses; others count on their years of experience to see them through; many try to move into management, where that sharp edge is not necessary. Labor is subdivided to accelerate the attainment of company goals. One consequence is enforced overspecialization, which nurtures obsolescence. When familiarity with new developments is required, many companies find it easier to bring in new talent than to help professionals keep up with the latest developments in their fields (Perrucci and Rothman, 1969:249). According to Ritti (1971:219–220) the problem of obsolescence does not lie with the individual but flows "directly from . . . management's definition of what 'engineer' means. The problem is more one of technical amnesia than of technical senility. And the solution must be found in the organization of work roles rather than in individual updating."

Typically, Route 128 engineers were rated obsolete by their managers when they reached the age of 37 (Dalton and Thompson, 1971:57–59). Gene Dalton and Paul Thompson described the process of increasing obsolescence as a "negative spiral." An engineer is kept at a dull job for a long time or is passed over for promotion; his performance is rated low; he is informed of his rating and his self-confidence drops, resulting in poorer performance and a lower rating, and so forth. In an effort to stay afloat he may resort to night courses, but by this time the downward obsolescence spiral is too far along for formal instruction to be of much help (p. 64).

Among Route 128 technical professionals, the problem of keeping up was widely regarded as a real one. I asked, "Is there a mid-career crisis due to the obsolescence of technical knowledge? Have you had trouble keeping up with your field?" Fifty-four percent responded affirmatively. Another third of the sample said that obsolescence was a problem for the narrowly trained, the highly specialized, the marginally skilled—but not for them. Fifteen percent said that mid-career obsolescence was a bogus problem created by management to keep the salary scale low. Years of experience increase problem solving efficiency, they claimed, and easily compensate for the new jargon of younger men, who, of course, can be brought in at lower salaries. Whether the obsolescence problem is real or made real by management, apprehension grows with age.

Futility and Waste

The knowledge that one's work is useful to others or has value for society is a critical dimension of occupational accomplishment, especially to detail oriented technical professionals. At the outset, scientists, technologists, and data systems analysts certainly expected such satisfaction to be theirs. But work had lost its purpose for many at mid-career. "How important is your work to society? What kinds of contributions do you make?" I asked my sample. Only 37 percent thought that their contributions to the economy were important. Only 43 percent thought that their contributions to scientific development were significant. Forty-eight percent felt that their work was necessary to national defense. Overall, 58 percent cited positive purpose to their work (23 percent were ambivalent and 19 percent were entirely negative). The failure of bureaucracies effectively to utilize slotted professional positions was one of the reasons for this decline in felt utility; war work was another.

Eighty-one percent of the sample spent all or part of their careers working under federal defense and aerospace contracts. These professionals developed atomic energy, nuclear warheads, and strategic missiles. Some were proud of these accomplishments; some felt guilty; others could point to indirect civilian "fallout" from their work—color television, miniature calculators, and electronics for medicine. Many were too involved in the minutiae of daily procedure to discuss ultimate utility. Yet most could detail instances of project duplication and gross inefficiency that they had personally witnessed and by which they were appalled.

Scientists and engineers want to be productive in concrete, measurable ways. They are involved, however, in a system that pays scant attention to these needs. Long before cost-plus contracting policies characterized defense based industries, Thorstein Veblen predicted that innovative engineers would become deeply disturbed by waste and inefficiency, inevitable by-products of surplus spawning capitalist economics (Veblen, 1933:142). Veblen accordingly foresaw in technologists a new revolutionary vanguard (pp. 71–82). My data showed that Route 128 professionals were disgusted by the waste they witnessed and by their lack of useful work, but they were not radicalized as Veblen in 1899 had hoped. Instead, these sources of disillusionment caused work alienation for some and intensified it for others.

Erosion of Professionalism

To be considered a professional was an important part of the reason why careers in science and technology were sought in the first place. Professionalism meant, at the beginning, acquiring the knowledge and training necessary to do difficult and challenging work. The fields of law and medicine provided in a general way the models for what these men thought being a professional entailed: their performance would be judged by colleagues; their work would serve people's needs; their competence would be recognized; and their autonomy would be assured. But scientists were never independent professionals, as doctors and lawyers were in the past, because they found themselves salaried employees in large organizations. Notions of the meaning of professionalism had to be altered. And in the pursuit of successful careers, professional goals were modified by or merged with organizational goals.

The astrophysicist or quality control engineer was not disturbed by midnight calls from sick patients. Instead, he had a general clientele—society. But the organizational structure in which his job was embedded impinged upon his professional autonomy in unexpected ways. To be a technical professional in postindustrializing society came to have various meanings among different types of professionals. But the illusion of independence in the application of skills and training had, by mid-career, been dispelled for all.

By 1972, almost two-thirds of my Route 128 sample no longer thought of themselves *primarily* as professionals. When presented with a list of possible self-designations—managerial personnel, professionals in general, technical people in general, those on salary or wages—only 39 percent (48 percent of the scientists and 32 percent of the engineers) chose the professional category. Conversely, when asked whether a successful career is more dependent on the pursuit of professional or organizational goals, only 13 percent (26 percent of the scientists and 9 percent of the engineers) picked professional goals.

To belong to a professional society has long been considered part of the professional career. Seventy-seven percent of the sample had joined at least one such society. But for only 5 percent had active participation been a meaningful part of their self-conception as professionals. The societies, according to 29 percent, were useful as a general way of keeping in touch with developments in the field. But 17 percent admitted to using the meetings primarily as a way of keeping up personal contacts and soliciting customers for their employers. Twenty-four percent found them of no use whatever.

Nevertheless, most of the people I talked with clung to the trappings of professionalism even as they abdicated recognized dimensions of professional commitment. Indeed, many used professionalism as a protective veil against the economic insecurity of their position as expendable employees: "Professionals have special things to contribute to any company." Or, "I'm a professional! In a way that really makes you different. No one can take your skills away." But all too often I could sense a void beneath these protestations, a longing for the never experienced feeling of what being a professional was supposed to have meant.

The technical elite had expected to be professionals, whatever their original conception of the term. Yet, by mid-career, two-thirds of the sample had developed what can best be described as mixed organizational and professional orientations. It was apparent to them that organizations impinge on professional autonomy and that what was promised had not been fulfilled. Their independence had been eroded by management. Their societies neither protected them nor represented their interests. Many feared to organize as professionals lest they lose what status claims they had. Some tried to borrow prestige from the corporate executives with whom they identified. In order to survive in the bureaucratic context, professionals had to adapt role expectations of previous years. The Golden Horseshoe spawned company men with professional titles, robots in ties with attaché cases.

Strategies of Adaptation

Many professionals exchanged on-the-job satisfaction for recognized symbols of achievement. Fancy titles brought prestige in the community, if not always in the laboratory. Good salaries paid for a nice home and a comfortable, upper middle-class lifestyle (which for two-thirds of the sample was considerably more than they had had as children). This process of adjusting to career disappointments by emphasizing the rewards that were obtainable was usually gradual. Some searched for satisfying work situations by frequently changing jobs during the sixties, when jobs were plentiful. Most made the best of conditions as they found them, did what was expected, and accepted the rewards offered. Then, as the years went by, there was a tendency to interpret success as satisfaction (70 percent of the highly successful said they had found satisfaction, as compared with 40 percent of the moderately successful and 20 percent of the less successful). But others were aware they had sacrificed past expectations to maximize present realities. They tried to bury their disappointments and coped as best they could.

Adaptation to disappointment was most difficult for a cluster of physicists and chemists with doctorates from the best schools who had hoped for fame even more than for fortune. They took Route 128 jobs instead of university positions because laboratory facilities were excellent, freedom was promised, and salaries were high. But great men are rare in any social context. And in this one, early dreams of dramatic discovery were thwarted by performance requisites of systems laboratories. These scientists were, as Barney Glaser (1964:129–135) has called them, the "comparative failures." In order to live with faded dreams of glory, they stressed the "fundamental" nature of their research, which was usually at the highest levels of technical responsibility. It was their work, they claimed, regardless of how it might have been restricted, that was the basis of any potential product development 10 years or so down the pike. A few of these people ascended to the management of an entire research department and so, in a general sense, could claim the division's work as their own. But substitutions for career expectations did not come easily. And to the degree that professional satisfaction had been denied them, these men deprecated the success they had achieved.

The quest for promotion up the management line was the other major strategy of adaptation attempted by technical professionals. This route was downgraded by some, but sought by most. Increased authority within the organization softened feelings of lost professionalism. A management position assuaged gnawing feelings of technical obsolescense. And higher salaries compensated for job dissatisfaction.

As a strategy of adaptation, the shift toward management roles worked best, of course, for the few who made it to the top. Company goals came to be redefined as professional goals. Success within the organization increasingly became interpreted as career satisfaction. Most, however, practiced intermediate strategies. Frequent attempts at compromise between professionalism and company interests were more common but less functional as a way of obliterating career disappointments. But for those who consciously continued to struggle against the system, as some did, disillusionment and bitterness were constant companions.

Satisfaction and dissatisfaction merged in various ways as people adapted to the working conditions they found along Route 128. People experienced dissatisfaction differently depending on how much they understood about the situations they encountered and how they chose to deal with them. At the same time, the cumulative impact of structural circumstances did not prevent all scientists and technologists from salvaging at least some degree of career satisfaction. Expectations may have been transformed but nearly half of the sample claimed that their skills were usually utilized. Even if underutilized some were nonetheless gratified by salary and position. Still others found ways to respond to this complex work context that created the sense of a meaningful career. Income, security, and status (macro) factors can counterpose on-the-job restrictions (micro) factors such as lack of challenge and underutilization. Ivar Berg, Marcia Freedman, and Michael Freedman (1978:63–74) reviewed relevant literature to show how macro, mezzo, and micro factors interpenetrate to affect job satisfaction. Indeed, along Route 128 in the 1970s both general and specific job related conditions in bureaucratized systems laboratories stimulated varied responses from technical professionals. These responses appeared in the data as four typical modes of adaptation, which, for purposes of explication, I have dubbed Superstriver, Routinized, Savvy, and Trapped.

Although satisfaction and dissatisfaction have many meanings, it is nevertheless possible in a general sense to classify these typical reaction modes according to the degree of substantive satisfaction. Superstriver is the most upwardly mobile type of organizational professional, hell-bent on success. His are the rewards of top salary, highest level supervisory position, and self-proclaimed satisfaction. Routinized accepts whatever conditions he must in order to maintain a successful career. Salary, position, and affordable lifestyle replace on-the-job challenge as his criteria of work satisfaction. Savvy is the scientist or engineer who understands the dynamics of the scene in which his career involves him. He is unhappy with many aspects of the Route 128 work world but has a strong sense of his own professionalism and takes satisfaction in his expertise. This brings him pride amid dissatisfaction at mid-career. Trapped is prototypical of the most dissatisfied professionals along technology row. Trapped never comes to accept the negative aspects of his work environment (as does Routinized), regardless of how much success he may have experienced. Trapped is painfully dissatisfied at mid-career and has long despaired the possibility of liberation.

Superstriver, Routinized, Savvy, and Trapped should be seen as central tendencies in the Route 128 data. They are personalized reactions to an institutional context. They help us understand how people cope with and adjust to complex and unanticipated career situations. They also help us to penetrate the façade of corporate efficiency and to focus our attention on the organizational dynamics of this highly technical society.

Superstriver

Stephen Howard was born in Philadelphia in 1937, son of a physician. He went straight through school, from a bachelor's degree at Princeton to a Ph.D. in chemical engineering from the University of Delaware in 1965. While still in school, he was attracted by Route 128 and the gracious Lexington lifestyle. Upon graduation he accepted a generous offer from the company of his dreams. He was a group leader within three years, a department manager earning $30,000 a year (plus bonus) within seven. Howard was 35 years of age when first interviewed in 1972. He was young Superstriver, ever devoted to the company. His loyalty increased as his position advanced.

Stephen Howard found his career always challenging. He did not view company goals as restrictive. "I always did what was expected of me and would do anything myself I ask of others," he said. Howard's department was working on a new film product. He was a manager who pushed his staff *hard* in directions he felt were necessary to meet scheduled organizational goals. And these goals, rather than the technical aspects of problem-solving, appeared to absorb his interest.

> Right now I'm managing a project on my own for the first time. I must make a good, strong showing.
> I am demanding a lot. I am running a short string. This project must not fail.

They are resentful that we are on their backs. They feel that they should be given goals and allowed to go themselves—but I can't allow them that. I do talk to them—to keep the dialogue open. I don't have the liberty of failing at this point.

Howard thought of himself as a manager first, a technical person second—and not primarily as a professional. He maintained token membership in the American Institute of Chemical Engineers. He was concerned with contacts, not papers, and found the American Vinyl Fabrics Institute a good place to make them. Company profit interests became *his own* occupational goals.

Howard was confident in his own abilities but was always anxious about his continued upward mobility. By 1972 his department successfully developed that all-important new product, and Howard was promoted to manage a larger department. In 1975 he was still pushing as hard as ever; those in his department were forced to meet development goals. He saw a company vice-presidency in his future.

I hope to move up as high as vice-president. I'm better qualified than most of the VP's we have here now. You have to be in the right place at the right time, otherwise you must give way to those with less ability. I have to make it up to where I really belong. Dedication to the company counts a lot too, and they know where I am on that score.

Superstriver (13 percent of the sample) comes to Route 128, assesses the scene, and determines, from the very start, that he will *succeed*. He makes the decision to shift from scientist or engineer to administrative staff early in his career: it looks like his surest way up. He calculates his every move so as to maximize his own upward mobility. He never considers on-the-job satisfaction as anything other than measurable success. He talks only about the supervisory and administrative aspects of his position, not about the scientific stimulation of the projects with which he is involved.

Superstriver thinks himself very successful and on the way up. Unlike most of the rest of my sample, Superstriver's father was well educated—an upper middle-class professional or manager. Superstriver was socialized in an atmosphere of movers (70 percent of the Superstrivers were recruited from the upper middle classes, compared with one-third of the sample as a whole). Superstriver is either relatively young, the gung-ho type on the make and on the move, or he is over 45 and earning more than $35,000 annually (in 1971). Superstriver is always moving up. Young Superstriver, a Stephen Howard, has many rungs on the success ladder still to climb. Established Superstriver has salary increases and a final move or two ahead of him—from divisional vice-president to company vice-president, from assistant director of research to director of research.

Organizational constraints, conflicts, and complexities are the essence of career challenge for Superstriver. He seeks to cope with these in ways that maximize his own organizational position. Superstriver does not merely provide what is expected of him by his superiors: he is the overconformist who more than fulfills institutional requirements, using them to realize his mobility aspirations.

Superstriver embodies the needs of large organizations for systematic control of all operations. From his perspective, company restrictions are a source of positive goals, which inspire professionals to pursue company objectives. Scientists and engineers need guidance and direction or nothing would be accomplished, he says.

Superstriver is the company man par excellence. He works for one, sometimes two, companies during the course of his career. If he leaves his first job, it is because a critical mobility channel seems blocked and he feels he must move on to move up. Superstriver is the consummate yes-man to his superiors. At the same time he minimizes substantive problems raised by scientific staff personnel. He deprecates the contributions creative professionals make to company goals. Sometimes he recognizes how restrictions frustrate competent professionals; mostly he does not.

Young Superstriver adamantly demands total staff compliance with organizational directives.

> Many scientists view themselves as creative who are really not. If you let them alone, it would be idle dabbling—they need goals and direction if they are going to accomplish anything. They would be lost if I let them wander off.

Established Superstriver minimizes the extent of staff-line tension by singing the praises of enlightened management; he talks of separate but equal promotional and salary scales for professionals and administrators, of the technical competence of his company's line personnel, and of his own efforts to understand and to keep communication channels open.

> There is a problem here: professionals should have a fair degree of autonomy, only give him broad limits within which to work—hard to do. But you can't give him an open field or he does totally irrelevant things. He needs freedom to create but you must also set limits—tough problem. Enlightened management can handle it.

Professionalism as such means little to Superstriver since company objectives *are* his professional goals. Superstriver's strong success orientation dwarfs the meaning that being a professional has for others. The term connotes neither a code of ethics, nor dedication to knowledge developments in particular fields of inquiry, nor feelings of camaraderie. Superstriver staunchly supports organizational policies. He is adamant, for instance, that companies are entitled to total ownership of an individual's patent rights. This is a common company practice that angers many scientists and technologists because it violates the boundaries of professionalism. Superstriver considers himself to be a manager first and a professional second. If he bothers with professional societies at all, as I suggested earlier, it is only to solidify contacts or to solicit clients for his employer. When Superstriver invokes professionalism, he does so exclusively as a reason for opposing unionization among scientists and engineers.

Superstriver personally avoids facing a mid-career obsolescence crisis by moving into high levels of administration and supervisory responsibility.

> It was never a problem for me. I moved into management and left the technical problems behind. People can keep up if they want to. You must put in more than 40 hours a week if you expect to be a professional.

He becomes a manager, removed from the details of laboratory procedures yet in a position to evaluate the performance of others, which he frequently does in terms of *their* obsolescence. Established Superstriver, a 55-year-old divisional vice-president, said, "We only have top quality technical people here. Either they gravitate toward management or become deadwood." It's possible for technical professionals to keep up, says young Superstriver, only if they select one narrow area. And of necessity they then lose touch with the rest of the field. But as for himself, gung-ho Superstriver wants to become a vice-president.

Superstriver maintains a positive posture toward Defense Department appropriations. His major arguments: (1) a strong deterrent keeps the peace; and (2) Defense is the only government department that knows how to fund advanced research and development. Superstriver recognizes that waste and duplication accompany cost-plus Defense contracting but he minimizes their importance. "There is inefficiency everywhere else you look" is apt to be his disclaimer. Superstriver is quick to point out consumer benefits from Defense expenditures.

Employment instability in the 1970s does not discourage Superstriver's ascent. But then he is securely anchored to begin with. When budgets are cut and layoff decisions are made, Established Superstriver often decides which people are to be laid off. And Young Superstriver, who so firmly upholds company policy, is usually not the man to go.

Only one Young Superstriver in my sample was laid off in the early seventies. He had a nuclear physics doctorate and superb credentials. At one point he had requested a transfer from a Defense to a NASA project, where he hoped his expertise in energy research would be better utilized. This transfer was refused. Subsequently he was laid off for reasons he could not determine. He was reemployed within a few weeks. By 1975, issues of theoretical substance no longer concerned him.

Insecurity, the lot of so many, is not shared by Superstriver. In the three-year interval between initial and follow-up interviews, 75 percent of the Superstrivers were still with the same company. They had moved up to higher levels of supervisory responsibility, as had been their intention. Success continued and so did satisfaction. Company policy was taken as gospel even more than before.

Routinized

Arthur Myers was born in the Bronx in 1932, the son of a paperhanger. As his way of making it out of the neighborhood, he went to college and majored in chemistry. He took a first job as a bench chemist in a local commercial enterprise and went to graduate school at night. Myers received a master's degree in metallurgical engineering in 1961 and moved on to a job in a large systems laboratory in upstate New York. By 1964 he was the manager of an $8 million titanium extrusion program. An expert in the new fields of defensive countermeasures and penetration aids, Myers came to Route 128 in 1967.

Myers was delighted with his position as project manager. He described his many responsibilities at length and with much pride. His middle management niche was critical to career and lifestyle. He ignored possible negative aspects of working under Defense Department contracts, and his opinions in all areas supported whatever behavior he thought others expected of him. He minimized the extent of staff-line conflict and organizational constraint.

> Scientists and engineers both need close supervision. Otherwise they wouldn't know what to do. They resent toeing the mark so they talk about tension. Just a lot of crap. There's really no difference between scientists and engineers either. Scientists just like to think of themselves as better. It's the job of the staff to do what they are told. The worker always has to get along with his boss. It's much easier that way. Once you make up your mind to the facts of life, the tension disappears.

Myers considered himself both a professional and a manager, but he had little patience for arguments about the importance of professional autonomy. Company objectives, he said, must always come before empty goals of professionalism. Companies were entitled to an individual's patent rights, he claimed, since they paid for his time and his equipment. Myers joined the American Society of Metallurgists but found meetings meaningless. The only ways to keep up with the latest developments, he said, was through in-house gatherings of the Association of Old Crows (a military electronics warfare group).

After working on various penetration aids programs for five years, Myers was laid off in June 1971. He was 39 at the time and earned $24,800. He had just built, but not paid for a swimming pool in what he called his "posh Lincoln setup." At our first interview he had been out of work for one year. Over the next three years he had bits and pieces of various kinds of jobs. None of them lasted more than six months.

In 1975 Myers was working on a trial basis as the plant manager of a medium-sized industrial operation. He was proving his worth to the company, he claimed, by applying systems controls to a commercial enterprise. He kept production up and expenses down, he said, by firing surplus employees. Myers could not admit to me, nor I think to himself, feelings of uneasiness at earning his living by putting others in the painful situation he understood so well.

Routinized (42 percent of the sample) conforms to all imposed behavior patterns as appropriate. He generally does what superiors expect of him, has a high salary, and at mid-career feels relative job satisfaction.

Routinized comes to Route 128 with genuine interest in science and technology that remains with him throughout his career. He is involved with the details of the projects he works on and describes them with interest, pride, and satisfaction.

Routinized is in his early forties. During the course of his career he has generally had three different jobs along Route 128. He held each one for five to seven years and then moved on for a salary increase or for what seemed to be a more secure position. Routinized attains a top staff position; sometimes he reaches middle management levels. He is a project manager, a senior engineering specialist, perhaps a principal engineer or a research group leader. He thinks of his career as successful, but not *very* successful because Routinized is not focused on reaching the top. He says he has reached his peak and does not want to move into top management or does not want to leave behind the excitement of problem-solving at the research level. Above all else, Routinized is a realist: he does not strive for what seems impossible to achieve. He assesses his chances and is happy to be earning $25,000 a year. He accepts the symbols of achievement his job provides and fears bucking the system.

There are aspects of working in advanced R&D laboratories that Routinized finds less than desirable but he accepts them and even tries to justify them. More often than not he likes his work enough to overlook aspects of his occupational environment that others find problematic. Constraints certainly exist when professionals work in large organizations, he says, but that's true all over and people should and can adjust. He tries to discount troublesome effects of organizational constraints: they exist in other companies but not here; they cause problems for other people but not for him. "I have as much freedom as I need. Organizational controls interfere but you have to accept them."

> Scientists and engineers have some sense of discipline and can adjust to goal directed operations that are part of commercial organizations. The organizational pressure bit is overplayed.
> High tension levels with staff are worse in low periods. You have to put more pressure on them to improve profit levels and they resent it.

In order to combat microdivision of labor (a problem he does not like to discuss), Routinized sometimes tries to move into management. He does so in the hope of gaining a broader view of the product or process being developed. This motivational pattern diminishes his perception of staff-line conflict. Should differences with managers become problematic, Routinized attributes the situation to personal rather than structural factors.

> Tensions are due to personality conflict not controls in the organization. It's possible to accept controls without tension. If I was told to work on something I disagreed with, I took it in my stride.

If conflict does erupt, Routinized—whether scientist or engineer, top staff or middle manager—ends up justifying the managerial point of view.

Mid-career obsolescence is a problem Routinized sees for others but refuses to face himself.

> Sure it's a problem. Few can do it. First you must decide where you want to keep up. I dug in, in special areas, where I needed to. Now that I'm in the direct management line, it's not so necessary. Only the very best can do it, if they are really willing to make the effort.

It is important to Routinized that he be considered a professional. Even though he deals with discrepancies between professionals and organizational goals by conforming to company expectations, he remains a professional by his own conception and uses the status connotation of this designation as frequently as situations permit. Routinized belongs to professional societies and gives papers if his company encourages him to do so by paying his expenses.

Routinized feels that his work significantly contributes to scientific and technological developments. This is true even though he usually allows himself to understand little about the larger context of his work. He overlooks what inefficiency he sees in the cost-plus defense contracting industries. Routinized favors large Defense Department appropriations. "Perhaps some fat could be trimmed" is as critical a statement as he is apt to make. If you ask him about the possibility of massive R&D funding in areas such as environmental protection or mass transportation, he tells you he would love it and would probably work twice as hard. But hoping for this kind of economic conversion, he tells you, is like "pissing in the wind." So Defense means his job, his security, and ultimately his sense of satisfaction. Routinized, a common type along Route 128, cannot rock the security boat in which his sense of satisfaction reposes.

Routinized plays the game by the institutional rules. Yet when contracts are lost and people are laid off, Routinized is not more likely to keep his job than are his less conforming colleagues. Despite long years of demonstrated company loyalty, 52 percent of the Routinized employees were laid off in the early 1970s. And by 1975 only 31 percent were still working for their original employers. After a few months or a few years, Routinized was usually working again but frequently at a lower salary or status (only 14 percent claimed to be working near previous levels). During the three years between interviews all but five of the laid off Routinized workers had changed jobs at least twice. Many worked with smaller companies on less sophisticated projects or at lower skill levels—from nuclear physics at Raytheon to junior high school math, from biochemistry to analysis of dog food for the U.S. Bureau of Customs, from section head of infrared electro-optic systems to computerizing accounting systems for the Massachusetts Department of Welfare.

Reemployed Routinized is always glad to be working again. He finds new ways to justify employer expectations. Bitter and insecure, he is nevertheless grateful to a system that allows him upper middle-class survival.

Savvy

Harold Brenner was born in Baltimore in 1927, son of a small shopkeeper. Brenner attended Johns Hopkins and received his doctorate in chemistry from the University of Pennsylvania in 1955. Synthetic organic chemistry was his field and has remained so for 20 years. Brenner prized his professional career more than his upward mobility. He remained a committed scientist but the tensions and conflicts of the bureaucratic context eroded satisfaction.

Brenner worked for three different companies during the first 10 years of his career—leaving each time because conflict with managers hindered the progress of his research. In 1965 he came to a Route 128 company with the best reputation in the business. In 1972, at the age of 44, Brenner was a senior research group leader with an annual salary of $28,000. He felt secure in his position because the products he worked on were critical to the company. But his anger at managerial intrusion into professional autonomy and scientific progress sapped justified gratification.

If you were to ask me what I talked about to my wife when I came home and she asked me how the day went—it is never the problems, the scientific problems in the lab but the personal problems, the political nonsense that one cannot avoid.

If integrity is important to you, you have to see it sacrificed every day because of the way the companies operate. The smooth political boys run the operations. Even if you don't agree with them you have to pretend to. Science, truth, integrity—always compromised by the slick, smooth organizational guy interested in profits. Never truth and creativity. The scientist always wishes for more freedom. Must compromise integrity to work. Must go along with the big boys who are not interested in the quality of the scientific enterprise.

Managers have narrow, personal, self-serving goals that often have nothing to do with science. They are involved with staying on the good side of the top people and often are entirely preoccupied with small, unimportant things.

The scientist is interested in problems; the manager is interested only in results. Managers have no patience with the problems. For example, our group discovered a new process. An outside company was making the product for us.

We asked them to use the new process and lower their prices accordingly. The company, at a meeting, played it down, criticized our work. Price bargaining was the only reason for the meeting, not discussion of the merits of the new process in scientific terms. The young Ph.D. who was really responsible for the new process was disturbed because the managers weren't concerned with the quality of his work. The manager came over a few weeks later and asked how things were going. This guy was upset and said so. A few days later this manager told another manager that this new Ph.D. was always complaining. "I wonder what's bothering him; he's always complaining," he said. The manager couldn't even see that the scientist *should* be concerned with the quality of his work.

Brenner coped with career disappointment by maintaining a strong sense of his own worth, regardless of the judgment of others. He came to terms with the problem of mid-career obsolescence by reaffirming his problem-solving effectiveness.

The language changes; the jargon changes. The man of 40 has superior techniques. He may be somewhat behind theoretically but he knows how to tackle problems; he feels technical self-assurance. The younger man is not used to attacking problems for himself. Older men tend to be frightened but they can really be more effective.

I went through this crisis. For years I tried to keep up with the vast changes in organic chemistry. I would spend all my evenings-trying to keep up. Then I saw the kinds of things that the younger guys were coming to me for—the kind of service I could give. I saw how unable they were of coping with problems. I've stopped trying to learn the new language. I no longer feel obsolete. I'm far more effective than the hot young guys.

In order to maintain his own professionalism, Brenner was active in the American Chemical Society. He attended meetings, gave papers, and worked on committees. He helped draft a set of employer-professional guidelines that the American Chemical Society accepted and some companies complied with. Brenner took his responsibility as a professional in highly technical society seriously. He wished social circumstances allowed for freer expression of creativity and imagination. He wished society funded science and technology rationally.

Savvy (17 percent of the sample) begins his career highly motivated to work toward breakthroughs in scientific and technological knowledge. He comes to Route 128 to work at the frontiers of discovery. He has every expectation of being inventive, creative, and always stimulated by his work. Savvy is a nuclear physicist, an electronics engineer, an organic chemist, or a computer systems expert. He is recruited from good jobs in other parts of the country or directly from MIT or Harvard. The prospect of living in cosmopolitan yet suburban communities is an important but secondary consideration. Starting salaries are good and living conditions are pleasant, but the glistening, overorganized systems labs are a source of irritation from the start. The exciting, rewarding career fails to materialize.

By the early 1970s, Savvy has been around Route 128 several years. He's in his late forties or early fifties. Sometimes he changes jobs once or twice, but more frequently he tries three or four situations in the hope of finding more satisfying work. Over the years he learns the ropes of survival in what he interprets as a bureaucratic, technocratic maze. He feels successful enough in terms of official position and annual income but frustration, anger, and disillusionment have replaced the optimism of graduate school days.

From the start he feels that advanced system laboratories are organized so as to prevent a creative person from functioning at full capacity. It is almost impossible to communicate good ideas to people who have the power to alter operational procedures, he claims. Management goals define research directions away from tangents Savvy feels might be most fruitful to pursue. And managers enforce profit and/or productivity goals that have nothing to do with science.

> Communications are unbelievable. I feel underutilization due to overspecialization. And you never see the end product, never have a sense of what you're working on. You write an honest report and managers try to take you down. They think you're too critical. You have to spend money you've been budgeted whether or not it makes sense. And you never do get a sense of how it all hangs together.

> Promotions are not based on what you know. Positions of responsibility are not given on the basis of technical competence—the smooth corporate image is the only thing that matters.

> Organization kills all creativity. Science can't survive in a jungle.

> I've always been underutilized. During most of my career, I felt like my father, the grocer—moving cans around from shelf to shelf but not interested in what was inside. I'm not really interested in my field anymore. As a physicist, I've been stagnating for years.

Savvy is frequently prevented from choosing the projects he works on. Sometimes he gets stuck for years writing a seemingly endless series of proposals from which he receives little or no feedback. Savvy comes to see imposed organizational objectives as insulators against the real world—as preventing him from seeing the relationship between the projects he works on and broader social issues and problems. Savvy learns that organization kills creativity and satisfaction.

Savvy understands organizational operations too well to think he can fit in easily. He also feels confident about his own abilities and resents those at high levels of supervisory responsibility who know less yet are in the decisionmaking positions. He sees his managers easily threatened as he asserts his skills.

> The real problem was that when managers couldn't control what I was doing it made them feel insecure. Their need for control is the critical thing. A few years back I had a good idea. Took it to Washington. It cut like butter. My manager was threatened and called me back. They try to take the prestige for your ideas. So they need you in one sense but are threatened by you in another.

> Managers are just put in the management slots. Usually they don't have the type of knowledge for the area they are working in. Companies feel it's easier to move the managers around than the technical people. So managers often make stupid decisions, even from the company point of view. The problem is critical.

> Sure I've had problems with managers. In the typical case, the manager wants the glory and pushes—even without knowing the details of the research.

> I don't trust managers. They can't deal with creativity. Creative men are kept on while the projects show a profit. But managers find that good people are a nuisance. They can't deal with them. The most creative people don't get good positions because they can't really be controlled. Managers should be able to do both—understand details of the work and supervise—but all too often they don't understand what their subordinates are talking about.

Mid-career obsolescence is viewed as a complex problem by Savvy. The knowledge explosion, as he sees it, makes it impossible for an individual really to keep up with new developments in his field. But companies, according to Savvy, use age unfairly to discriminate against workers with accumulated seniority. Firms cite obsolescense, says Savvy, as an excuse to replace an older man with a young hotshot at half the salary. Savvy sees a subtle relationship between years of experience and the ability to tackle problems, on the one hand, and new knowledge, on the other.

> Obsolescense depends on the man, depends on how specialized he is. By the age of 45 you need muscle and connections and a reputation. If you don't have a professional reputation by then, times are rough.

> Experience keeps you from becoming obsolete. Defense managers are removed from the technical problems—they become obsolete. Success in America is a title, but then they lose contact with the details and *they* become obsolete. The defense industries encourage this.

A mature technical professional, Savvy works out ways to cope with these circumstances.

Savvy's identification as a professional is strongest among Route 128 people. The freedom to exercise independent judgment based on one's credentials and proven ability is a major component of professionalism for Savvy. Such freedom does not usually prevail in bureaucratized systems labs. Savvy is offended by organizational incursions into his professional autonomy. In his estimation, companies do not sufficiently reward professionals for their creative contributions. In his estimation, for example, an individual's patent rights should not be owned by his employer.

Savvy realizes that professionals need protective organizational clout. So he participates actively in professional associations: he volunteers for committees; he runs for office; he tries to activate the societies to protect the interests of their members. Savvy-Engineer says that his societies are controlled by the companies who pay membership dues and expenses. Savvy-Scientist says his societies are dominated by a combination of old guard academics and corporate representatives. From this perspective, professional associations do not address the economic or occupational concerns of the vast majority of their members. Therefore, they do not bolster a sagging sense of professionalism in the face of increasing organizational encroachments. Since existing organizations do not protect the interests of technical professionals, Savvy hopes new kinds or organizations will emerge. But given what he knows about engineers, he does not really expect this will happen.

Dehumanization, Savvy finds, occurs on many levels in R&D labs. The more insightful Savvy becomes, the greater his sense of distress. He is disturbed by the lack of institutional supports for science and technology. He has a sophisticated understanding of federal government expenditure patterns for research and development programs. He is adamant about the need for a total revamping of funding priorities. Savvy is upset by the irrationality he sees—cuts and additions that make no sense in terms of long-range technological needs or preserving national scientific manpower resources. Savvy is more concerned than others about the waste and inefficiency he witnesses in the defense industries. His hopes of contributing to social progress disintegrate into qualms about working on weapons of war, aggravating his growing job dissatisfaction.

Savvy is distinguished most from others along Route 128 by the security he feels in himself as a professional *independent* of the demands of employer organizations. He is sure of what he knows and regrets his underutilization. Erosion of professionalism is the major cause of his mid-career dissatisfaction. He longs for the autonomy that he thinks his skills and knowledge merit.

Savvy has a better understanding of the social underpinnings of his occupational role than do others. But insight does not help him keep his job. Savvy may have indispensable skills but he is also the troublemaker who knows too much and can be difficult to control. Fifty-nine percent of the

Savvy employees were laid off in the early 1970s, and security was short-lived for the others: by 1975 only 12 percent still retained their previous positions. Instead of comfort and security at mid-career, Savvy faced anxiety, instability, and downward mobility.

However, he remains confident about his own abilities. Savvy plays the Route 128 game as best he can, takes the success symbols he is offered, and utlimately settles for the jobs that are open to him. Yet he feels had by the system he expected to change. His career is not all it should be, but he knows the fault is not his own.

Trapped

Arthur Fulton was born in Atlanta in 1924, son of a postman. He served in the Army during World War II. Fulton went to New York University on the G.I. bill, taking a B.S. in physics and a master's in electronics engineering. He worked in a well-endowed New York laboratory before he came to Route 128 in 1960 to computerize military communications systems. He changed jobs once more in 1965. The company was different but the job remained the same. Fulton at age 48 earned $28,000 a year, but his salary locked him into an unpleasant work situation.

> No sense of satisfaction now. You can't use your skills; you can't handle enough of a project to see the end of it—can't control much of it. There are always so many frustrations. Everything stinks but the money.

Fulton had no feeling of accomplishment. Impersonality in large organizations troubled him. The routinization of his assigned tasks demoralized him. The great tragedy, he said, was that "less qualified people could do what I'm doing. There is no job satisfaction. I feel like a prostitute in aerospace."

He described waste and inefficiency as constant features of the defense industries that employed him.

> The work I was doing was premised on a projection of USSR bombing capability. While working there, a guy came in for an interview, a Ph.D. with top credentials, who showed me that by the time the defense system I was working on was adequate to defend under the projected probabilities, the specific problem would have long since passed away. We were operating on the basis of falsehood. We couldn't know what point the Russians would be at by the time we would be finished.

Yet Fulton favored vast Defense Department appropriations because the arsenal was the deterrent and the contracts paid his salary.

Fulton thought he was loyal to his employers. He never instigated fights with managers. And over the years he compromised his professionalism in favor of company goals as circumstances required. He was nonetheless let go in 1974. Fulton was out of work for several months when salvaged by a renewed contract flow. At 51 Fulton earned a lower salary than he formerly had and received no fringe benefits; he was frightened and angry but *stuck* even more than before.

Trapped (28 percent of the sample) is the most blatantly dissatisfied type of technologist found along Route 128. He begins his career, as do so many others, expecting stimulation as well as remuneration. The Golden Horseshoe seems to offer both. He takes his first job as low level staff and moves up a notch or two—to reliability engineer, principal research engineer, or research physicist. But by his late forties he is stuck in an "adequate" slot he thoroughly dislikes. His salary, about $20,000 in 1971, is higher than national averages for men in his position; it allows him a home in the right kind of neighborhood and sustains his newly acquired, all-important lifestyle—but barely. Yet it is the degree of success he achieves that traps him. He must put aside past hopes for a stimulating career and settle for what he has.

Trapped finds microdivision of labor and tight organizational constraints at his first job. He describes his work as drudgery. He is bored and disgusted with the waste of his skills. If he changes jobs, he merely replaces one formatted task for another. After several years his feelings of overspecialization become unbearable. He estimates that only a small portion of his time is spent solving scientific or technological problems. He has no sense of accomplishment because his work is such a tiny part of a vast, complicated matrix he is barely able to conceptualize. For years he feels like a cog in a wheel.

> The problem with working in large organizations is that you can't get to the bottom of things. You can't see something you've worked on all the way through. When you have a good idea you can't communicate with the key people because they are too removed. It's a waste of time trying to get things done. You know what should be done but you can't get to the guy with enough authority to let you do it. It's damned frustrating.

> Managers frequently didn't let me do what I knew should be done. There is competition with other departments. You must try to make your department look good at any cost. Most especially I resented getting as specialized as they forced me to become.

> The biggest problem is that it's all so impersonal. An engineer in a company is just another number. There is no relationship that binds guys to the company. And the company certainly doesn't care about you. Real job satisfaction is so removed. I don't feel a sense of accomplishment about anything.

I don't really like what I do but I'm not stagnating either. How else could I earn almost $30,000 a year? I have children in college, and all of this to keep up. My son is an artist. I envy his freedom. But sometimes my work is interesting, too. What other choice do I have?

Despite his college degree and professional title Trapped feels like an assembly line worker. He is frustrated and bored at mid-career. Trapped is oppressed by bureaucracy even more than by antagonisms with managers. His career is a series of restrictions by the specifics of project designations. Locked into bureaucratic routine, he stays for the money.

I love engineering but only do it 5 percent of the time. Most of my time is spent on administrative work—scheduling, budgets, cost estimates. I've been with this company 17 years. I guess that's what happens. Sometimes I wonder if anyone ever even reads all of these proposals.

Trapped is disillusioned and questions his professionalism. Earlier dreams of career success had been tied to expectations of creativity, independence, and autonomy. As these expectations diminish, so do feelings of being professional. And Trapped resents the lack of recognition for his many years in a bureaucratized lab: "Companies treat professionals as though they were on a production line. I used to think of myself as a professional but society and owners treat us like workers." But Trapped needs his job. Disappointed though he is, he tries to be loyal to the company. He plays both sides and hedges his bets. He is as likely to favor as to oppose company politics and reward systems.

Demoralized by feelings of eroded professionalism, Trapped doubts his own abilities. He fears obsolescence but denies this fear. He blames organizational policies for his dilemma, but he also blames himself. Trapped goes through the motions of participation in professional societies; however, he sees them as another useless part of the total context in which he is enclosed.

That Defense Department contracts support his work is only one of the many factors that confine and confound Trapped, yet he favors the defense industries because they provide him with work. And however distasteful he finds his job, he can envision no other. He talks about the waste he sees but needs his job more than he prizes efficiency. War work is only a minor source of Trapped's career disaffection. The instability of Defense contracts troubles him more.

Trapped is caught between previously held commitments to professionalism and notions of the social utility of his work, on the one hand, and the priority of organizational goals and the defense industries, on the other. His self-conception as a professional needs institutional supports: these are absent. His career becomes a drag. He gives up claims to professional autonomy and social responsibility and tries to circumvent management restrictions in small ways. But lost are the hopes of making important contributions to technology and society, of being someone who really matters.

Trapped feels increasingly stagnant, tense, and anxious. But unlike Savvy, Trapped has little understanding of the institutional parameters of his situation. He goes along with a system that oppresses him while letting him taste affluence.

Like so many others in contemporary society, Trapped is disappointed with his career as a salaried professional. He is locked into a work situation that lacks stimulation. But he makes the best of it. There is no evidence that his job performance is less acceptable. When cutbacks come, Trapped is no more vulnerable than his Routinized or Savvy colleagues. Fifty-seven percent of the Trapped workers in my sample lost their jobs in the early seventies. By 1975 only 18 percent still held previous positions. These few no longer felt secure; "There is talk that the electronics division will be cut. At my age I'll really be in trouble."

After two months or four months or a year, unemployed Trapped finds another job. Sometimes it is similar to the one he lost but it lacks security. Even when the job lasts, fears that supporting contracts will soon expire are always present. At upper age levels men are forced out before their pension plans mature. Sometimes they manage to find jobs that supplement benefits, but skimping by at age 55 is not retirement in comfort and leisure.

Unemployed Trapped spends the 1970s coping with job changes, stretches of unemployment, and subsequent downward mobility. He loses his job and is rehired perhaps three or four times. Despite inflation he works for at least 25 percent less than his former salary. Some settle into underemployment. Others float around the fringes of smaller companies, sporadically unemployed.

Occasionally layoff liberates Trapped. After 20 years of being a tired organic chemist, he becomes an investment counselor with a large brokerage firm. After 10 years of being a physicist in a systems lab, he invents a best-selling bicycle rack. This is Horatio Alger, Route 128 style—and just as rare. Most who try independent business ventures fail. Usually the lost Route 128 job is mourned despite its disadvantages. It is difficult for people, trapped by circumstances about which they understand little, to find new ways at mid-career.

Superstriver, Routinized, Savvy, and Trapped personify characteristic patterns of response to organizational structure. They are not confined to Route 128. These are modes of adaptation to impersonal occupational environments. Superstriver subordinates satisfaction to success. Routinized consciously exchanges achievement symbols for feelings of career gratification. Savvy has personal resources that uphold his sense of self-worth despite daily circumstances. Trapped's career has gone sour but he has neither the ability nor the opportunity to change its course. These characteristic modes rarely exist in isolation. Savvy, for example, frequently feels like Trapped; one major difference between them is commitment to a field of study. Routinized behaves much like Trapped in response to daily requirements; but Routinized accepts all whereas Trapped has difficulty deriving gratification from his forced accommodation.

Trends

The rectangular buildings that house Route 128's bureaucratic systems labs are virtual beehives of complex human activities. A complex web of interdependent functions forms the work environment of scientists and technologists, as it will increasingly for all of us. As work worlds in postindustrial society become more complex, patterns of response will grow more varied.

The culture and ethos of large organizations differ according to company goals. Yet institutional interdependence in mass society engenders similarity of structure and process. Bureaucratic contexts vary and impose different kinds of restraints on professionals. And the logistic needs of different categories of professionals vary, as do the resources that people bring to their jobs. But salaried professionals must all work out ways of adjusting to what they find on the job.

Academics who work in universities, for instance, face conflicts and tensions different in form but similar in intensity to those experienced by industrial scientists and engineers. Young professors begin their careers expecting rewards for excellence in teaching, their primary function. The long process of earning the Ph.D. indoctrinates universalistic goals of the discipline to which most are initially dedicated. They think that creativity and brilliance matter. Very soon they learn the ramifications of organizational conflicts within the Ivory Tower. The sources of stress in academe were last studied systematically by Theodore Caplow and Reece J. McGee in 1958. Findings from *The Academic Marketplace* increase in significance with heightened competition for scarce jobs in the seventies and eighties.

> For most members of the profession, the real strain in the academic role arises from the fact that they are, in essence, paid to do one job, whereas the worth of their services is evaluated on the basis of how well they do on another . . . . Most professors contract to do teaching services for their universities and are hired to perform those services. When they are evaluated, however, either as candidates for a vacant position, or as candidates for promotion, the evaluation is made principally in terms of their research contributions to their disciplines. . . .
> Today, a scholar's orientation to his institution is apt to disorient him to his discipline and to affect his professional prestige unfavorably. Conversely, an orientation to his discipline will disorient him to his institution. . . .

Brilliance, especially in the young man, is suspect unless it is turned into the universally acceptable coin of productivity. . . . Anyone who attempts to establish a claim to prestige based on his intelligence but not supported by the accepted evidence of his usefulness becomes a threat to his colleagues. . . .

There are factions in all faculties, and at least some of the factions are the same everywhere. In each of the ten universities it is a simple matter to trace the lines of schism between:

Young Turks	and	Elder Statesmen
Teachers	and	Research Men
Generalists	and	Specialists
Conservatives	and	Liberals
Pro-administration	and	Anti-administration
Humanists	and	Scientists
Inbred	and	Outbred

Most of these fundamental divisions are likely to be represented in any good-sized department. (Caplow and McGee, 1958:82, 85, 164, 192–193)

Young professors must abandon previous expectations about the independence of teaching and scholarship to the realities of "publish or perish" and campus politics. Work tasks are not narrowly formatted as in systems labs but time demands are stringent nonetheless. Faculty members must deal with the frequently conflicting pressures of professional commitment (as once understood) and job survival. Accordingly, varieties of Superstriver, Routinized, Savvy, and Trapped can be found in every academic department.

Salaried professionals in every field face problems particular to the organization in which they are located. Women face on-the-job problems perhaps even more intensely. All encounter the organizational denial of individuality. This denial, aggravated by a lack of personal recognition and oppressive organizational constraints, is most difficult to deal with. Those who cannot cope with impersonality have neither successful nor satisfying careers. Superstriver adapts to the bureaucratic context by depersonalizing all he encounters. He accepts the structure and becomes part of it. He embodies the goals he imposes on others. He feels less and less as he climbs higher and higher. He compromises professional autonomy from the start without realizing he sacrifices anything. Tensions are smoothed over by the skills of enlightened management and public relations terminology. Neither war work nor firing others engenders guilt. Since he lacks a feeling of personal responsibility, anything can be justified in the name of success.

The fate of introspection in the modern labor market is best represented by Savvy. Savvy understands much about the personal, organizational, and institutional dynamics with which his career is intermeshed. He has an independent sense of self-worth: he knows he has achieved success on the basis of his abilities. His insights decrease satisfaction; introspection sharpens feelings. Route 128 Savvy is disturbed by war work. He feels guilt. His sense of social responsibility deepens. Savvy understands why managers interfere. Sometimes he compromises. Sometimes he argues. He's troubled because professionalism and autonomy have lost their meaning in the impersonal bureaucracy in which he works. Savvy is as modern as Superstriver. He holds to impersonal goals: (1) dedication to honesty in the conduct of research and in the development of products; and (2) the ultimate integrity of scientific truths. He is troubled because these goals are so frequently dismissed as unimportant by government as well as by organizations and individuals.

Superstriver represents the impersonal goals of achievement and success within specific organizational contexts. Savvy represents more universalistic goals of knowledge advancement. Conflicts between Savvy and Superstriver are the classic battles that will continue to characterize the postindustrializing process.

The career patterns of Routinized and Trapped demonstrate the continued priority of status attainment among salaried professionals. Success demands conformity in an other-directed society. Both Routinized and Trapped accept institutional expectations, altering their behavior and their attitudes accordingly. Both trade feelings of work satisfaction and professionalism for symbols of success and lifestyle rewards. Trapped feels cheated in this bargain. He remembers the independence he once hoped for. Routinized does not. Many variants of accepting organizational norms and goals are possible. Personal goals and feelings, however, are always suppressed in the process.

Major trends among professionals who work in large organizations are (1) declining individuality, (2) decreasing introspection, and (3) heightened employment insecurity. Furthermore, work dissatisfaction and employment insecurity are apparently related in an ascending spiral. Dissatisfaction, as we shall later see, is one of the factors associated with termination. Among my Route 128 sample as a whole, a higher proportion of the dissatisfied (65 percent) than of the satisfied (39 percent) were laid off in the early 1970s. The lost job was both mourned and hated as long as unemployment lasted. This pattern was reversed only if relatively successful reemployment followed the bout with joblessness. In such cases, the tendency toward the Routinized pattern increased.

6

Losing a Job, Trying to Find Another

The other day I encountered the man who fired me. He is an affable, bright man, and on the eve of retirement. Many months ago he told me I had outlived my usefulness, and he wished me well. The other day he said he knew what I had been through. When I said he didn't, he looked just a little startled. He does not, never did, like to be contradicted. But I knew he had never been without work. I told him that physically and spiritually I and all members of my family had been wiped out. Then he asked why I was having such trouble finding a new job.

The easiest, possibly even the only truthful answer would have been this: "No one wants me." That is the way I feel, of course. (Paranoia, depression. I used to think these were modern conveniences that only others afford.) But I told him what I know: My age, sex, and salary needs work against me. So, of course, does the shortage of jobs. Then he turned to talk with another passerby. He meant well, though. ("Fired at 46," 1977:33)

Who Is and Is Not Laid Off

When layoffs are as massive as they were along Route 128 in the early 1970s, professionals of all types can be affected. Impressively credentialed Ph.D.'s, along with marginal mechanical engineers, crowded unemployment offices. In the face of such apparent irrationality, it was often difficult to determine why some were laid off while others were retained. The unemployed themselves, by and large, claimed that layoffs hit widely regardless of proven worth or ability.

> People were kept on in reverse ratio to their competence, no matter what they try to tell you.

> I wasn't an in-boy. You know, in the tennis group or the bridge group. I wasn't one of the buddies.

> It didn't matter how good you were. A friend of mine still with the company told me that all the troublemakers from the managers' point of view are gone, so that must have been one of the criteria.

The retained, on the other hand, especially those in high supervisory positions, sometimes regretted firing loyal employees but usually viewed those laid off as a less qualified pool. An examination of factors such as educational attainment, field of specialization, age and years of experience, salary, career stability, position within organizational structures, and attitudes toward work partially supports both positions. Tough times disproportionately affect some categories of professionals.

Amount of education and formal training influenced overall layoff vulnerability. The master's degree was the median education for Route 128 people. Among those at this level, formal degree made little difference (54 percent were laid off; 46 percent were retained). The importance of credentials was apparent at the extremes. The bachelor's degree holders who counted on years of experience and perhaps some evening courses to prove their continuing worth were in trouble (67 percent were laid off; 33 percent were retained). A doctorate in science, engineering, or applied mathematics, other things being equal, provided security (21 percent of the Ph.D.'s were laid off; 79 percent were retained). When a company cut its staff in half or closed its doors, as did the NASA facility in Cambridge, nothing helped and Ph.D.'s were let go along with others.

Field of specialization and even area of expertise within a field influenced likelihood of layoff. With the educational level held constant, scientists were generally less likely to be fired than engineers (39 percent and 53 percent, respectively). Engineers who had been forced to work in a single area for many years were expendable if a new process or procedure appreciably altered the field. Certain types of technologists, such as reliability engineers, were considered a luxury easily dispensed with to cut costs. Particular subfields within physics or chemistry suddenly seemed played out. Technical professionals caught in outmoded areas of specialization had no less foresight than others. There was no way a reliability engineer or a solid state physicist could have predicted changed labor market conditions earlier in his career. Broadly trained scientists, usually considered more flexible, had greater occupational longevity. But companies often wanted "focused specialists" to solve immediate problems in given situations. Moreover, when budgets were tightened, basic research was cut sooner than was development. Under conditions such as these, scientists fared no better than others.

Age or long years of experience did not help people hold their jobs. Thirty-one percent of my unemployed sample had worked as technical professionals for 21 years or more before being fired (as compared with 21 percent of the retained who had at least 21 years of experience). Years on the job mean time away from school and frequently removal from the latest developments in a field. The experienced were a financial liability to their companies because they commanded higher salaries and because their pension plans neared vestment. Firms, using the excuses of knowledge obsolescence or poorer job performance, were apt to fire men over 45 years of age first. Sixty percent of the unemployed, compared to 40 percent of the retained, were between 45 and 56 years of age—the period of greatest vulnerability.

Knowledge obsolescence was recognized as a problem, at least for others if not for oneself, by almost everyone in the sample. Nevertheless, 61 percent of the unemployed, compared with 43 percent of the retained, said that obsolescence was *not* the reason older men were fired first. My study included no on-the-job measure of efficiency or performance aside from the qualitative descriptions of the people I interviewed. Resumes were frequently impressive and almost always adequate. Paul Thompson (1972: II-2) identified the major difference between those laid off and those still employed as the management performance rating of engineers: 34.8 for the unemployed, and 54.8 for the employed.[1]

Age discrimination in both hiring and firing is unstated Route 128 company policy. Fear and insecurity increase with advancing age, and for good reason. Advancing age is related to termination vulnerability more consistently than any other single factor. Seventy-five percent of the 1972 employed who were subsequently laid off were between 42 and 58 years of age. Reemployment prospects were dim for this group. Seventy-three percent of the terminated who were over 40 in the early 1970s never found

[1] Firms generally do nothing to help older technical professionals with the vast proliferation of knowledge. They might vary job assignments to promote stimulation. They might institute released time or sabbatical programs. They might even attempt to apply new techniques of computerized information storing and transmission to the problem of obsolescence itself (Dalton and Thompson, 1971:64–67). None of these innovations was tried during Route 128's time of austerity.

Stanford University has developed videotape courses, now used by Silicon Valley firms to train young engineers and acquaint older ones with new processes and techniques (Lenzner, 1978:73). Whether such courses can break into the "downward obsolescence spiral" identified by Dalton and Thompson (1971:64) has not been established.

jobs at former levels again; whereas 64 percent of the under 40 unemployed subsequently found satisfactory reemployment. There are no labor unions or other organizational protections of seniority rights or tenure for professionals who work in bureaucratized R&D labs. Full payment on pension plans is always considered a nonproductive cost. Even in better days, companies never estimated future pension payments for more than 20 percent of their professional employees. As people reach the time when pensions are to be fully vested, they become cost liabilities. An early retirement package, presented to long-term employees at age 55 or 60, is a cheaper way out. Many employees who thought they had already earned a comfortable retirement were forced to alter expectations drastically.

In combination, certain other circumstances, conditions, and attitudes—vulnerability or organizational position, prior employment instability, job dissatisfaction, cynicism about superiors, ambivalence about war work—help further to explain why some professionals were laid off while others were retained. We have seen how Superstriver knew how to maneuver for position (only 17 percent of those in my sample were fired). Job security ranked high among the reasons technical professionals pushed toward managerial positions, yet in the crunch middle managers (mostly Routinized) were vulnerable (50 percent of those in my sample were laid off in the early seventies).

Program managers and project managers found that administrative skills themselves were not as highly valued as they had been led to believe. They avoided facing mid-career obsolescence but became removed from the details of laboratory procedure. They sacrificed a sharply honed problem-solving edge for mobility. Top management, however, frequently found this group expensive and expendable. Staff personnel (Routinized, Savvy, or Trapped) generally had little organizational protection (56 percent of the top staff and 54 percent of the regular staff were laid off). The only retained professional staff who had some degree of security were those whose work was deemed crucial for company survival at the time.

> *Program manager.* Had complete responsibility for financial and technical aspects and the planning of multimillion dollar contracts. Laid off in 1970 at the age of 46. Annual salary was then $24,000.

> *Project manager.* Was responsible for new concepts for penetration aid devices and delivery systems—headed proposal teams, assigned duties to others, responsible for final proposal, cost analysis in detail, and presentation to Defense Department representatives. Laid off in 1971 at the age of 41. Annual salary was then $24,800.

Job hopping along Route 128 during the 1960s predisposed professionals to layoff in the 1970s. While contracts flowed freely scientists and engineers with credentials and/or experience could float. As positions were always available, those who were disappointed by the lack of professional challenge, angered by intrusive managers, or distressed by organizational restrictions could try to find better situations. But when abundance ended in the seventies, companies fired first those whom they had hired last. Occupational instability correlated with layoff probability. Eighty-two percent of those who had held five or more different jobs through the course of their careers in the fifties and sixties were among the unemployed in the seventies. Three or four different positions during a 15- or 17-year career was modal for my sample. These typical technical professionals had a 50 percent chance of holding their jobs in the seventies. Only people with highly stable career profiles who worked for one or perhaps two different employers had a better than average chance of lasting through tough times. But 37 percent of the most stable were terminated nonetheless.

> *Engineering specialist.* Worked for the same electronics firm for 15 years. Had an important role in the first anti-missile program. Laid off at age 44.

> *Senior staff engineer.* Worked for a large, New York based company for 21 years. Lured to Route 128 by the optics firm where he worked for 12 years. Laid off at age 58.

> *Staff physicist, section head.* Worked on systems analysis of infrared, electro-optic lasers in same division of same company for 18 years. Laid off at age 56.

More of the unemployed than of the retained disliked their work assignments. Forty-seven percent of those laid off in the seventies claimed that their skills had been underutilized and spoke of their jobs as "stagnating," "boring," or "drudgery" (compared with 25 percent of the retained). The retained, on the other hand, were more likely to express positive attitudes about the tasks they had to perform. Two-thirds of them said they were "on the frontiers of developing techology," "challenged," or "happy with professional growth" (compared with 41 percent of the terminated).

Ninety percent of each sampled group admitted that at least some degree of conflict between managers and staff is inevitable in bureaucracies. More of the unemployed (63 percent), however, than of the retained (45 percent) claimed to have personally experienced persistent staff line tension.

Cynicism about the technical capabilities of top management is shared by many jobless professionals; 69 percent of the unemployed (contrasted with 45 percent of the retained) did not agree with the popular assumption that those who become vice-presidents are talented and able as well as ambitious. The *real* criteria for becoming a Route 128 vice-president, according to 42 percent of the unemployed, were characteristics of the political operator—"smooth," "cool," "yesman to all superiors." Ability, they said, had nothing to do with upward line mobility (only 18 percent of the retained shared this attitude).

Working on weapons of war, especially during the anguish of the Vietnam years, was an added source of uneasiness for many Route 128 professionals. They had a vested interest in military spending but were cross-pressured by cosmopolitan and humanistic values. Forty-one percent of the sample maintained positive attitudes toward the defense industries; 29 percent were positive about some aspects of defense industry operations but negative about others; and 30 percent flatly opposed defense industries and their role in society. The negatively disposed were somewhat more likely to lose their jobs than others: 63 percent were laid off. This compares with 48 percent of the ambivalent and 44 percent of the pro–Defense Department people who were laid off.

Dissatisfaction with tightly controlled work environments, coupled with organization related tensions and negative attitudes toward war work, built up friction in many technical professionals over the years. This combination of factors correlated with probability of layoff. But sometimes those who accepted work conditions and unquestioningly conformed were fired. In so many cases, accidental circumstances—the shift of a contract from Massachusetts to California or Arizona or the transfer to a new department that suddenly lost its funding—caused a particular layoff.

Initial Encounters

To be *fired* is insulting and painful, especially for credentialed professionals. They find it hard even to imagine how carefully nurtured careers into which so much time, effort, and affect has been invested can suddenly be disrupted. By the summer of 1970, Route 128 people knew that the job market was tight but most thought that experience and outstanding records of achievement would protect *them*, if not others, from layoff. They were surprised by the swiftness with which long years of company service were ended, sometimes with brutal impersonality.

I was laid off when things for me were at a high point. I invented the mechanism that held the lifeline onto the astronauts' space suit that was actually used on the Apollo missions. I received two awards.

I had just returned from a successful trip to New York. I thought the president was calling me in to give me a raise. When I walked down the hall, the only thing running through my mind was how much the raise would be. I was shocked when I was told that I had to leave. Traumatic is not too strong a word to describe my sense of shock.

The promotion I'd been waiting for had just come through with a $30,000 salary. We bought our dream house. I was told I had to leave on the very day we moved in. After the movers left, my wife and I were sitting in the kitchen. And I had to tell her I just lost my job.

Two-thirds of the rational professionals of Route 128 tried to explain their termination in general terms: "Contracts were cut"; "My whole department was cut"; "All research people were fired." Such explanations did not help them deal with their own predicaments. Despite the recognized need for company cutbacks in the face of canceled contracts, half of the unemployed felt that termination in their *particular* case was not justified. Most thought that the scope of layoffs was determined by top management. However, *who* was to go, they claimed, was usually the decision of their immediate superiors. This was where personality conflicts, jealousies, and political factors frequently entered the picture.

The general manager had a budget he had to get down. He thought I was the best solution to his budget problems. He was stupid. In my case the layoff was to- tally unjustified. I've done too much for the company in the last 15 years.

Department heads made across-the-board cuts. I had told my boss that I wanted to work on commercial development of lasers. Several months before my layoff they shifted me to this project. Then the company cut all commercial work that was not self-supporting. There was no commercial market for laser applications at the time, so I was fired. Things were tough but management couldn't shift the best people around. They should have kept me. My layoff was in no way justified by their financial troubles.

Termination notice was usually abrupt, except where federal Civil Ser- vice regulations (as with NASA employees) or established company policy (as with the Lincoln Laboratories) provided a cushion. Fifty-three percent of the unemployed had only a few hours, or at most a few days, to assemble their possessions. Length of notice did not vary with years of ser- vice: 75 percent of those who had worked 11 years or longer with their company were given from a few hours to no more than a week in which to leave; 29 percent had from two to four weeks' notice. More generous organizations allowed "surplused" men to use company facilities, for a time, to help locate other jobs. But companies wanted those they laid off to leave without a trace as quickly as possible. Managers frequently acted as if the terminated would try to abscond with company secrets. In some in- stances those on notice were denied use of their own notebooks. People of proven company loyalty complained that management should have informed them as soon as the dismissal decision was made instead of waiting until the last possible moment.

Equally painful was the immediate withdrawal of civility and friendship from peers. Even colleagues of many years avoided lunch or conversation. "They acted as though I had a contagious disease," said several of the terminated. It was in fear and embarrassment that the retained left unsaid "Sorry friend, but better you than me."

During the three years subsequent to my first series of interviews, 33 percent of the unemployed group were laid off twice; 17 percent were laid off more than twice. And from 1972 to 1975, 14 percent of the previously employed group were also terminated.[2]

People who survived a first and perhaps a second series of layoffs felt both uneasiness and confidence that the company recognized their importance. Then as the age of 40 approached, when an expected contract failed to materialize, or the time for vesting of full pension benefits neared, they, too, were let go.

> I thought they needed me. I made it through the '71 and '73 layoffs. Had to hire and fire hundreds, perhaps thousands of men during the last four years. We were waiting for a contract we didn't get. My closest colleague died of a heart attack right on the spot the day he knew we lost it. Then after 14 years they told me on Friday afternoon not to be back on Monday. My wife asked me how I got my things out so fast. I had had them ready. I was shocked at the time but must have known all along.

> I had been with the company for 27 years. Always did what was expected of me. We had to close a division. We had to fire many qualified chemists—and I held the axe. Soon after my fifty-fifth birthday I was forced into early retirement. The early retirement package was a far cry from what it would have been had they let me stay on to 65.

In the seventies society of specialists some Route 128 companies hired management consulting firms to help with the "outplacement" process. TH, Inc., a Manhattan based firm, for instance, taught executives how to conduct "exit" interviews and then immediately interviewed outplaced professionals to give them a chance to "venticulate" against the consultant instead of the company from which they had been fired (Spiegelman, 1973:1, 10). Some of these personnel entrepreneurs supposedly provided reemployment counseling. The use of public relations firms however, rarely mollified the terminated.

Successful professionals who are fired at age 40 or 50 are rudely torn from their social context. Psychological preparation for an experience such

---

[2] An additional 20 percent of this group had moved out of the Boston area by 1975. They were either laid off or transferred. A few probably relocated voluntarily.

as career interruption is virtually impossible. Scientists and technologists were no better prepared for sudden termination in 1975 than they were in 1971, although they surely should have been. And as cutbacks in many areas of the economy brought unemployment to teachers, administrators, academics, and executives, individuals were always surprised when personally hit.

Job Search

> I did everything I could to find another job. But there were just no jobs for electronics engineers. I must have sent out hundreds of resumes—no replies. Rejected everywhere I turned. Part of the trouble is that I don't have many contacts except for the people who used to work for me. When you're with one place for 16 years you don't have people who can write for you. Something must be wrong with my resume. I've tried to change it around. I guess I don't know how. I don't know what to do. For the first time in my life I feel completely helpless. How do I live with this terrible feeling. What the hell am I going to do?

Job finding skills, unneeded before, were not cultivated. During the late 1950s and through the 1960s, technical professionals were flooded with offers from fancy firms. If a particular job was unsatisfactory, all that was necessary to find another was a walk across Route 128, a single phone call to a friend, or one visit to a headhunter. Technical professionals could write contract proposals more easily than personal resumes. They could hype a new product or process but had no experience selling *themselves*. Those laid off in the seventies did not know where or how to begin the search for reemployment.

Coming to Terms with the Situation

First of all, they had to overcome embarrassment and admit to their families, their friends, and especially themselves that *they*, recently so successful, were actually out of work. Some were too ashamed to confide in their families. One engineer was out three months and told no one. His wife called the office one day to let him know that her checking account was overdrawn. The surprised secretary told her that he was no longer with the company. That night when he came home she confronted him and they wept together. An unemployed physicist spoke of his neighbor:

> He was a well-known department manager, an important man. He must have been making at least $40,000. He was out of a job for six months before he told his wife. In the meantime, she kept right on spending. Their debts kept accumulating. Finally they were forced into bankruptcy. They left town in the middle of the night. No one has heard from them since.

I learned from employment crisis groups how difficult it is for professionals to admit their need for work. Although those who appeared at these meetings were an activated minority, even they had trouble discussing why they had come. The Lincoln Job Opportunities Group was more likely to focus on company policy than personal problems. The Association of Technical Professionals decided in steering committee strategy sessions to emphasize the importance of organizational clout for the employed, even more than for the unemployed. These patterns changed as unemployment persisted in Lincoln, Lexington, and elsewhere. But first unemployed professionals had to face facts squarely: they had been *fired* while others were retained. They were of less value to employers than they had imagined. Ultimately they were forced to seek help from family, friends, professional associates, and state institutions. And gradually, as they explained their needs to others, they admitted to themselves that they were jobless.

Resumes and Interviews

Route 128 professionals applied to the job search the rational mind set that had worked so well for them in the past. They prepared resumes and sent them out to every firm they thought might possibly need their services. Sixty-two percent of my sample mailed from 50 to 300 resumes. The others sent resumes only if they thought they really had a chance.[3] Most firms never bothered to reply. Few men were called for interviews.

> I wait for the phone calls. Wait and wait. If I push it and call myself I get the standard brush-off: "Thank you for your resume. We will get back to you as soon as we can." And I know that means never. I can't just keep calling. It's the hopelessness of it all that gets you down.

And if they came, interviews brought discouragement more frequently than employment.

> One night a VP called and asked me about a job from a resume I'd sent. I went in and a personnel man was there. Gave me a stupid test. I told him I was supposed to see the VP. He told me to go away; they'd call me if they needed me. It was dishonest. Companies interview a lot of guys to get ideas to see how to run a job. The personnel men you see don't really know the work. How can they hire the best man for the job? The whole thing stinks. That's why I hate big companies.

> Had an interview the other day with a small company. The engineer who interviewed me actually told me I was lying about my qualifications. I told him he

[3] The median number of resumes sent was upward of 50. The median number of interview requests was three.

could check my references. But he asked my salary. I broke it down by the week, which was the mistake. It's more professional to give it by the year. Maybe that's why he was so sure I was lying. You can imagine how angry I feel every time I think about it.

I was out for a year, had given up hope. But I saw this ad in the Sunday paper for a job that was perfect for me. I sent a letter and my resume. They called me for an interview. I thought the job was mine. The family sat around with me and waited for the phone call. It never came. Someone told me later that a younger man was hired for the job. It was all nothing but a phony PR stunt to make the company look like they hire older men.

Contacting Friends

The unemployed called their friends, people with whom they had worked who knew their abilities, and professional acquaintances they knew from conferences. Usually they sensed uneasiness at the other end of the wire. Sometimes there was a polite brush-off. Frequently calls were not returned.

None of my friends were there in the crunch. They were firing older guys and hiring others. I was willing to take anything. They know how good I am. But they don't even talk to me.

The unemployed felt isolated from colleagues. They felt alone in their search for work. This loneliness increased, just as it did among jobless workers in the Great Depression, as they realized that hundreds, perhaps thousands, of qualified people competed for every position that might be theirs.

Department of Employment Security

At the outset, unemployed seventies professionals fully expected assistance from official help institutions. They registered at local Massachusetts Department of Employment Security (DES) offices. These federally funded state agencies are charged with three tasks: distribution of compensation checks, job placement services, and compilation of unemployment statistics.[4] DES offices in Route 128 communities were swamped with hun-

---

[4] U.S. Department of Labor funding of state DES agencies depends upon their placement rates. Released DES statistics are consequently suspect. (The Massachusetts DES claimed placement rates of 9.2 percent in 1972, 8.6 percent in 1973, 14.4 percent in 1974, and 18.0 percent in 1975). "At DES a placement means that a person got hired and stayed on the job for at least one day." ("Employment Office Fails to Find People Work," 1974:11).
Employers complain that state DES offices do not service *their* needs.

dreds of new registrants daily. They processed people quickly and impersonally and provided checks to the eligible. DES personnel had little time to make job referrals.

A top management official at DES said: "That's the absurdity of the whole thing. DES very rarely makes referrals from the unemployment line. They can barely service the people who walk in the doors looking for work." ("Employment Office Fails to Find People Work," 1974:11)

Professionals dreaded the weekly (biweekly by 1978) wait in line for $72 or $86—in the early seventies—and $95 or $114—in the middle seventies—to feed their families. They resented "superficial," "impersonal," and "insensitive" treatment from state employees.

You stand in unemployment lines—people drive by and look at you like you are shit. They're not supposed to be for people like me.

It's humiliating. You feel like cattle. Who would have thought I'd be standing in line for hours, sometimes fighting to keep my place, for a meager check. It's painful. Hard to talk about. It takes me the rest of the day to recover.

People who work there are below average in intelligence. They degrade you. They are rude, cold, insulting. They treat you like it was their money they were giving away and you ought to be grateful.

Experiences at the DES were always degrading for scientists and technologists, accustomed to feeling needed. Class and status attributes of recent years were stripped away and all at once these professionals were brought back to the working-class milieu from which they had fought so hard to escape. This was perhaps the basic source of their humiliation. Some deliberately dressed in suit and tie, they said, to distinguish themselves as professionals. Forty-four percent of those I interviewed expressed intense resentment of state employees, their social inferiors, from whom they nonetheless had to beg assistance. The rest of the sample felt

---

I have to spend a lot of money in the newspaper instead of getting people free through DES and we're paying taxes for these services," said Mary Rizzilano, personnel director for Cambion, which makes electronic parts. (Stewart, 1975:52)

The New England Regional Commission's Task Force on Capital and Labor Markets reported:

This has resulted in some estrangement between business, the potential client, and the DES. Business and the public generally have come to see DES not as places to seek employment, but, instead, as places to get unemployment compensation.

The unemployed worker is the victim. . . .

. . . Far too many businessmen consider DES as nothing more than a way station to welfare.

As a result, the communication between DES, which should provide the job applicant, and business, which needs the worker, has seriously deteriorated. (Stewart, 1975:52)

humiliation but struggled to retain professional objectivity. Their general attitude: "All you can expect is your check and you get it"; "They're not trained to deal with professionals"; "You can't expect them to help you find a job."

> Routine bureaucratic, vacant advice. Told me there were no jobs at my level. They handed me the check. Curiously it felt demeaning. So out of their realm to deal with people like me.

> The girls were polite enough. But after all those years I went to school and all those nights I spent developing my knowledge—the idea of standing in line and taking a handout from people like that was really tough. I dreaded every Friday morning.

Route 128 Professional Service Center

Unlike factory workers, past or present, who have found themselves jobless, unemployed seventies scientists and engineers *had been* widely regarded as important people. The "tragedy" of their unemployment made national headlines. Heralds of the new society had special needs and deserved special attention, the media maintained. With much political fanfare, a Professional Service Center, supported by Department of Labor funds, opened in January 1971 in the heart of the Route 128 belt. Promises were elaborate: a computerized job bank, counselors, psychologists, and financial advisors. The unemployed flocked to the center. Here they found new forms of rejection and disappointment—nothing but another computerized, bureaucratized mess. Eighty-seven percent of my sample sought help from the center; the others heard it was so bad they thought it useless to try.

> I went to that center three times. That whole matching and placement process is stupid and ridiculous. They couldn't find the right holes to punch. Only had me as a manager, but what about my degrees in metallurgy, chemistry, and engineering?

> They never knew what to do with my resume. Printouts are ridiculous. Too many people apply for each entry—two or three thousand. Listing not specified enough, so you can't tell if the job really fits you. Everyone applies for everything. So the good jobs never get listed here. How can the firms be bothered?

> I've never been so humiliated in all my life. I waited a long time for this slick, young jerk to interview me. He looks at my resume, sees my degrees, my former positions. Then says, "Okay, Len, let's see what you can do." *Len!* They don't even call you mister. They take away your dignity before they start. I walked out and never went back.

The center's placement record was dismal. The unemployed were not wrong in their assessment.[5] During the first 18 months of operations, the director claimed only 535 "reportable" placements at a cost of $301,000. By 1975, a new director claimed about 20 placements per week. "They don't listen to us," said a counselor who was there from the start. "They come in once and never return. We tell them it takes months to place a professional. We tell them to come back weekly. But many are in such a fog we can't get through."

Most professionals tried the center soon after layoff. They left disappointed and depressed. If all else failed, some returned. Occasionally, out of desperation, they took a low paying job that scarcely utilized their talents. A few in my sample eventually found placements: one as a technician at $8,000, another as a mechanic at $10,000. There were no listings for solid state physicists, electronics engineers, or research chemists who were as yet unwilling to move down rapidly.

An estimated 80 to 90 percent of professional level positions are reportedly filled through in-house channels. Good jobs were rarely listed at the center or advertised in newspapers. Yet 65 percent of the unemployed answered ads they knew might well be phony. Some went to companies directly—usually to be told that the job was filled. They kept trying anyway, like those who walked the streets in the Depression 40 years before them.

Private Agencies

Some professionals sought help from private employment agencies. Management-paid specialized placement agents, most helpful in previous periods of prosperity, were useless in the crunch. Headhunters, *Electronics* noted, always oriented toward recruitment for management (their employers), never focused on the problems of unemployed professionals (Halstron, 1972:107). Headhunters rarely returned the calls of people over 40, even those they knew and had personally placed in the past. To be unemployed, even in these difficult times, was itself a stigma.

> If you're unemployed, you're considered unemployable. They let you know, in no uncertain terms, that companies are looking for people good enough to hold on to their jobs. If you have a job, they can get you another. But then who needs them?

Some had enough cash at the beginning of their job search or were desperate enough later on to pay for help. Sunday newspapers listed the following kinds of ads from private employment counseling services.

[5] A survey by the Associated Industries of Massachusetts indicated that only 3.7 percent of the companies contacted said that job openings and applicants were properly matched by the DES (including the Route 128 Professional Service Center) (Patterson, 1972:34).

Job hunting
    If you qualify for a $12,000 to $65,000 job send us your resume now and let us help direct you to the missing majority.

Discouraged
    About your inability to find the right job: It's not surprising. The *best* jobs are seldom advertised and even more infrequently appear at employment agencies. . . . And that's where we come in.

The career game
    It shouldn't be a gamble. If you know how to market your skills, how to use your abilities, you *can* get interviews—fast.

Career positions
    Are hard to get. An extensive job search is futile if you are not prepared for the interviewing and hiring process. And those who aren't will have no second interview—not ever knowing why.

If an individual responded, most firms asked him to come for an interview and to bring his wife. The first two consultations were usually free of charge. So-called consultants generally looked conservative, like middle-aged insurance salesmen. They attempted a subtle sale. During the first session, called the "probe," the potential client was asked to explain in writing all that he hoped the agency would do for him. What each provided amounted to a personal plea for help. During the consultation, called the "close," the client was promised the assistance he asked for—everything short of actual job placement. By law these counseling firms are not permitted to maintain job listings or to promise placement. If the client signed, he was promised help (for up to five years if necessary) until he found the job he was looking for. The client paid a fee—in advance—based on his previous salary, usually about $1,000. The fee in advance was an important part of the process, agency personnel claimed, because it motivated people to work harder at helping themselves. Finally, the client was assigned a counselor who might be a psychologist, an ex-clergyman, or a businessman (he could change counselors or even get a rebate if dissatisfied after the first few sessions).

The relationship between client and counselor was usually the crux of the process. Vocational and personality tests were administered. Feelings of confidence in the counselor developed. Then a process of positive programming began. The client was asked to list all the achievements of his life. The counselor picked out the "success factors"; perseverance, innovation, creativity, discipline, courage. Together they developed a resume. The client was encouraged to develop personal contact networks. The counselor initiated this program of positive focus, providing guidance and above all sympathy. One placement professional I interviewed explained his role.

I help them define objectives. I help them focus their resources around their "blue sky" job. I help to reinforce a positive self-image, which helps them find a job. The mind can work like a computer. You get them to focus on the job they want. You get them to dig out all the information they can about the job. The mind stores it and directs them to the job. Positive programming is the key. Another aspect is that I can sympathize with them. This cuts their loneliness and helps with the image problem.

Private counseling agencies helped two men in my sample feel better about themselves; one found temporary reemployment; the other established himself as an independent consultant, with subsequently fluctuating fortunes. Most of the men in my sample who paid for such services were dissatisfied. Some claimed outright dishonesty.

Self-help Groups

Employment crisis groups—self-help groups—that emerged in the early seventies were another possible avenue for people seeking assistance. Image building was part of their purpose; mutual support was another. Only a small percentage of my random sample sought out such a group. A few people gained perspective, which helped them cope. A few made contacts that they hoped would lead to jobs. Most who came once, however, never returned to a second meeting.

Self-help group activists tried to co-operate with VEST (Volunteer Engineers, Scientists, and Technicians), a Department of Labor supported organization. NE-VEST, in the New England area, openly appealed to the unemployed to participate in self-appraisal and job development ("Waltham Session to Aid Jobless Space Engineers," 1971:5). NE-VEST was organized in cooperation with the DES at the Route 128 Professional Service Center. Unemployed technical professionals were required to volunteer time to do the work necessary to maintain group activities in exchange for NE-VEST's assistance. The center provided space and phones. A program of workshops began in 1971 and continued through the decade.

NE-VEST was beset by organizational problems because the most active volunteers placed themselves in jobs and left the group; these volunteers also fought with self-help group organizers whom they and DES personnel considered too political. Federal and state funding was threatened and then curtailed in the mid-seventies, but the Route 128 center continued to provide support facilities and the workshop program survived. For a time professional societies successfully solicited employed members to train as leaders, and sessions with the unemployed were held at various locations around Route 128. After 1976 the program was confined to the center and broadened to include all types of unemployed professionals. I interviewed NE-VEST volunteers, workshop facilitators, and professionals who had attended the workshops, and I observed several sessions. Those who took advantage of the sessions found support and useful information therein.

The facilitator opened the first session with attempts to elicit feelings shared by jobless professionals seeking work. When the words "depression" and "desperation" were mentioned people nodded agreement but usually offered little about themselves. "Friends think there is something wrong with you," said the leader of one group I attended.

> In our society we're told to get a good education and then get a good job. We're told we *ought* to be working. Some of us think that selling is a dirty word. We must redefine ourselves as self-employed people who are selling a product: ourselves.

The unemployed were encouraged to talk to their families, to explain that the siege was apt to be long (six to nine months), and to request their help—for instance, to ask them to stay off the phone so calls could come through but to screen calls if necessary. They were advised to economize in all areas but to keep the telephone and health insurance. They were told that unemployed people are apt to suffer physical illness and need health coverage more than in the past.

Subsequent sessions concerned details of the job search. People were asked to prepare lists in a data book as if they were the product to be marketed. They were asked to index each chapter:

1. Places I earned money
2. Hobbies and leisure activities
3. Formal education
4. Special interests/areas of expertise
5. Achievements—things I've done that have made me feel good about myself
6. Accomplishments—things I've done that others have admired
7. Dreams
8. Personal and professional contacts

Focus and resume reconstruction were emphasized. Participants criticized and advised each other. The facilitator discussed "shotgun letters" in answer to job advertisements: "Tell them *only* what was requested; do not give away possible *de-selectors.*"

> You can never tell in advance what de-selectors are operating—age, education, school attended, previous experience, previous salary, sex, race, religion, employment status. Avoid personal data until you get an interview.

The unemployed were given tips: insist on personal rather than telephone interviews, make a dry run to the potential place of employment, and research the company's contract flow. They were told to work full-time (at least 30 hours a week) at finding a job. They were warned against career consultants.

The last of the basic sessions examined the interview process. Role-playing techniques were used to defuse fears of new situations and to help people gain perspective on self-preservation through experiences as interviewer and interviewee.

The workshops seemed to bolster the self-confidence of those professionals who attended them regularly. My observations were confirmed by Douglas Powell's study, which compared a sample of 22 scientists and engineers who went to such seminars with a matched sample from the Route 128 center who had not. Powell found that people who attended meetings had more positive feelings about themselves and conducted a more active job search than those who did not. After 90 days, 11 men from the workshops found jobs, compared with six from the control group (Powell, 1973:165).

The Lucky Break

Most unemployed technical professionals looked for work as hard as they could for as long as they could. They tried every method they thought realistic and stopped only when all seemed hopeless. This point was reached sooner for some than for others.

> I worked full-time at it in the beginning. Sent hundreds of resumes; only got one interview. Called everyone I knew. Went to every group I could find. Even went to headhunters. Finally I realized I was just too old. I know how hopeless it is. I sleep late. Work on my ham radio. Spend some time looking around trying to start up my own business.

> I was working as hard when I was unemployed as when I was working. Harder. Went all over every day looking for work. Would drive up to companies and leave resumes. Would knock on doors myself. I had to work at side jobs to supplement unemployment compensation. Fixed TVs, worked on automobiles, and even cleaned boilers. Kept working and looking.

> At first unemployment was a full-time job. I went to DES, to the center—nothing for people at my level. Sent over 100 resumes; only a few replies—nothing for research physicists. Called my friends. Then things slowed down. I would type some letters; waited for phone contacts during prime hours. Painted the house. Finally one of my teachers at MIT found a research job for me in one of their labs.

It took seventies professionals about six months to find work. Median length of unemployment, the first time around, among scientists and engineers in my early seventies sample, was five months (for 26 percent it took three months or less; for 37 percent it took four to seven months; for

37 percent it took nine months to three years). Other studies confirmed these findings. Median length of unemployment among scientists and engineers who had been laid off while working on NASA contracts was seven months (U.S. Department of Commerce, National Technical Information Service, 1971:viii). Median length of unemployment among Thompson's (1972:II-14) sample of Route 128 engineers was six months. Public and private employment service personnel, NE-VEST facilitators, and self-help group activists all cautioned the jobless to prepare for a concerted six-month search.

The unemployed tried both formal (DES, the center, agencies, ads) and informal (friends, personal contacts) means in the job hunt. None of the institutionalized methods brought measurable results. Route 128 center officials told me that their reported placement rates of 19 or 25 per week in 1976 were an underestimate since "we don't hear from people after they start working." Private counseling services publicly claimed placement rates of 80 to 98 percent, after 16 to 20 weeks, if clients conscientiously followed prescribed programs. When I asked for documentation, agency personnel admitted that their effectiveness was "difficult to measure" and that "accurate statistics were hard to get." NE-VEST claimed that their seminars placed 20 percent of the people who "followed through." I found that each method helped a few, but reemployment, especially at levels considered adequate, was secured in the main through an individual's network of personal and professional contacts, as Table 6-1 illustrates.

> I got a call, out of the blue one day, from a young man who used to work for me. He is with a small company. He knew I could help him with a problem they had. I went in on a one-shot consulting agreement. They got a big contract from a foreign government. I've been there ever since.

> It didn't take too long to find another job. I was luckier, not better, than many of those still out. My old boss moved to another firm. He needed me. Called me on Friday. I was back again by Monday.

> A friend of mine found a job for me with a friend of his whose company got a major contract. They needed some top level people quickly.

Scientists and engineers in the 1970s believed in the social institutions that had put them in positions of comfort and importance. They believed, most of all, in the rationalized world of computer technology made possible in part by their own contributions. But these institutions and procedures failed them. Operational requisites of bureaucratized systems labs caused on-the-job dissatisfaction. During the job search, dissatisfaction turned to bitterness. These men felt trapped by impersonal methods of employee selection. They found it impossible to cut through the personnel

Table 6–1
Job Search Methods

	Ways Help Sought	Most Helpful Method[1]
Friends and personal contacts	89%	50%
Direct application to firms	67	10
Private employment agencies	56	6
Massachusetts DES	71	4
Route 128 Professional Service Center	85	2
Newspaper ads	68	6
Professional journal ads	33	0
Assistance from former employers	23	0
Professional societies	15	0

[1] Twenty-two percent remained unemployed and found no method helpful.

staff to talk with project leaders, who could evaluate their utility. They found that formalized methods of securing reemployment did not work, at least not for them. The straightforward ways resulted only in repeated rejection. And even the Professional Service Center, supposedly tailored to their needs, was at best seen as a sham. Indeed, the center was a particular target for their anger because it symbolized the failure of technologized society to meet the needs of people—and, in this case, the needs of the very people who helped create that society.

Government did nothing for unemployed professionals except to fund the Route 128 center and a few token programs in other parts of the country in the early seventies. By the mid-seventies, the full impact of nationwide unemployment obscured needs of professionals as a special category. Jobs programs promised by politicians aimed at the working classes. Inflation rather than unemployment was the economic problem of public concern later in the decade. The unemployed professional who looked for work in the seventies felt alone.

Reemployment

Experimental physicist, age 32
    Laid off in 1970 . . . out a few weeks . . . took lower paying position but still in physics. Laid off again because when things got tough for the company I had been the last hired. Took crash course in programming. Now I'm a programmer with this large insurance company. I earn less money and there's certainly much less to look forward to.

1975. Still with the same company. We're doing systems analysis for insurance application programs. The company is in transition to more system programming and they want me in this transition. Feel good about my job. Sometimes I feel underutilized when I have to do nit-picky clerical things that I can't give to someone else to do. But I guess these kinds of things go with any job. Really glad I picked what I did—to retrain for and to work for. This is one of the few places around really hiring.

Electronics engineer, age 45
    I worked for that company for 15 years—first anti-missile program . . . designed antenna systems, vehicle and aircraft tracking systems. Last two years before layoff, I went to a Pacific island test site on a top secret, highly classified project. . . . I went so I could save money to buy a house. But when I came back I wasn't solidly plugged in. Never expected to be fired. Real hardship . . . out a few months . . . took many engineers on the market so I took a job as a technician. Worked for this small outfit for five months . . . It went out. So bitter and depressed. I couldn't live that way anymore. I took another technician job for even less and repair TVs at night. You take what you can get. You pull yourself together. With kids around you have to manage somehow. You could say I'm in commercial electronics. Takehome pay is 45 percent less than 128.

1975. He was called four times. I tried in the evening and on weekends. His children told me that they never knew when he would be home because he had a few different jobs. His wife was never available. Obviously they managed to keep their Needham home.

Solid state physicist, age 54
    Laid off in 1970. I was out four months. They took me into ADAPT [federally funded program held at MIT to teach unemployed Ph.D.'s urban applications of their knowledge]. I was placed in a job with an urban department of public works in another city . . . left family here. . . . The job folded. It was fortunate though because I had to come back to Massachusetts. I found a job computerizing accounting systems for the state. I make about 20 percent less than my previous salary. Not exciting research, but interesting work . . . will be glad if its lasts.

1975. Working for a different division of the same state department. I'm still underpaid. I'm no longer a physicist but I guess I'm doing well considering. . . . I just have to hope the job continues. A new commissioner was appointed . . . wasn't sure for a time exactly what would happen. Things seem to have settled down.

Eventually most technical professionals found reemployment of one kind or another. But career stability seldom followed the first layoff. After weeks, months, or years without work, 24 percent of my original unemployed sample were reemployed once and kept that job, 34 percent were laid off and reemployed twice, 4 percent established viable independent enterprises, 16 percent were laid off and reemployed three or more times between 1970 and 1975 amid episodes of joblessness, 10 percent were never really employed again, and 12 percent involuntarily left the Boston area (some for jobs but some to move in with relatives). Between 1972 and 1975 my original retained sample, the control group, now three years older, had problems keeping their jobs. Six percent were laid off and unemployed in 1975, 8 percent were laid off and reemployed, dissatisfaction and fear caused 6 percent to change careers, and 20 percent left the Boston area.[6]

Among the many obstacles to reemployment, the stigma of unemployment itself was particularly difficult to overcome. Achievements of the past were discounted as experienced people were considered overqualified for the jobs that existed. They could not be hired, according to management, because they would "always be looking for something better." Fear of knowledge obsolescence grew: "How can you keep up if you're isolated from work and colleagues?" As the months went by, many lost faith in themselves and came to doubt their own employability.

On the whole, reemployment was more difficult for engineers than for data systems analysts or scientists. People with master's degrees faced a tighter market than did Ph.D.'s or bachelor's. Men with over 20 years' experience with one or two firms and those with highly unstable career profiles—the extremes—remained unemployed longest. Professionals in higher income brackets, as well as top staff and middle managers, also had more trouble than others.[7]

The biggest barrier to reemployment was age. The older technical professional was more likely to be laid off to begin with, more likely to be unemployed for longer periods of time, and less likely to be reemployed at all.[8] Thirty-one percent of the men I interviewed who were over 45 at first layoff failed to find jobs. Many of those who did were forced into low level slots or demanding but very temporary positions.

The kinds of jobs professionals took usually paid less, were often less interesting, and were always less secure than those they held at the turn of the seventies. There were two dimensions to underemployment: the level of challenge and skill utilization and salary. Sixty percent of the reemployed took technical positions at lower levels than their previous jobs had occupied. Knowledge utilization in these cases was sometimes total but more likely partial or absent—from a project manager in a large defense electronics firm through three years of sporadic employment to manager of a middle-

[6] The retained remained the more stable group. Sixty percent held their jobs throughout: some moved up in their companies; some had to change task orientation—a frequent pattern was from basic research to hardware development.
[7] Thompson (1972:III-14) also found reemployment more difficult for people at opposite ends of the skill and interest continuum. Those most interested in engineering as well as those with low performance ratings were jobless the longest.
[8] The federal government surveyed the effects of contract fluctuations and/or cancellations on displaced defense and aerospace technologists during the late 1960s and early 1970s. Age discrimination was cited by every such study as the major obstacle to reemployment (Bain, 1968:17; Loomba, 1967:51; Mooney, 1966:12; Ross .and Ross, 1968:98; Thompson, 1972:III-10; U.S. Arms Control and Disarmament Agency, 1969:22, 96; U.S. Department of Commerce, National Technical Information Service, 1971:65).

sized commercial plant on a trial basis; from data systems analyst to junior high school math teacher; from reliability engineer to the night shift in a knitting mill; from technical vice-president of a major firm, followed by three years without much work, to staff physicist; from principal engineer to programmer; or from mechanical engineer to insurance salesman. Thirty percent of the reemployed fared better than this, managing to locate jobs generally comparable to those they lost, at least in terms of skill utilization—from advanced systems development to nuclear energy projects; from principal engineer to project manager; or from aerospace engineer through a research stint at a university laboratory to military engineering projects. These were the fortunate minority but their salaries did not always match their responsibilities. Ten percent of the reemployed essentially hired themselves. They tried independent business ventures: one thrived; two survived; others called themselves consultants with a few days' work now and then from old friends.

Reemployment did not bring prosperity to seventies professionals. Seventy-eight percent of my original sample had taken jobs by 1972. Of these only 21 percent claimed full employment in economic terms; 28 percent took "bearable" cuts (1 to 15 percent), 10 percent sustained substantial reductions (16 to 25 percent), 24 percent went back to work for even less (26 to 40 percent), and 17 percent suffered salary cuts so drastic (45 to 66 percent) as barely to replace unemployment compensation. Over the next three years, new defense contracts and federal funding of energy research and medical electronics made it possible for some (usually the younger men) to change jobs for higher pay. Despite a general economic recession, which by 1975 adversely affected commercial employment opportunities, 57 percent of the mid-seventies reemployed said they were doing fairly well financially (even if they feared their jobs were temporary). Twenty-eight percent remained underemployed as schoolteachers, computer programmers, or engineers with small, struggling commercial companies. Fifteen percent were still in dire straits. These figures do not include those who were jobless (22 percent in 1972; 10 percent in 1975). And estimates of salary reduction were not corrected for the bite of inflation. A majority of the profesionals who were dislodged in the seventies had to face downward economic mobility.

Success stories among the unemployed or the retained who changed careers were rare. One 37-year-old physicist went from laser research with a large Route 128 firm into business in his own garage. He invented, manufactured, and marketed a gadget that caught on. In a year his income doubled; in three years it quadrupled. His success was more than financial; he had found liberation.

> There's a feeling of control over my personal situation. Always wanted to be on my own. Stay away from anything that has government support—squeeze on tax dollars caused by big defense contracts not healthy for the economy. Big

business is trying to cut me out but I've been anti–big business all the way so didn't have much of an overhead from the beginning. My machinery is antique but I can make the bicycle racks much better and cheaper than the big companies so I should be okay. I'm saving as much as I can. I guess you really never know.

He was pessimistic, however, about the prospects of his former colleagues: "You have to be a self-starter. Most of the guys aren't. They're dull. No real spark. No new ideas."

There was usually newfound satisfaction in task diversification. One 58-year-old engineer, who had been disgusted by routinized proposal writing, was without work for three years. His brothers finally provided the capital to help him start a business.

I do all the technical work to get the sound track on a film. Four hundred customers now. Doing about as well financially as before layoff. Really good to be working and using your abilities. . . . Some new customers but the old ones don't come as frequently. This is still a one-man show. I pick up and deliver and do all the technical and secretarial work. It seems that everyone takes at least 90 days to pay their bills.

Despite dissatisfaction, most professionals, unless forced, were afraid to change careers in midstream. Those who had the courage to do so gave mixed reviews. One bored chemist found success and satisfaction as a stockbroker but described the hazards he saw for others.

I was involved in investments as a hobby all along. The opportunity to work for a large investment company listed on the New York Stock Exchange came up and I decided to take the chance. This is more of a test of your own worth. I can be more independent. I can show my stuff. It's actually fun. Many of the people here had formerly been technical people of one sort or another. It's difficult to make it here. There is a very high mortality rate. You can't become an instant broker.

One optical physicist, disgusted by the irrationality of defense contract fluctuation left well-paid but uncertain employment in 1975 for optometry school.

They have a two-year program for Ph.D.'s in science. Full-time—straight through the summers. The only secure future is in health services. People should get out of science and research. I'm not going to do research in optometry. I want to practice. I don't think of it as giving up my skills—just using them differently.

I kept in touch with this man over the years. He loved optometry school. When he finished he had no capital to open his own office and had to work part-time for someone less qualified than himself. He was struggling to find a way to break out on his own. He had financial problems but few regrets about leaving Route 128 research.

These successful mid-career changes were atypical. More common among the financially solvent survivors were (1) people who sacrificed commitment to fundamental research for short-run applications projects, (2) people who buried former resistance to war work and shifted from energy or space to missile systems development, or (3) people who relinquished exploration of technological frontiers for less interesting but more stable commercial employment. The reemployed found that American society had not fully forgotten its experts. Civilian industries paid for their services when they could afford to do so. Forty-six percent of my reemployed 1972 sample took initial jobs, usually at low salaries, in the commercial-industrial sector.[9] These kinds of jobs were less available later. Once again professionals out of work had to track the contract flow to technology row. They had to learn where and how to peddle expertise—military hardware and computer software remained the surest ways.

[9] Twenty-nine percent of the others found jobs in the defense industries; 7 percent were supported by federal non-defense contracts; and 18 percent found jobs in state or local government, schools, or junior colleges.

7

Experiencing Unemployment: Economic Survival

I was out for six months. I'm a programmer now working for 25 percent less than before. We're still in there but our sights are much lower now.

Things were very tight when I was out. I got $1,000 in severance pay and weekly unemployment compensation checks. My wife works as a relief nurse on weekends for $100 a week. We feel we just made it. Had to take a $1,500 loan.

I was a physicist-engineer. We looked forward to a large salary when we bought this house. My salary as a programmer is not going to soar. There has been a change in our expectations, especially on my wife's part. And it took time to get used to. Can't dismiss the disappointment. We both work. We're adjusting. Have learned to deemphasize material things. My wife would never go camping before. We always had to rent a cabin. I got her to go camping, if she wanted any vacation at all this year. She actually enjoyed it. We've changed in other ways, too.

The first time I was laid off I was out 13 months. I had two months' continuance pay, $4,000, and then compensation checks. Wife went to work in a department store; she brought in a little. We had heavy expenses to begin with. Bills came in immediately. We had to take loans.

You find you can live on less. I don't know how we did it. We bought no

133

clothes, spent much less on food, only paid the interest on the mortgage. Each month I thought we couldn't go on and yet we made it through. We wanted food stamps; couldn't get them. We used to have beautiful things in this room. We had to sell everything dealers would buy just for food and utilities. None of us had a medical checkup for two years. There was a time when I washed windows during the day and was a guard at an electronics plant at night. No sleep.

Finally another engineering job came through. It was a long commute and 35 percent less than the $26,000 I'd been making before. The job lasted a few years. Found another job closer to home this time. Still earning less than before.

I've been unemployed for about a year now. Had some severance pay and compensation checks, $81 a week—pays for the food. Savings all gone. Wife works. She brings in enough to keep us going. Trying to get a loan so my older daughter can go to college. Just about at the end of the line. But we'll never go back to the Bronx. We *must* keep this lifestyle.

I'm up there now and won't sink back. I'm too afraid to let myself think about it. It just can't happen.

Middle-aged professionals lost their income security with the first notice of termination; reemployment rarely restored fringe benefits or retirement plans. Their economic troubles persisted for at least as long as they were out of work. The last paycheck was not followed by immediate economic crisis among 1970s professionals as it was for workers unprotected by union benefits or among the unemployed in the Great Depression. But status loss was as difficult for many to bear as economic hardship had been for others.

Dwindling Financial Resources

Most Route 128 people had resources that helped them manage for a time, as Table 7–1 indicates. Ninety percent of those I interviewed received from several hundred to several thousand dollars in severance pay. One week's wages for each year of company service was standard policy in the early 1970s; this had been halved by 1975. Then they collected unemployment compensation. Eighty-four percent obtained weekly checks ranging from $72 to $96. These increased to $127 in 1978 for people with dependents who had been in the higher income brackets but eligibility then lasted for 30 weeks with no extensions. Most had savings and some had income from investments. Seventy-six percent gradually used up savings or liquidated holdings to meet living expenses. In addition, some of the older professionals, in what must be a new American anomaly, survived by combining unemployment compensation with dividends from shares they held

Table 7-1
Financial Resources Available to Unemployed Professionals

Types of Resources	Percentage of Unemployed Professionals Utilizing Each Type
Severance pay	90%
Unemployment compensation	84
Savings and investments	76
Wife's salary or wages	72
Temporary jobs	45
Loans; remortgaged house	20
Funds from pension plans	20
Assistance from extended family	12
Small inheritance	6
U.S. Naval Reserves; veterans' benefits	4
Rental property	4

in the very companies from which they had been fired.[1] Most of the men were married to educated, skilled, creative women, who if not already employed generally found jobs quickly. The wives of 76 percent of my sample worked: 48 percent had either full-time or substantial half-time professional level positions; 24 percent worked from 10 to 40 hours a week but rarely took home more than $100. By combining these resources, unemployed seventies professionals managed for longer than any of them at first had imagined possible. Ultimately, just how severe the economic impact of unemployment was for the professional and his family depended largely on the number of months that elapsed before he found another job and on the kind of job found.

Living Through an Economic Crisis

Six months was about the average period that technical professionals in the early seventies were jobless. This was enough time, in most cases, for a real financial crunch to begin. Twenty-two percent of my sample were still unemployed at the time of the first interview. Most of the others went back

[1] When Route 128 firms were rapidly expanding in the 1960s many gave valued employees bonuses in the form of stock options. This practice continued: Silicon Valley firms expanding in the mid-seventies used "stock ownership heavily to attract employees" (McElheny, 1976:D1). If technical professionals subsequently were laid off, bitterness grew with the amount of their dividends. During the peak layoff year of 1971, Raytheon, for instance, had the "highest sales and earnings per share in any year in the history of the company" ("Record Sales by Big Employers," 1972:1). Loomba (1967:107) also found that firms involved in aerospace layoffs had large profit margins during the high layoff periods.

to work after varying lengths of time (from three months or less to 18 months or more) for lower salaries than they earned before (as detailed in Chapter 6). Most of these people did not keep the new job for very long. Only 24 percent of those reemployed by 1972 held the same positions when I spoke with them three years later. A minority made changes for the better but many (the last to be hired) were laid off again and again as contracts expired and the economy slumped. Gradually they experienced economic catastrophe.

For 21 percent of my sample the economic effects of unemployment were *not* severe: those who were reemployed within a few months, whose severance pay was generous, whose savings were not depleted, whose new job brought a good salary, or whose new job lasted. A vacation might be canceled or major purchases deferred, but the standard of living essentially remained unchanged. Most of these people were the younger men in my sample. But financial pressures were also eased for older professionals whose wives earned substantial salaries and for those few middle-aged males who had independent incomes from investments.

The fear of losing everything and having to struggle for survival was greater for many (22 percent of my sample) than the economic pressure actually experienced. Anxiety outweighed the economic crunch, especially among those unemployed four to six months in the early seventies. They spent less on food. They scrimped on everything that outsiders would not notice. All nonessentials were cut. Savings kept them going. But they agonized over every dollar they spent. They made it through, but the strain, they recalled, was greater than the deprivation.

> Laid off in 1971. Out for six months. Had $1,425 in severance pay. Compensation checks covered the food and some of the utilities. We never paid the oil bill. Bought nothing. Borrowed things from friends for the children. Used all savings. Tremendous anxiety. Would have been wiped out in one more month. Found job teaching physics in a junior college. Had to take a 25 percent cut in salary. [Still held same teaching position in 1975.]

> Laid off in 1970. Out for six months. Had $3,200 in severance pay. Collected my compensation checks. Spent less on food, clothing, everything. No frills like going out to dinner or entertaining friends. Had to use $5,000 of savings. We were never in real need. The pinch was more in psychological terms. [Reemployed at 15 percent salary cut for nine months. Out again. Working with friends in a small firm. Income only somewhat less than before, but no fringe benefits or security.]

Their new jobs, however, did not always last.

> Was unemployed four months the first time. Reemployed at $15,000. Unemployed twice since then; out a few months each time. No severance pay.

Requalified for compensation checks. Used all our savings. Had to borrow from wife's family to pay daughter's college tuition—we'll never be able to pay them back now. We cut back on everything. The worst of it was the anxiety. What if our savings run out? They did, but I got a job just in time. Never thought I could survive it again. But somehow we did, twice. If my wife wasn't working we never would have made it.

First laid off in 1970. Out for months. Took job as junior high school science teacher at $8,500. I like teaching but can't make it on that salary. Received $3,500 in severance pay. Used all savings. Wife helps by giving piano lessons; makes a few thousand a year. Together we've been making $11,000, and I used to make almost twice that before myself. My salary is a little higher now but so is everything else. We live in constant fear but somehow skimp along. If I could get a summer research job things would be better. I had one all lined up by a friend of mine for the old company. But when they found out it was me the job was gone. Company policy not to hire part-time people who had been laid off. All the anger returns.

Many men in my sample were again unemployed by 1975. Their chosen careers virtually over, a gradual lowering of living standards set in. The hallmarks of upper middle-class life were forgotten. They bought no stylish clothes, once an important symbol of status. Only necessities were purchased—from Sears, not Bonwit's. Older professionals discarded expectations of the comfortable retirement for which they had saved and planned so long, a painful adjustment during middle adulthood. Their wives at age 55 or so took full-time jobs as secretaries just to make ends meet. Hopes for travel and luxury, so recently held, were bitterly buried.

Laid off at the age of 56 in 1971. Out nine months. Financial security went. Wife had to go out to work. Used all savings to pay children's college tuition. Finally took job as programmer at $12,000. With both of us working we just break even. There's nothing left to retire on. Then that job went. Fortunately I found another. Who knows how long this will last.

Younger men with increasing family expenses were forced to depend on their professional wives. The so-called extra salary often became the mainstay. They tried to hold on to their homes so that their children would *feel* middle-class. They no longer made full mortgage payments. Banks allowed unemployed professionals to pay only the interest and suspended payments on the principal. But finally, some were forced to sell their homes. They bought smaller ones or rented apartments in the same communities if they could. Others were forced to move away. Some remembered their parents' struggle to survive the Great Depression and tried to emphasize their values, as the credit card, status symbol lifestyle quickly slipped away.

Laid off in 1970. Used up severance pay. Wife takes substitute teaching at $21 a day when she gets called. Tried to keep the same life-style. Bought nothing. Parents paid the morgage.

When I felt that we were about to hit bottom, I took this job as a mechanic. I earn $12,000. They say I can move up. Must find a way to keep this going.

Professionals unemployed for longer than a year usually endured acute financial crisis, (one-third of the sample). Some took temporary jobs. Others started their own businesses. Most of these failed, further depleting their resources; a few limped along—a basement fix-it shop, a sheet music–guitar repair store—providing activity to fill the endless days but little income.

Unemployed professionals learned to live on very little, as we have seen. They tried to get food stamps, but these were not available in suburban communities in the early seventies. A few took advantage of monthly surplus food allotments from designated distribution centers—flour, sugar, powdered eggs, and milk; canned meats and vegetables—so foreign to upper middle-class people accustomed to prime meats, imported cheeses, and gourmet trimmings. Many were eligible for surplus food but considered it junk they could not eat and did not know what to do with.

Debts increased. They sold valuable possessions to pay long overdue bills that could not be deferred without dire consequences—gas, telephone, electricity, automobile insurance. They liquidated all bonds and other securities. They cashed in life insurance policies.

Health insurance was a major problem unless coverage was provided through a group plan at the wife's place of employment. Twenty-seven percent of my sample had no health coverage for varying lengths of time. Fear of accident or illness was justifiably acute. One of the engineers I interviewed suffered a heart attack soon after he was first laid off. He survived but had to borrow $10,000 from his brother to pay hospital bills, an enormous debt he saw no way of ever repaying. The middle-class unemployed were not eligible for Medicaid. Anxiety increased, and with no job in sight, some were forced to carry individual health insurance, inadequate coverage at high rates, but as necessary as food and shelter.

I've been out of work for two years now. Had $3,000 severance pay. It went quickly. Even the compensation checks stopped. All savings gone. Had to take loans; can't pay the interest. We don't buy anything. We support ourselves on very little. I had to take out my own health insurance; relatives pay premiums. I did everything to bring in some money—was a carpenter, did some work as a tax consultant, ran a bus line for two months, ran a floor polishing service. I don't see how we will live and still we do.

There was strong resistance to geographical mobility among these supposedly mobile professionals. Even though many were told of jobs in other parts of the country, they feared that employment was unstable everywhere. They told stories about friends who had moved for jobs that were filled by the time they arrived and about friends who sold everything and moved thousands of miles away only to lose their jobs six months later. But the fear of moving was also based on what slender claims to informal sources of support they felt they had. Networks of professional contacts, what status remained in the eyes of friends and neighbors—all depended on previous occupational position. Only 10 percent of my unemployed sample did move in desperation for insecure jobs outside the Boston area. A few of the most desperate moved in with relatives, as had so many of their parents 40 years earlier.

Skidding and Clinging

While experiencing financial struggles over this four-year period in the seventies, unemployed professionals clung to status claims of the recent past. Jobless professionals could hold on to an upper middle-class social station for a year, sometimes two, before downward social mobility began. They denied this descent to themselves, as well as to others, as long as they possibly could. Sixty-seven percent of the unemployed I interviewed experienced reductions, frequently drastic, in their economic circumstances; yet only 44 percent considered this to be downward mobility in any sense. Even these people found many ways to disguise the implications of job loss. Skidding and clinging appeared as part of the same process. When forced to accept lower standards of living, to relinquish symbols of success, or to sacrifice prestigious patterns of social participation, unemployed professionals emphasized *values*.

> We are part of a sort of professional-academic class. Education, graciousness, ability to like people and meet them on their own terms, our values, our sense of what is just and moral—these are the things that make us what we are. We can't lose them.

> This isn't moving down because I'm interested in a new lifestyle now. I feel an identity with the youth culture. We've become vegetarians. I'd like to run a health food store.

The long-term unemployed professional ardently emphasized those things that remained: "We think the same and act the same and still live in the same house, so you can't say we've moved down."

If unemployed men came to question their continued residence in upper middle-class communities, their wives usually did not.

> I don't know what we're still doing here. The neighborhood is too expensive considering what I make now and how much we lost during all those months

when nothing was coming in. We should be leading simple lives. My wife won't even discuss it. I don't like to think in terms of economic differences and social classes. Your education and your values make the difference—the things you believe in.

Some were forced to sell their homes, which other than their careers were the major link to life along Route 128. Two families after much anguish sold elegant homes in 1972—one for $150,000, the other for $85,000. They each bought smaller houses in the same communities, trying to retain what status they could for themselves and especially for their children.

It was painful to put that house up for sale. We put so much of ourselves into it over the years. But we can manage the upkeep on the smaller place. Our friends are here. We don't want to move away.

Didn't really need all that space anyway. Had one party here last summer. Couldn't afford one since. Our friends all have more money than we do. Don't think of class in terms of money.

Those who sold their homes in a desperate quest for capital admitted only that extra space was wasteful.

We don't classify people in terms of money. Things like appreciation for literature and music are the qualities that make the difference. We enjoy these as much in our apartment. We don't need that extra space anyway.

The pain of selling personal possessions is a universal result of prolonged unemployment, as was noted by Depression researchers (Bakke, 1940:a 259; Zawadski and Lazarsfeld, 1935:228–229). This experience was especially difficult for seventies salaried professionals, a "new middle class," in Joseph Bensman and Arthur J. Vidich's (1971) terms.

When nothing remained of income, possessions, lifestyle attributes, or occupational prestige, nevertheless education, values, and asserted appreciation for culture inhibited acceptance of downward mobility. Even the most hard-pressed unemployed professionals managed music lessons for younger children. College plans for older children shifted from Harvard or Brown to the University of Massachusetts or Northeastern, but their education was never in doubt.

Values notwithstanding, some nonetheless were driven up against the wall by economic necessity and were forced to accept the altered social reality of their downward mobility. One engineer reemployed in 1972 who could not yet face his situation said, as he left for the night shift in work clothes with dinner pail, "We still have middle-class values. We live in the same house. Our kids take piano lessons." The following year, after that job, too, was lost, denial was no longer possible. He was forced back to

Brooklyn to live with in-laws. Similar experiences of downward mobility, although not typical, were probably more common than records reveal.

Like so many along Route 128, many members of the new middle-class are people who have rejected their parents' traditional values. This rejection occurred as they moved upward rapidly on the basis of college education and career. They sought new values and lifestyle models, which were "college diffused but skin deep patterns of cultivated, genteel leisure" (Bensman and Vidich, 1971:133). Together with their neighbors in suburban communities they acquired highly valued possessions and displayed appropriate in-group behavior in a quest for status. Bensman and Vidich caricatured their lifestyles: "culture vulture," the sophisticated, avant-garde consumer of high cultural items; "country gentleman," who is concerned about skiing, golf, sailing, fresh air, and health; "cultured academic," who lives near a campus community and emulates pipe-smoking, intellectually oriented role models; "fun-lover," an active type among younger men, "who specialize[s] in being on the move and who convey[s] an impression of being 'in'—influential in science, technology and administration" (pp. 145–147). Bensman and Vidich depicted the espoused interests of the new middle class in literature, art, and music, for instance, as "artificiality, superficiality and inauthenticity" (p. 137). The majority of Route 128 professionals I interviewed fit this description: pretension mixed with uneasiness as they frequently drew my attention to paintings, etchings, musical instruments, record collections, and stereo equipment. Some offered detailed descriptions of antiques or furnishings once possessed but now gone or pointed out the Oriental rugs that were being moved out from under them. Their distress in such situations was always acute.

An unemployed professional's self-esteem, damaged by career interruption and economic loss, was buttressed by claims to newly made status for as long as possible. Personal identity seemed tied to the possession of status symbols. Self-conception noticeably withered with the loss of such possessions and the deprivation this loss implied, all the more as they tried to deny what was happening. Most of the unemployed in my sample were never destitute. But social and psychic damage resulting from the extent of economic loss was clear at every stage of adulthood among those affected by the new unemployment of the 1970s.

8

Experiencing Unemployment: Self, Psyche, and Family

An aerospace engineer, out of work for two years, began having a dream that had long been the fondest memory of his childhood: "It was the World Series, bottom of the ninth, two outs, bases loaded. I was up. Everyone was screaming. The pitch came. It was a great pitch—right down the middle. I hit a home run. I knew it as soon as it left my bat. That sound always woke me up. But now, since I lost my job, the dream isn't the same. The circumstances are, but the outcome isn't. Now the pitch comes right down the middle of the plate so slowly I can almost count the stitches on the ball. But I can't swing the bat. The ball floats by and I'm just standing there with the bat on my shoulder. The umpire calls, 'Strike three.' I didn't do anything. I couldn't even swing at the damn ball." (Shaw, 1976:26)

Shifts in equilibrium toward dependence, narcissism and anger have serious consequences, not only for the unemployed engineer himself, but also for his relationship with his wife and children. . . .

The wife's needs are no longer being met; she may be forced to go to work herself and, furthermore, discover that she likes it. Her own aggression may be mobilized and directed against her husband, leaving him open to her long repressed, hostile, devaluating and castrating wishes. . . . He may become more depressed, anxious or actively hostile toward his wife. . . .

There is uncertainty about the future and an increase in anxiety in the family which threatens the child's basic need for constancy and security and intensifies his own anxiety. (Newman and San Martino, 1972:3-4)

Work worlds are pivotal places where adult self-realization occurs, where society measures one's worth, and where family social status finds its base. All people have trouble coping with job loss, whatever their age or family circumstances. Professionals, cut from career in their forties, feel a special sting. The middle years are usually a time of reassessment and painful self-appraisal. Disruption at this stage of life threatens a man's sense of self-esteem as well as his relationships with wife and children. Love and support from one's family, always important, become crucial under the strain of unemployment.

Among out-of-work 1970s professionals loss of income wreaked havoc with lifestyle and status claims just when the needs of growing children increased family expenses. Symptoms of psychic distress were always apparent and often severe. Anger and frustration were brought home to teenage children, already rebellious, and wives resuming careers or pursuing advanced education. When father lost the job that made possible the house in a good neighborhood, with-it clothes, symphony tickets, summers on Cape Cod, and winter skiing in New Hampshire, the together family of four in the ideal suburban home was badly shaken. Sometimes normalcy never returned to individual self-conception, psychic organization, or family interaction.

Career Interruption and Mid-life Crisis

It was with older patients that I had the greatest difficulties—that is, with persons over forty. . . . It seems to me that the elements of the psyche undergo in the course of life a very marked change—so much so, that we may distinguish between a psychology of the morning of life and a psychology of its afternoon. As a rule the life of a young person is characterized by a general unfolding and a striving toward concrete ends. . . . But the life of an older person is marked by a contradiction of forces, by the affirmation of what has been achieved, and the curtailment of further growth. His neurosis comes mainly from his clinging to a youthful attitude which is now out of season. (Jung, 1939:66-67)

For the great majority of men—about 80 percent of our subjects—this period evokes tumultuous struggles within the self and with the external world. Their Mid-life Transition is a time of moderate or severe crisis. Every aspect of their lives comes into question, and they are horrified by much that is revealed. They are full of recriminations against themselves and others. They cannot go on as before, but need time to choose a new path or modify the old one. . . .

In many cases the marker event is not the result of a man's voluntary effort or choice, but is a result of circumstances beyond his control (such as war, economic depression and the illness or death of others). His current developmental period does not influence the time of this event, but it does shape his adaptation to it and the influence it has on his subsequent life. (Levinson, 1978:199, 56)

Stress and turmoil particular to the middle years was first recognized by C. G. Jung (1939), later by Erik H. Erikson (1950), and most recently by Daniel J. Levinson (1978) and his colleagues at Yale University. Jung found traditional dictums of Freudian psychoanalysis inadequate as he groped for ways to treat mid-life patients. Jung identified a qualitative shift in the psychic dynamic as people experienced the "noon" and "afternoon" of their lives, whatever their heritage of unresolved conflicts from infancy and childhood. He wrote of the "stages of life" and chose age 40 as the critical turning point.

> It must be remembered that despite all similarities, resistance, repression, transference, "guiding fictions" and so forth, have one meaning when we find them in young people, while in older persons they have quite another. (Jung, 1939:76)

He sought to help his patients achieve a psychic "state of fluidity, change and growth, in which there is no longer anything eternally fixed and hopelessly petrified" (Jung, 1939:67).

Erikson (1950) saw "generativity versus stagnation" as the central duality of adulthood. His "eight ages of man" present a series of polarities, each of which has to be experienced and surmounted if an individual is successfully to meet the crisis of the subsequent stage. Erikson conceptualized stages of physical maturation combined with stages of psychic development and examined both in relation to social and cultural supports and restrictions. He perceived of adulthood (the seventh stage, age 40 through 60) as the time when the mature individual must be concerned with "establishing and guiding the next generation" and his "relationship to his production as well as his progeny" (pp. 267–268).

> Generativity . . . is an essential stage on the psychosexual as well as on the psychosocial schedule. Where such enrichment fails altogether, regression to an obsessive need for pseudo-intimacy takes place, often with a pervading sense of stagnation and personal impoverishment. (Erikson, 1950:267)

Erikson exposed the hurdles of the middle years and argued that resolution of adulthood's crises requires substantial modification of family role responsibilities as well as occupational role expectations.

"Mid-life crisis" became a popular expression, a buzzword, in the 1970s. Levinson's *Seasons of a Man's Life* built on the work of Jung and Erikson and focused serious contemporary attention on problems of adult socialization. Levinson divided the life cycle into four partly overlapping, age sequenced "eras":

1. Childhood and Adolescence: age 0–22
2. Early Adulthood: age 17–45
3. Middle Adulthood: age 40–65
4. Late Adulthood: age 60–? (Levinson, 1978:18).

Between each era there are critical transition periods, which usually last four or five years (three to six at the outside); in these transitional times people are faced with the developmental tasks of evaluating the past and establishing a "life structure" for the next era (Levinson, 1978:19, 51). Life structure, in this view, integrates elements of self and society—"class, religion, ethnicity, family, political system, occupational structure" (p. 42).

The mid-life transition, occurring in Levinson's scheme at age 39 or 40, usually a crisis, was apparent in all of Levinson's subjects during their early forties. This is a time when most men experience a decline in their physical prowess, their sharpness of intellect, and the urgency of their passions. They question every aspect of their lives and are often pained by what they see. Many are immobilized. As Jung (1939:70) found in his patients, the ordinary expression for their situation is: "I am stuck."

Men are forced to reexamine the early adulthood structure they have established—its gratifications and disappointments—as well as the psychological residue of childhood. Levinson found that whether or not the mid-life transition was experienced as mild, disruptive, or traumatic, men between the ages of 40 and 45 made major changes in their lives for better or worse. Sometimes the shift was sharp, the "marker event" (divorce or recommitment to marriage, leaving or finding a lover, job change or a break in career pattern). Sometimes there was a series of seemingly minor changes (in the quality of personal and sexual relationships, in orientation to work tasks) that when examined closely "make a considerable difference." The capacity for development in the forties sets the stage for the subsequent 15 or 20 years of middle adulthood (Levinson, 1978:61).

The first "developmental task" of the mid-life transition is to "reappraise the past" and come to terms with "de-illusionment."

> The process of losing or reducing illusions involves diverse feelings—disappointment, job, relief, bitterness, grief, wonder, freedom—and has diverse outcomes. A man may feel bereft and have the experience of suffering an irreparable loss. He may also feel liberated. (Levinson, 1978:193)

There are four polarities, identified by Levinson, that men must resolve along the way to "individuation" and middle adulthood fulfillment.

The "young/old" polarity is pivotal. Each man must come to terms with his own mortality and the meaning of his life. His "legacy" in terms of possessions, relationships, and the worth of his work becomes a major concern (Levinson, 1978:216–221).

> For many men at mid-life, work is the most significant component of the life structure and the major source of the legacy. . . .
> During the Mid-life Transition he must move toward a more realistic view of his occupational legacy. (Levinson, 1978:219)

Resolution of the "destruction/creation" polarity is particularly painful. The middle-aged man experiences the frustrations of social constraints most keenly. His anger merges with what feelings of unconscious guilt and aggression he carries from childhood. The mature mid-life male must understand something of his own destructive potential and establish a new balance between life and creativity, on the one hand, and the more negative aspects of his existence, on the other.

> In reappraising his life during the Mid-life Transition, a man must come to a new understanding of his grievances against others for the real or imagined damage they have done him. For a time he may be utterly immobilized by the helpless rage he feels toward parents, wife, mentors, friends and loved ones who, as he now sees it, have hurt him badly. And, what is even more difficult, he must come to terms with his guilts—his grievances against himself—for the destructive effects he has had on others and himself. . . .
>
> His developmental task is to understand more deeply the place of destructiveness in his own life and in human affairs generally. . . . If he is burdened excessively by his grievances or guilts, he will be unable to surmount them. (Levinson, 1978:223–224)

The "masculine/feminine" polarity and the "attachment/separateness" polarity are hurdles of mid-life individuation enumerated by Levinson. Heterosexual men must come to terms with their fears of homosexuality and weakness. The desire for power can now merge with greater feelings of compassion and sensitivity (Levinson, 1978:230–237). Self-worth and social rootedness should each come to have new meaning.

> A major developmental task of middle adulthood is to find a better balance between the needs of self and the needs of society. A man who attends more to the self, who becomes less tyrannized by his ambitions, dependencies and passions, can be involved with other individuals and perform his social roles in a more responsible way than ever before. . . .
>
> A man in early adulthood is full of intense desires: to win, to be right, to achieve the noble Dream, to be highly regarded by those who matter. . . . With further development in middle adulthood, some of these desires fade away. Those that remain have a less urgent quality. They can also be realized more fully. He can be more loving, sensual, authoritative, intimate, solitary—more attached and more separate. (Levinson, 1978:239, 243)

Levinson found that the gratifications and deprivations of the middle years are molded in the highly varied ways that people deal with the polarities of individuation and the developmental task of de-illusionment, which together form the mid-life transition. The process is always stressful, and development does not always occur.

> It is not at all certain, of course, that development will occur in middle adulthood. For large numbers of men, life in the middle years is a process of gradual to rapid stagnation, of alienation from the world and from the self. Severe decline and constriction are common enough so that they are often seen as part of normal middle age. (Levinson, 1978:26)

Levinson, Jung, and Erikson each studied the psychological and sociocultural transitions that are ordinarily part of middle-age development. Each of them understood the importance and the many meanings of work for ego expansion and self-conception among mid-life males. To deal with job dissatisfaction, or de-illusionment, is an integral part of the process of adult socialization they each described. We saw how mid-career technical professionals along Route 128 coped with the tensions and conflicts they experienced in bureaucratized system laboratories when we examined their characteristic modes of adaptation in Chapter 5—from satisfied Superstriver to dissatisfied Trapped. Whatever the pattern of mid-career adjustment professionals in my study followed, it was radically disrupted by layoff, unemployment, and repeated rejection during the job search.

Job loss at mid-life is a triple whammy because it comes at the time of greatest self-doubt, interrupts economic stability, and intrudes on family relationships just when the process of self-appraisal is apt to be most stressful. Unemployment was the marker event in the lives of many professionals I interviewed. Job loss halted development during the mid-life transition and scarred middle-age adjustment.[1]

Unemployment hit 28 percent of my sample as they were in the stage Levinson termed "becoming one's own man" (ages 34 to 39). Instead of attaining the "social rank, income, power, fame, creativity, quality of life" (Levinson 1978:59) they had envisioned, they lost their illusions. In some cases unemployment brought on the mid-career crisis a few years early. Circumstances forced a few positive attempts at career change. For the most part the younger men in my sample were reemployed sooner than their older colleagues. Routinized and Trapped forced themselves to remain in harness even when underemployed. Depending on the degree of economic strain sustained, their overall adjustment seemed easier than it was for others.

Forty percent of my sample lost their jobs in the midst of the mid-life transition (between the ages of 39 and 46). These were the people whose obvious anguish during our interviews was greatest, regardless of their economic circumstances. Whether Routinized, Savvy, or Trapped, these men were most willing to detail their painful struggles with self-conception and family responsibilities. Unemployment seemed to be their marker event, and few found liberation in future reemployment. The vast majority remained dissatisfied, struggling and underemployed.

Thirty-two percent of my sample reached middle adulthood (over the age of 46) before their first layoff. All of them regressed to the transitional crisis so recently resolved. With economic stress and suspension or termination of the centrally important career, the legacy, to use Levinson's term, was endangered or lost. Renewed periods of agonizing self-

---

[1] Surely Levinson's (1978) conceptions are limited by his male, middle-class data base (75 percent of his subjects were executives, biologists, and novelists). Nonetheless, he identified stages of development apparent along Route 128.

evaluation sometimes lasted for years. A few possessed the psychic resources to cope, adapt, and find fulfillment in their fifties. Most suffered acutely as long as unemployment lasted. For those who found jobs again, and many men in their fifties eventually did (usually underemployment by their previous standards), resignation restored a Routinized pattern, pierced by bitterness.

Life cycle theory provides a framework that helps us understand the impact of even a six-month career interruption on mid-life professionals. Yet *age* was not the sole determinant of an individual's ability to cope with the adversities of unemployment. The event of unemployment itself somewhat altered the age specific sequence of Levinson's stages. Reaction to job loss was also influenced by (1) economic strain (as we have already seen), (2) psychological resources, (3) religious and ethnic heritage, and (4) established patterns of family interaction.

Psychological Impact

> In addition to its obvious economic function and social value, useful work has important psychological significance, as an outlet for neutralized aggression, and as a means to enhance self-esteem. Work functions to support defenses against basic anxiety and depression; it serves as an antidote against thoughts of infantile helplessness and encourages in the worker a belief in his own competence. Loss of employment is associated with disruption of carefully constructed adaptive defenses and leads frequently to regression, depression, anxiety, loss of belief in one's adult competence and a re-emergence of infantile conflicts. (Newman and San Martino, 1972:2)

Unemployment was a living hell of fear, anger, loneliness, depression, and despair for the seventies professionals I interviewed, much as it had been for jobless workers in the Great Depression. Well-placed scientists, engineers, and data analysts were stunned, literally shocked, to find themselves suddenly out of work. Virtually all initially experienced job loss as "traumatic" or "ego shattering." The pain of that event was so intense that detailed descriptions were often difficult to elicit. As time went on, loss of accustomed work routine, loss of the economic function, loss of the ability to provide for one's family, and repeated experiences of rejection resulted in erosion of self-confidence and in psychic disorientation. Unemployment was not an experience any were prepared to cope with.

Symptoms of Distress

Most professionals began the job search with energy and a degree of confidence, which faded quickly as their understanding of crowded market conditions increased. Typically they were turned down—over the phone or through the mail—or never contacted. People who prided themselves on their rationality became increasingly disoriented as they exhausted expected channels of securing employment. Their carefully laid plans of a lifetime were smashed seemingly beyond repair as their financial resources disappeared and they began to doubt themselves and their own abilities. The people I interviewed never became immune. The experience of unemployment was worse, if anything, each time around.

> Traumatic. Never had to look for a job before; always had offers. Was put down constantly. Never put down in my life like I was during those six months. They wouldn't believe my resume. One personnel manager actually told me I was lying. I told him to check my references. He didn't. Unimaginable ego blow. After a few months of this I went into deep depression. It's hard to stay up when they keep putting you down. (1972 interview)

> I found an ad in the newspaper that was a perfect fit for me. I answered it with a letter and my resume. They called me for an interview. It went well. They called me back for a second interview. They called my references. I know I was a finalist because one of my referees told me. I wanted that job so much I could taste it. The lab was a dream set up for me. They never called me back. We waited. We were afraid to use the phone. They never had the decency to send a letter. After several weeks one of my referees called the manager. They filled the position with a much younger man. They must have kept me in the running to show the government they didn't discriminate by age. (1975 interview)

Some suffered serious illness (4 percent of my sample had heart attacks; 4 percent were hospitalized for ulcers). They all experienced high levels of tension, which resulted in explosiveness and depression for as long as unemployment and uncertainty continued—and in many cases well into the years that followed.

Sometimes dryly, sometimes emotionally, 82 percent of the unemployed I spoke with described their psychological reactions as poignant, memorable experiences.

> Personal demoralization. Shock of being laid off and losing everything just at the time when we were looking forward to easy retirement. Very tense. Very nervous. Hard to handle such drastic change in your life.

> Very depressed for a long time. I even forgot my children's birthdays. I was even depressed after I started working again. I'm only just beginning to come out of it.

> Personally I know I'm in very bad shape. I'm a failure in engineering and can't think of anything else. Floundering. Lost. Something must be wrong with me. Don't know exactly. Do you think a psychiatrist could help me?

The worst part of it is the self-image problem. I'm running a shorter fuse. Would be worse if income was zero. To a large extent you are what you do. You kind of lose track of who you are. Erosion of self-esteem and confidence.

Many described their symptoms of distress—tension and anxiety, lack of control, anger and depression, demoralization and personal desintegration. Professionals spoke of the anger they couldn't contain, of episodic rage, of aggression misdirected at wives and children. Idleness and loneliness spurred personality deterioration. Goal directed, task oriented technical professionals, accustomed to accomplishing useful things, felt useless and helpless with nothing to do that mattered. Communication became increasingly awkward—with former colleagues, unemployed friends, nuclear and extended family. Dinner talk was difficult. They tried to prevent well-meaning family or friends from asking them how they were feeling or what they were doing. There was little chatter at the meetings of the employment crisis groups I attended. There was no conversation between people waiting in line for compensation checks. Quietness was the first thing I noticed each time I walked through the doors of the Route 128 Professional Service Center. I saw people in trouble—alone. Many withdrew in apathy—gained or lost weight rapidly, smoked heavily, drank excessively. And the people I talked with did not include the most desperate cases who refused to be interviewed. Newspapers in 1971 reported five suicides of jobless Route 128 engineers. Attempted suicides, breakdowns, and hospitalizations were often discussed at employment crisis group meetings.

Stages of Adjustment

There were no clearly delineated phases through which Route 128 people passed in gradual adjustment to joblessness. Instead, there were variable stages, often truncated, that many professionals experienced as they attempted to deal with their troubles (comparable in general to the mood sequence described by Zawadski and Lazarsfeld [1935:235]). Eighteen percent of the unemployed I interviewed spoke of qualitative stages in their emotional reaction to layoff and unemployment. These stages probably occurred more frequently than the people I talked with recalled. In fact, when questioned about personal tension, many were so overcome by feelings of pain and anger that they were unable to describe a sequence of stages they may actually have experienced.

Those who mentioned separate stages said that shock, disbelief, numbness, and denial came first. Few used the word "fired" to describe their situation. Euphemisms shielded the blow: "laid off," "displaced," "surplused," or "temporarily furloughed pending recall" (Rice, 1970:28). They spoke of the plight of others rather than themselves. As reality penetrated consciousness, anger quickly followed—at government, at companies, at managers, at families, at themselves. With continued rejection, anger turned to depression. Depression brought feelings of hopelessness, despondency, withdrawal, and lethargy. Forty-one percent of my sample spent much of their time, they said, in aimless anxiety, feeling apathetic and immobilized. They described endless hours of sitting in the same chair, staring out the window or at the television.

Apathy and despair were, however, punctuated by periods of active job search. The long-term unemployed or drastically underemployed sometimes spoke of the impossibility of sustaining anger and bitterness. Instead they tried to gain control of themselves and were usually successful, but for only a time. Their rationalizations were easily pierced and if reemployment attempts proved unsuccessful, rage and destructive tendencies toward self and others remained dominant patterns.

> I went through different phases. Dazed at first. Then very angry. Then very depressed. Then you get around to rationalizing and pull yourself together. Still feel very anxious. This job could go tomorrow and no savings left now.

> I was too shook up at first even to look. I thought I'd have no problems with an MIT degree, young, relatively low salary level. But when the first leads fell through I began to get anxious. As the months went by and the savings were getting lower and lower and all leads went nowhere, I was quite depressed. I was in pretty bad shape for a long time. But I managed to start looking again. Lucky to get hired. Guess it was because I came cheap.

> It was so unexpected. I was so depressed. Why are so many of my friends still working and living at high levels? At first a few called. Then they stopped. No one really cares about anyone else. Tension always so high—waiting for the mail, for the phone to ring. The worst part is the terrible tension. You get so depressed. But you can't go on living like that. You have to believe in something. I had to pull myself together. That's when I took this job as a repairman.

Only with great difficulty, if at all, did professionals adjust to lowered expectations. Most who experienced a series of layoffs were more fearful, not more flexible, with each episode. And after years of struggle, with no job in sight, desperation, withdrawal, and physical and psychological disorientation usually occurred.

Oftentimes the emotional stress of unemployment was most dramatically revealed after people were working again in jobs that offered some security. The full impact of the unemployment experience was visible only when circumstances improved. There were, among the reemployed sample, two cases of mental breakdown severe enough to require temporary hospitalization. Others sought treatment. And the incidence of illness, high blood pressure, and heart attack was startling. Among these cases were surely many instances of delayed reaction to unbearable strain.

Introspection

The experience of occupational dislocation had such a powerful psychological impact on all of the professionals interviewed that at first similarities among them disguised individual differences. Some of the unemployed professionals (approximately one-third of the sample) had personal resources to help them deal with adversity. These were people who gleaned strength from previous years of insight into their own psychological problems, as well as into the workings of social institutions. They had a perspective that ultimately surfaced to provide a measure of personal control so that they could deal realistically with altered circumstances. Initially, introspective professionals experienced what others did—shock, anger, depression, and apathy—but the length of each stage was truncated. They denied less, rationalized less, and managed better. Most unemployed professionals (approximately two-thirds of the sample), however, were unable to rise above their fear and despair. These people showed little psychic strength, and less social insight. Defenseless against their anger, they exhibited symptoms of severe distress. Adjustment to altered life circumstances among these, the vast majority of professionals, remained elusive.

The effects of unemployment were so profound for professionals that introspection itself increased with the length of their joblessness. Pain brought insight that pierced protective denials of the past. No longer was it necessary to praise a company that found one superfluous or to glorify institutional systems that failed to provide support. Many unemployed professionals began to come to terms with postindustrializing society in new ways. For the majority, however, manifest insight lasted only as long as unemployment. Necessity forced reemployment, often at lower levels and usually with far less security, but frequently in familiar industries. Reemployed professionals felt rescued from a perilous future. They clung to familiar denials with renewed ardor.

Ethnic Differences

As a criterion for differentiating among the psychological reactions to unemployment, introspection was affected by two other factors: religious and ethnic background. Protestants, Catholics, and Jews of various class and ethnic origins were all as likely to be represented in the unemployed sample as among Route 128 professionals as a whole. Overall 42 percent were Protestant, 39 percent were Jewish, and 17 percent were Catholic—figures determined by parentage, if not current religious affiliation. Most of Route 128 unemployed had distant ties to organized religion: two-thirds of the Protestants, half of the Jews, and one-forth of the Catholics claimed nominal affiliation or none at all. Only the Catholics (63 percent) attended church regularly. Yet most people did not disclaim their ethnic heritage. In many cases traditional roots seemed to influence reactions to unemployment.

The Protestants had parents who were Episcopal, Universalist, Methodist, or Lutheran. Most were from middle-class families with strong traditions of individualism and a worldly oriented achievement ethic. Unemployment challenged previously held notions that hard-working people could control their life circumstances. The unemployed were enraged by their newly felt helplessness. There were numerous instances of severe psychological disorientation and of acute alcoholism eventually requiring clinical intervention. Tensions within families increased. Nine percent of couples were eventually divorced. Unemployment among Protestants, however, markedly increased introspection. More important, insight into self and society, once heightened by joblessness, was more likely to last through reemployment—and even underemployment and downward mobility—than it was among other religious groups. The few instances of relatively graceful, self-conscious skidding in the data were middle adulthood Protestants from middle-class families of origin. Those were cases in which newly acquired perspectives seemed to rekindle feelings of self-reliance, damaged but not destroyed by months or years of joblessness.

Jewish sons of the Great Depression, grandsons of eastern European immigrants, who became scientists, engineers, and data systems analysts had moved up fast and far on the basis of education and career. Education, sanctified as an end in itself by ethnic tradition, became the modern passport to professional career and economic security. Jewish professionals in the 1970s had faith in the value of their education. They felt a special sense of entitlement to good jobs and liberated lifestyles, which were merited, they thought, by their knowledge, training, and cosmopolitan ethos. Whether their mode of adaptation to working conditions in bureaucratized systems laboratories was Routinized, Savvy, or Trapped, they felt sure of their ability to provide the good life for themselves and their families. Unemployment unhinged economic and social security, desperately sought and so recently attained. Joblessness had devastating psychological effects. Cut off now from communal supports of the past, they felt betrayed by the rational system they had come to trust. Fear, sometimes terror, was openly expressed in every interview. They vividly detailed the symptoms of their distress—hypertension, colitis, uncontrollable anger, neurotic patterns traced to childhood conflicts. Emotively they confronted deep pain. They talked freely of family fights, demanding wives and troublesome children. Ten percent of the Jewish families dissolved during the three years between interviews. Yet many of the unemployed, despite episodic explosiveness, were openly supported by sympathetic families in a mutual fight for survival. During the months of joblessness and anguish, introspective tendencies, often already present among Jewish professionals, were always heightened. But the need for security was so great among them that reemployment at any level buried new insights. They worked hard to develop mechanisms of denial—survival as worthy members of the new middle class—whatever the cost.

Catholic professionals seemingly sustained the trials of unemployment most easily. Always polite and cooperative, they were difficult people to interview. They spoke of stress and tension in tight, terse phrases. Deeper feelings were well hidden from me and perhaps from themselves; Catholics were less introspective than either Protestants or Jews. Catholics were at least as upwardly mobile as the rest of the sample. Most of them had working-class fathers. Most of them were children or grandchildren of Irish or Italian immigrants. It was hard work, their parents' and their own, that made upper middle-class status possible, as precious to them as it was to others. Yet they seemed to lack a sense of entitlement to high salaries and affluent lifestyles. Unemployment brought disappointment to some, pain to others, but most could continue to function as if things were as they were meant to be. They spoke of being upset but never described neurotic symptoms. Wives seemed to accept their husbands' situations and actively did what was necessary to keep families together. Husbands mutely pursued job leads. They tried to disguise, rather than confront, what tensions they surely felt. In only one case was separation contemplated, then finally rejected. When interviewed again in 1975, most Catholics were unemployed or had taken jobs much below previous employment. Yet they were adjusting to downward mobility (rarely verbally acknowledged) with a stoicism not present among their Protestant or Jewish colleagues.

Legacy of Self-blame

Notwithstanding the general tendency toward temporarily increased social awareness among most of the sample, industrialized capitalism engenders feelings of self-blame in its unemployed victims. This was true even in the Depression. One-third of the nation was then unemployed but two-thirds, presumably the better workers, had jobs. Alfred Winslow Jones's pioneering study of class consciousness during the industrial conflicts of the thirties demonstrated that workers, even militant unionists, shared the achievement ideology of the middle classes (Jones, 1964:

330-332). Then, as now, the awareness that people may be fired through no fault of their own revealed resentment of the system and feelings of powerlessness but failed to diminish feelings of shame. With unemployment less massive among the seventies professionals than thirties workers, its effects were more easily internalized as personal problems. Seventies professionals blamed themselves for not being good enough, for entering industry instead of a university, for putting up with years of dissatisfaction. They were angry at private companies but more often at the government, the system. They felt powerless but could not pinpoint root causes. Bureaucracies are faceless, thus blameless. Professionals were isolated from supportive social relationships that might have helped them target legitimate aggression. Neither employment service personnel nor psychiatrists used societal variables as explanatory devices to help the unemployed. Counselors told clients how to market themselves. If the pitch did not land a job, guilt deepened. Traditional techniques of therapy drew patients' awareness to their unresolved infantile conflicts rather than to the failings of economic institutions. The unemployed continued to blame themselves and to vent their anger at available scapegoats, their wives and their children.

Family Dynamics

The husband's successful professional career was the fulcrum of upper middle-class family life in the 1960s. The wife, usually college educated, raised the children and managed the right kinds of social contacts and community relationships. She learned how to acquire and appreciate symbols of newfound status, while the husband worked hard, succeeded, and brought in the money needed to make it all possible. They maintained a façade of togetherness—a well-groomed wife deriving prestige from her husband's career; two or three children taking lessons in everything; a tastefully appointed suburban home. The wife often played the role of "special woman" to her husband.

> The special woman is like the true mentor: her special quality lies in her connection to the young man's Dream. She helps to animate the part of the self that contains the Dream. She facilitates his entry into the adult world and his pursuit of the Dream. She does this partly through her own actual efforts as teacher, guide, host, critic, sponsor.
>
> Like the mentor, the special woman is a transitional figure. . . . The special woman can foster his adult dependency, his incompleteness and his need to make her into something more than (and less than) she actually is. (Levinson, 1978:109)

Through the nesting years, her primary task was to stay at home in order to mold model children. She was guided by Dr. Benjamin Spock's *Baby and Child Care*, her bible. To develop her children's every potential, as Philip Slater (1970:63) noted, was "rooted in individualism and achievement ideology."

> Spockian parents feel that it is their responsibility to make their child into the most all-around perfect adult possible, which means paying a great deal of attention to his inner states and latent characteristics. The consequence of this is what is superficially defined as greater "permissiveness," but from an internal perspective is actually more totalitarian—the child no longer has a private sphere, but has his entire being involved with parental aspirations. (Slater, 1970:75)

By the late sixties older children questioned their parent's values. Many adopted alternative lifestyles in order to resist what "they regard[ed] as the hypocrisy of their parents" (Bensman and Vidich, 1971:137). By the seventies many wives sought individuation through graduate school and careers of their own. All the while, the husband's income, still the basis of it all, was surely taken for granted. When his paychecks suddenly stopped, new tensions erupted. Old myths were destroyed. Fragmented family functioning was often reestablished, but things were rarely the same as they had been before.

Unemployment immediately strained marital relations. Ninety-four percent of the Route 128 sample spoke of increased tension with wives. A majority mentioned problems with children as well. They traced disruption of family interaction patterns directly to job loss. Conflicts with wives were described as severe, really severe among 52 percent, and so severe among another 12 percent that separation or divorce was contemplated.

> Tremendous tension with wife and children. I was severely depressed for so much of the time. Maybe she couldn't help me, but she never even tried. For that whole first horrible year we were always angry at each other—the kids, too.

> I thought the marriage was going to break up. I applied for a job in Detroit. If it had come through I would have left. I don't think she ever understood what I was going through even though she was sometimes sympathetic on the surface. She was always at me—I didn't really know what I wanted to do; I wasn't trying hard enough; I wasn't together.
>
> It was hard on the kids. All that tension. Our little boy is still acting out in school.
>
> Things are better now. She found a job she likes. We try to live from week to week. We try to cheer each other up.

Mutual Resentments

Jobless professionals felt entitled to strong support at home. Usually they found initial sympathy, which waned as unemployment continued. Husbands found fault with wives for not understanding what they were experiencing, for not supporting them emotionally, and for denying them love and affection at a time when they needed it most. Some said their wives were too upset by threatened status loss to face economic reality. They felt scapegoated by anxious wives who blamed them for their joblessness and accused them of not trying hard enough.

> She is always nagging me for not being aggressive enough and for not helping more around the house. She was worried that I wasn't looking hard enough—said I was letting her down. Spending was limited. She resented the restrictions.

> She says she has faith in me and keeps on spending as though I was working. She absolutely avoids facing economic reality. She won't adjust. There are lots of fights. It's getting worse.

> She blames me for not having a job. She says I don't look hard enough. She blames me for not being motivated in engineering so she can keep her comfortable status world. I can't get through to her. All she understands is that I've stopped bringing home the paycheck. She wants us to see a marriage counselor. I'm thinking of moving out.

Counselors at the Route 128 Professional Service Center confirmed these assertions. Lack of support from wives, they said, was a major problem for unemployed men.

> Wives usually don't understand or help. They make the problem worse. They don't believe men are looking because they see all the jobs listed for engineers in the *Globe* every Sunday. But only two percent of those jobs are real. Most don't exist or are filled when listed. They list them publicly because they are forced to do so by law. But the wives don't know this. They don't believe their husbands.
> The wife of one of the men we're trying to place told him she was leaving if he didn't find a job. He went to register for a special retraining program. He returned to find the truck moving out all of the household possessions. So he lost his wife and all his worldly goods, too.

Oftentimes, if women found work and their husbands did not, resentment intensified. Route 128 professionals had employable wives: 87 percent had more than a high school education; 39 percent had bachelor's degrees; 27 percent had master's degrees; a few were attorneys; one was a physician. Where women took employment, whether as teachers, nurses, secretaries, or saleswomen, or where they substantially increased their working hours, enormous conflicts were apt to erupt. Relationships were less strained if women already had careers and were working or if they remained at home: 42 percent of the families in which the wife had a new breadwinner role experienced intense conflict as compared with 17 percent of the families in which the wife had been working and 16 percent in which the wife continued to stay at home.

The worst part of the day for many of the men with working wives was watching the wife go off to work in the morning. The prospect of facing, for the first time, the issue of role reversal, of undertaking childcare and housework, was typically felt as yet another form of degradation. Although 76 percent of my unemployed sample had working wives, there were few attempts at exchanging traditional roles. Only 9 percent agreed to try a substantial reversal of family responsibilities even for a time.

We changed roles for several months. She took this selling job and I stayed home. She soon became a buyer—earned $120 a week. She thinks she's a "success"! I did all the housework—everything she used to do when she was home all day. I accepted the notion that if someone was willing to pay for her services and not mine that it was fair.

Twenty-four percent claimed that they shared household responsibilities with working wives in certain areas.

My wife's a librarian. She likes having a professional career. She went back to work a few years ago to help with the burden of the children's college tuition. Now that I'm at home so much I cook the meals, do the shopping, most of the cleaning, too. Not laundry. We do the dishes together.

Sixty-seven percent said that there was no shifting of family duties. Some felt guilty about not fulfilling their wives' changing expectations, rarely recognized as needs.

Didn't do much around the house. Felt guilty that she was working. Not easy to accept role changes. I did some of the shopping. Sense of worthlessness was overwhelming.

Some played subtle games of resistance.

I do a little housework. I hate dishes. I'll be reading or studying and she'll interrupt with silly things like taking out the trash. She makes me feel guilty. I do a little more, then get angry. The more I do, the more she expects.

Others recognized that their wives were overburdened yet claimed nonetheless that women object to seeing husbands so demeaned.

I feel so badly that she has to go out to work. She is tired all the time. But both of us just break even. No other way now. I don't bother much with domestic work. My wife really doesn't want me to. She was embarrassed one day when she came home and found me vacuuming.

Many simply refused to assume any of the tasks regarded as the woman's domain.

I never stay around the house and do woman's work. It's important to keep your morale up.

Wife tried to operate a small catering service for a while. I won't touch any of the money. She can use it for herself. Insulting for a man like me to take money from his wife. Didn't work around the house. She never asked. I never thought of it.

Wife's salary is our source of steady income. Has been for three years now. She can handle the household duties. Once I washed the windows. The rest of the work is hers.

I asked the men to specify how much they helped out with shopping, cooking, cleaning, childcare, and laundry. No more than 2 to 5 percent of the husbands assumed full responsibility in any of these areas. About half helped out somewhat; the others did not help at all. Shopping was least resisted by suburban males (54 percent did some; 2 percent did all of the shopping). Husbands with small children and working wives had to help if money for babysitters was lacking (57 percent did this sometimes; 3 percent took full responsibility for daytime childcare). Some dusted or ran the vacuum cleaner once a week. Dishes and laundry were most avoided as work for women only. Working wives in the 1970s, much more so than in the 1930s, expected help with chores and greater decisionmaking authority within their families commensurate with new breadwinner responsibilities, but jobless husbands perennially have trouble fulfilling changing role expectations. So 1970s women were angry, and they expressed their anger to their husbands and in private to me.

Marital tension, common to the years of mid-life transition, are seriously compounded when husbands are unemployed and wives work. Jung found that the psychic needs of men and women shift during the afternoon of life.

There are many women who only awake to social responsibility and to social consciousness after their fortieth year. . . . One can observe women . . . who have developed in the second half of life . . . an incisiveness which push the feelings and the heart aside. Very often the reversal is accompanied by all sorts of catastrophes in marriage; for it is not hard to imagine what may happen when the husband discovers his tender feelings, and the wife her sharpness of mind. (Jung, 1939:124)

Levinson documented increasingly strained relationships between the so-called special woman and her husband after many years of marriage.

A couple can form a lasting relationship that furthers his development only if it also furthers hers. If his sense of her as the special woman stems mainly from his wishful projections and hardly at all from her own desires and efforts, sooner or later the bubble will burst and both will feel cheated. If in supporting his Dream she loses her own, than her development will suffer and both will later pay the price. Disparities of this kind often surface in transitional periods such as the Age Thirty Transition or the Mid-life Transition. (Levinson, 1978:109)

If the woman embarks on a career of her own, problems intensify.

> The more liberated woman tried to form her own specific Dream. If she gets seriously involved in an occupation, she and her husband must make tremendous efforts at mutual accommodation and individual development. Acknowledging and managing the disparities between their Dreams is a crucial problem in the relationship between lovers and spouses. It is hard enough to form a life structure around one person's Dream. Building a structure that can contain the Dreams of both partners is a heroic task indeed, and one for which evolution and history have ill prepared us. (Levinson, 1978:110)

When the husband's job loss hastened the development of the wife's career, marital crisis frequently ensued. Unemployed middle-aged men experienced an awakened desire for supportive love and tenderness. But many women, disappointed in their husbands and involved in building their own careers, had new needs and were less available than they had been before. The absence of an idealized love object often became an additional source of pain for jobless men and for the women I talked with as well.

Most wives were sympathetic when their husbands were first laid off. Usually they remained supportive as long as he actively looked for work. Sometimes she understood that his continued job search might be useless and that each rejection enhanced his pain. Sometimes her own financial fears and acute status anxieties blocked empathy. It was his withdrawal into apathy, however, that triggered her deeper resentments.

Wives came home tired after working all day, whatever their jobs. Arguments about the dirty house, the piled up dishes, and even neglected children commonly erupted. Bitter fights destroyed the sympathy that they once may have had for the husband's situation. The wife of an unemployed engineer wrote her account in a letter to the *Boston Globe* (Goodman, 1971:A29). She claimed that after 14 months of unemployment the marriage bargain—"I take care of you if you support me"—was broken. She described a happy marriage complete with two cars, split-level house in the suburbs, and an annual salary of $18,500. There was some real affection, she claimed, that gradually dissolved. After the severance pay was gone she took a boring secretarial job in order to keep food on the table while he sat sulking in his living room chair in front of the television. She had the responsibilities of childcare, job, and housework, she said, and wished that he would forget he was an engineer and do anything to help support them. She threatens divorce. Her story is not uncommon.

Sex Declined

Reliable data are always difficult to obtain in the sensitive area of sex. It was evident, however, from comments volunteered by several of my respondents that sexual enjoyment, unquestioned in the past, became problematic. Men complained that they needed expressive sex in their lives but that wives no longer responded: worried women were frequently not in the mood for lovemaking.

Husbands who ceased to provide the bacon gradually lost their conjugal rights. Some men sought sex with other women, but more often sexual rejection was but another component in an overall pattern of increasing demoralization among the jobless.

> Unemployment is a form of castration—by wife and by friends. Unemployment is a form of rejection and in a society where the job is everything, the man without a job is not a man. He is castrated and that means sexually, too.

There was evidence that sexual activity declined even in what seemed the better marriages. Sensitive women know that masucline prowess is apt to decrease among depressed males in their forties or fifties. Some women who said that they still loved and respected their husbands deliberately refrained from initiating sex. They worried that their husbands would have difficulty performing and hesitated to risk humiliating them in still another way. But all women who talked about their sex lives, even in cases of self-proclaimed devotion, did so with ambivalence.

> I'm afraid to encourage him too much. He's so depressed all the time, he probably wouldn't be able to get it up. I don't want him to have to face another kind of defeat. Besides, I'm tired by ten at night and ready to go to sleep. I have to be up and out by eight in the morning to get to work on time. I can't sleep until eleven like he can.

Children Affected

Marital crisis inevitably affects dependent children. Parents, caught in a net of interpersonal conflict and financial stress, struggled to preserve their children's claims to upper middle-class status. Even when confronted with economic catastrophe, we saw how professional parents refused to relinquish suburban residence, children's music lessons, art camps, and above all expectation of good colleges for able offspring.

> Our son is a junior at Princeton and our daughter is just entering Bryn Mawr. We had saved for their education. And are using that money for food now. Don't see how we're going to do it, but the kids are going to stay in those schools. Loans, they'll have to work, whatever.

Parents were pained at their inability to provide for the needs of growing families. They sought scholarships from music schools, art camps, and universities. Younger children were often oblivious to their family's financial struggles but teenagers resented the lack of new clothes and spending money. It was the psychological fallout from parent's experiences, however, not financial constraints, that had the most impact on children's lives.

Crisis intervention clinicians at a mental health center established to service children's emotional problems in one of the Route 128 communities analyzed their cases over a two-year period in the early 1970s.

> Anger, originating from parents' individual personality disturbances and from their disrupted marriages may be displaced onto children who become scapegoats. . . . Job loss alters the role relationships in the family; the father may be seen as a devalued object, homebound and without status. For a boy, identity formation is threatened as his antagonism about identifying with a devalued male may lead to partial identification with an achieving female. The father's increased presence in the house and the mother's relative absence may intensify anxiety in an adolescent girl and become a factor leading to running away, promiscuity and other behavior problems.

> As we attempted to intervene therapeutically with these families. . . . we found that they tried initially to continue a pattern of middle class striving and self-reliance and did not, at first, focus on job loss as an upsetting factor. Feelings were displaced onto various family members, especially a child who became the focus of the family's frustrations. (Newman and San Martino, 1972:4–5)

Sixty percent of the unemployed fathers in my sample admitted increased tension with their children, the result, many said, of their explosiveness and depression. In only 2 percent of the cases where fathers were home did relationships with children improve. Other unemployed professionals claimed not to know how their children were affected.

> I'm never sure just how the children are taking it. I think they see it all in very different ways, for they are not at all alike. One is a sphinx, one seems almost (although not intentionally) removed, and one sees it all. But they know I spend most of the week in my chair. Only one of them has said that I no longer talk, and I frown when others are talking. ("Fired at 46," 1977:33)

Usually children heard parents quarreling and, worse, they often became the objects of misplaced hostility. They were picked on for minor transgressions previously unnoticed. Contact was apt to bring contention under circumstances such as these. As one of the wives I spoke with described it:

> He would watch them closely and give them a hard time over every little thing. Our daughter would say something he didn't like at breakfast. He would start her day by yelling at her. He never ate breakfast with the family before. They weren't used to having him around, bothering them all the time, picking at things he never noticed or cared about before. Our son ate breakfast in the living room with the newspaper; he couldn't stand all that yelling.

Adolescent children trapped in an atmosphere of tension often came to question the values and beliefs of their parents. They questioned the importance of advanced degrees and the long years of struggle necessary to earn them, and they questioned the value of marriage if parents in trouble were torn apart by dissension.

Stages of Adjustment

Stages of family adjustment to prolonged unemployment and/or subsequent underemployment were evident among Route 128 families over the three-year study period in the 1970s. Soon after initial layoff, tension and fear destroyed accustomed patterns of communication. Expressions of mutual resentment and hostility, often involving the children, disrupted the façade of normal relationships. Usually, conflicts intensified as economic disaster loomed closer. Of the families that endured financial crisis, 44 percent experienced tremendous tension and contemplated separation (compared with 17 percent of those who felt the economic pinch less severely). Men in economic crisis households, and especially men whose wives worked, frequently lost their positions of authority and even the love and respect of their families. Mutual support was withdrawn. Sometimes fathers moved to jobs in other cities. These were the times of greatest family disorganization.

> I was five months without work. Headhunters wouldn't even talk to me. All the bills piled up. I was afraid and so was she. We were on each other all the time. I just couldn't take it. There was this job in my field, 700 miles away. I took it. Moved into a small, dreary apartment. I was miserable. Didn't expect to feel like that. I called home every other night after eleven. My wife kept saying that she and the kids hated the quiet as much as the fighting. After nine months of this I came back. Took this programmer job with a small commercial company. It's a real comedown in lots of ways. Somehow, over the last two years, things at home seem to have simmered down.

Many families of course weathered the storm. Two characteristics were evident among this group: (1) there was role equalization between husband and wife; and (2) there was a new quality of generalized flexibility about social position.

> I was fired under unpleasant circumstances and smarted for a long time. And we began to worry about finances all the time. She was angry because she said I didn't know what I wanted to do and didn't have enough ambition. She was worried about her job. There were state funding cutbacks and her position was in danger. We couldn't take the strain much longer.
>
> I applied for a training program in D.C. I would have left her if that had come through. But it didn't.
>
> I did some of the cooking and childcare, some of the shopping, too. I always did some—guess I do more.
>
> Hard to take personal rejection when you see stupid guys with good jobs. The tension almost broke us up. I guess we hung in there because neither knew

what else to do. A job finally came through and things got better and better. When I was laid off again eights months later, things weren't so bad. She lost her job, too. Both of us found others. We both feel more flexible about things in general. I think we have healthier attitudes.

————— * —————————

It was a personal blow. I did what I could to find work but nothing came through. She was very upset. She felt cheated. She had planned to start graduate school in the fall.

She said she would leave if I didn't go out and find a job. Gradually she came to realize that others were unemployed, too, that it really was bad. And she found a job herself. She started in sales, became a buyer, and is on her way to junior manager. She has a career. She seems more satisfied. With a life of her own she leaves me alone.

For a time we actually switched roles. I accepted the notion that no one was willing to pay for my services but that my wife was worth something to the department store. Now we're both working and pulling together. Are we happy? That's hard to say. I guess we worked things out.

Gradually, if grudgingly, husbands accommodated to the needs of their working wives. They began to accept their wives' decisionmaking authority and assumed more of the household responsibilities. Sometimes wives successfully forced such changes. In all crisis families that stayed together, husbands eventually went along with role equalization whether they liked it or not. Still, the tension was there even over the phone: "He can't talk to you now. He's fixing the washer. He's doing some chores," she said. In a few cases the role reversals went full cycle for a time.

He does the housework, vacuums the rugs, cleans up. I come in and he wants me to admire how clean the living room looks. I'm tired and couldn't care less. He wants approval and I want a martini. Of course I want him to help out. I just wish he didn't need constant appreciation.

With husband's reemployment, at whatever level, roles did eventually equalize. The women's movement, coupled with the widespread need for a second income among middle-class families in the tightening economy of the 1970s, made helpful husbands more fashionable in suburban communities. Reemployed men did shopping or cleaning; some even did laundry or dishes. Wives, for their part, blamed husbands less and the job market more for employment instability. With dreams of glory gone, they were grateful for underemployment so long as they could manage to hold on. Some wives asked me, when I contacted their husbands in 1975, whether other people's circumstances were similar to their own. They needed assurance that the adjustments they had made were really necessary.

In a small minority of the families I interviewed, overt tensions were less obvious and transitions went smoothly. In none of these cases did families suffer dire economic hardship. Some marriages were strong enough to withstand unemployment and lowered expectations. Here husbands and wives seemed to understand each other's problems. Despite loss of paycheck, father retained a position of importance within the family. Of course he was distraught about his situation, but he was aware of the emotional needs of his family. Husband supported wife's desire for professional gratification. He did most of the shopping, cooking, and cleaning. He searched for meaningful things to do. He built a room over the garage. He repaired cars for friends. And family members still looked to *him* when making major decisions while he urged *their* independence.

Permanent Disruptions

Many families never adjusted to the radical effects of the major breadwinner's prolonged unemployment, especially where economic pressures were severe. Divorces may have occurred frequently in Route 128 communities in the seventies, but none of the fully employed professionals I spoke with (as close to a control group as I could get) had split from their families during the three-year interval of my study. On the other hand, 38 percent of the early 1970s economic crisis families (16 percent of the unemployed sample as a whole) were separated or divorced by 1975.

Sometimes the separation had begun while the husband was out of work.

> Unemployed for just about a year now—financial crisis, marital crisis, too. She regards me as a failure because I don't bring home the paycheck. Our marriage is on the rocks. She is so afraid of losing this house and this neighborhood. The community is everything to her—more important than I am.
>
> Between marriage problems and the fights and the lack of money, things are rough—on the kids, too. She wants me to move out—out of the house, out of her way. She thinks they'll all be better off without me. I'll miss the children.

In other cases families managed to marshall emotional and material resources to cope with the problems at hand; yet resentments and antagonisms persisted. Later, after reemployment, when the crisis abated, people parted. Intense conflict had destroyed the faith each had in the other, the faith that had sustained their relationship. Unemployment triggered the disclosure of feelings too damaging to self and psyche to be forgiven or forgotten later.

> We are two very different people now. We don't have the same attitudes about sex. I need emotional support. I need to be mothered. She doesn't want sexual experiences on a meaningful level. Nice, superficial lovemaking isn't enough for me now; maybe it never was. There's no passion left in our relationship. Feelings of castration last.

There was a letdown, if anything, when I started working again. This "nice lady" can't help me. . . . Maybe my needs are neurotic, as she claims, but I feel them just the same. We just can't make it together anymore. I wonder now why we married in the first place.

Families in the so-called new middle class are increasingly held together by a status oriented lifestyle, funded by father's (and mother's) career. My data revealed that the ties that bind the American new middle-class family are so tenuous that in the space of several months, unemployment can tear the fabric of affection and respect. Unemployment caused less extensive but similar patterns of family disruption among workers in the thirties. Some Depression families, pressed by years of economic privation, trod the conflict-crisis-readjustment path traveled in the seventies. But survival was then defined in terms of subsistence, not status. Father's power over the family diminished if he could not pay the bills; yet though authority relationships shifted, role reversals were rarely contemplated. Time-honored traditions went far toward protecting the father's position of authority from the corrosive effects of his joblessness. Men resented working women but few women worked and fewer questioned domestic responsibilities. Readjustment was therefore easier than it was in the seventies.

Rapidly emerging middle classes in the fifties and sixties had shed traditions of their parents in a frantic quest for cultural patterns appropriate to newfound status. Father's position in the seventies was based solely on his record of actual achievement—tradition alone no longer sustained his position—and working wives wanted a more equal family division of labor. Almost immediately the unemployed husband became a devalued object to his wife and children. Though he expected the love and respect of his family to help him through troubled times, too often such support was withheld. In the past so much of his emotional resources had gone into the relentless pursuit of a successful career that the family had been neglected. At the same time, they had been absorbed in the status anxieties inherent in the pursuit of an upper middle-class lifestyle. When crisis came, there was no reservoir of affection and psychic stamina for unemployed fathers floundering in a shifting economy.

9

Experiencing Unemployment: Institutional Dimensions

The power elite is composed of men whose positions enable them to transcend the ordinary environments of ordinary men and women; they are in positions to make decisions having great consequences. . . . For they are in command of the major hierarchies and organizations of modern society. They rule the big corporations. They run the machinery of the state and claim its prerogatives. They direct the machinery of the military establishment. They occupy the strategic command posts of the social structure, in which are now centered the effective means of power and the wealth and the celebrity which they enjoy. (Mills, 1957:3–4)

C. Wright Mills's once controversial *The Power Elite* (1957) described decisionmaking in bureaucratized mass society as a working convergence of top officials in critical institutional spheres. Mills wrote of an informal and therefore "illegitimate" power structure of which professional functionaries as well as atomized publics were largely unaware. Whether or not one subscribed to the specifics of Mills's theory, it was obvious that most scientists, engineers, and data systems analysts shared an ideological malaise. They thought little about underlying institutional realities. The highly technical demands of their rigid task assignments obscured the human and/or societal worth of their work (Leventman, 1976:84). They assumed

167

that the system was supportive until it failed them: it took unemployment in the 1970s to awaken awareness.

Karl Mannheim, in *Man and Society in an Age of Reconstruction* (1940), foresaw patterns I witnessed along Route 128. Mannheim, in the tradition of Max Weber, elaborated several meanings of rationality. Central is his distinction between *substantive rationality*, the capacity of individuals for introspection and penetrating insight, and *functional rationality*, socially induced impersonality that results in actions calculable by an outside observer (p. 53). Mannheim argued that functional rationality, necessitated as it is by bureaucratic complexity, would increase while substantive rationality, or what he called "self-realization," would decrease in advanced industrial society. Mannheim saw functional rationality as the dominant trend, especially among people in professional and administrative roles (pp. 55–56). He also believed that there are times when substantive rationality will increase (p. 57); in these rare periods of "unorganized insecurity," depression, and widespread unemployment, people pressed by circumstances will probe the social arrangements that ensnarled them (Leventman, 1976:85–87).

The functionally rational professionals of Route 128 encountered precisely the kinds of consciousness raising crisis conditions described by Mannheim. Experiencing unemployment, just as Mannheim envisioned, did markedly increase their substantive rationality. Eighty-four percent of the jobless scientists and technologists I interviewed in the early seventies displayed greater insight about the inner workings of economic and/or political institutions; 60 percent were increasingly critical of the enhanced role of military institutions (Leventman, 1976:93).[1] Regardless of how long insight lasted and whether or not attitudes changed, unemployment affected what professionals came to know about power structures and policies that circumscribed their careers and altered their lives.

Private Enterprise

> By settled habit. . . the engineers. . . are a harmless and docile sort, well fed on the whole, and somewhat placidly content with the "full dinner-pail" which the lieutenants of the Vested Interests habitually allow them. It is true that they constitute the indispensable General Staff of the industrial system, except as employees in the pay of the financiers. . . . they have without much reflection lent themselves and their technical powers freely to the obstructive tactics of the captains of industry. (Veblen, 1933:135)

---

[1] Each respondent was asked several questions about each major institutional area at different times during the interview. The above percentages include all people whose answers to any item relevant to the respective institutional area showed that they accepted less and questioned more.

In manner and appearance, most unemployed technical professionals emulated management, much as they had in the past. What anger they felt at the system was more often directed toward government than at industry. Jobless engineers continued to justify the pursuit of profit by vested economic interests. Many felt that companies have to do whatever is necessary to survive and prosper in the competitive game imposed by industrial capitalism.

They were far less apt to fix primary responsibility for the seventies employment crisis on business (4 percent of the unemployed compared with 8 percent of the employed) than on government (78 percent of both samples). They condemned federal policies for trying to control inflation by increasing unemployment and criticized the government for lack of planning.

> The whole basis of handling technology is wrong. Nixon is deliberately dismantling the scientific establishment. He doesn't really see the importance of science and technology. He is criminally stupid about it. It was an intentional policy to try to cut inflation with unemployment and with the unemployment of scientists and engineers especially. He is cutting space in the same way—stupid.

Responding to termination and joblessness, however, many scientists and engineers reexamined company practices that they had accepted without question before.

In one area or another, pro-business attitudes of unemployed professionals were gradually chipped away, at least for a time. On the issue of the company's right to own individually earned patents, for instance, 22 percent of the unemployed (compared with 14 percent of the retained) asserted that patents should belong to people not companies. They also felt that scientists and engineers are entitled to a share in the profits companies make on their ideas and that individuals should be allowed to market their own inventions when their employers do not want to develop them.

One-third of the unemployed (compared with one-fourth of the retained) complained that companies had not dealt with them fairly. Despite the general recognition that companies were in trouble, 46 percent of the unemployed, as I previously noted in another context, felt that layoff in their particular case was not justified. They were offended by the "impersonality" and "inhumanity" of employers to whom they had been loyal. "Termination was needlessly abrupt," said many. Others spoke of age discrimination, imposed obsolescence, and the pension plan "rip-off." Knowledge obsolescence was "absolutely not" the reason people were laid off, claimed 61 percent of the unemployed (compared to 43 percent of the retained). Many noted that companies plan to pay retirement benefits for no more than 20 percent of the professionals they employ: "They lay off people just before pension plans are vested." Highly paid professionals felt victimized by budget cuts that replaced them with less experienced people who came at half the price.

They had me working nights for no extra pay in addition to the full day. When they had no more need for the training program I ran at night I was laid off, but the day job was still there. They could get someone to fill that job for less than they were paying me.

Unemployment increased antipathy toward the owners and operators of advanced systems labs. The expression of these kinds of feelings brought the freedom to question company policy. Even if subsequent reemployment restored feelings of obligation to employers, rational people had to remain somewhat doubtful of reciprocal corporate responsibility.

In those times of uncertainty, the defense industries, as distinct from corporations in general, frequently became the object of special scrutiny. Unemployment led many scientists and engineers to ponder the role that defense contracting firms played in the overall economy, in the development of knowledge, and even in the protection of the nation. While ambivalence toward these industries ran through the data, unemployment was apt to increase negative evaluations of firms like Raytheon, Sylvania, Avco, and McDonnell Douglass. Thirty-seven percent of the unemployed (compared with 22 percent of the retained) had such negative attitudes. "Evaluate the contributions of the defense industries to the general economy," I asked. Only 31 percent of the unemployed (compared with 43 percent of the employed) gave very high positive ratings. "How much do the defense industries contribute to the development of scientific and technical knowledge?" I asked. "Very little," said 36 percent of the unemployed (compared to 16 percent of the retained). Even the basic national security function of these industries was discredited by 35 percent of the unemployed (compared with 29 percent of the retained).

Technical professionals knew that defense industries, supported by government, provide jobs, but often they described these jobs as "useless," "empty," "building crap that doesn't work." Many viewed these industries as part of an overall system that is "sloppy," "overbureaucratized," and "not to the national good." Troubled scientists and engineers resented the control that these industries, embedded in an irrational and inefficient system, exercise over technological progress.

It is shameful that the defense industries finance the technological establishment. Terrible that the military had the power of life and death over technology itself. Companies are only interested in profit—not technological advancement.

Jobless professionals were more likely than others to attribute tremendous power to the defense industries and to the economic and political institutions that support them as well. The unemployed had good reason to understand this power: they personally felt its effects. Sometimes they testified to the intermeshing of these critical institutions, as described by C. Wright Mills, John Kenneth Galbraith, Seymour Melman, and others. "Do you think there is a military-industrial complex which threatens democracy in America?" I asked. "Yes," "absolutely," or "certainly out of control" were the responses of 37 percent of the unemployed (compared with 14 percent of the retained).

> I hold to the Galbraith view, profits alone are not the dominant thing. The whole process of funding R&D is ridiculous, wasteful. We must stop kidding ourselves about free planning and company competition. It's bullshit. Lockheed is part of the government. The Vietnam war proves it.

> Military-industrial complex exists but not in a formal sense. I met several times with Navy scientists, legislators, and other industry executives. They are in cahoots with each other. They talked about mutual investments.

> The defense industries run the economy with the government. If the government pulled out, the scene would be different. Capitalism couldn't exist without the military and the government—almost unimaginable.

Many of the unemployed were ambivalent. While the crisis raised social and political consciousness, the need for work exerted cross-pressures to temper negative opinions of defense contracting firms. When asked whether the then $86 billion defense budget was justifiable, 60 percent of the unemployed (compared to 45 percent of the retained) agreed that it was. The unemployed sometimes voiced opposition to the arms race and frequently complained about the lack of fiscal accountability involved in cost-plus Defense Department contract awards. But to cut the budget, they feared, would harm their own chances of employment. Some argued that even though "the whole thing is a boondoggle" and "foolish things are done," there is no alternative to massive military spending because "we must keep up parity with the Soviet Union." Others claimed that the Defense Department's budget was justified because Congress does not otherwise adequately fund advanced research and development. Sometimes they couched their support of Defense funding in national security terms. But the need for personal security was a powerful influence that permeated ideological perspectives.

Confused Class Consciousness

> Many of the problems faced by technical employees are identical with those of other workers—salary, fringes, job security and the lack of a grievance mechanism. In recent years, their problems have increased because salaries are not keeping pace with the cost of living; long workweeks with no overtime pay are common; work assignments are determined unilaterally by management; changes in American industry, like the cutback in space expenditures and

government research contracts, have caused severe dislocations and widespread layoffs.

Their problems are, in short, the same as the problems of all workers without unions. Yet while unionism among teachers has grown spectacularly and such professionals as musicians and newspaper reporters long ago reconciled their "professional standards" with trade union protections, the nation's scientists and engineers are still wrestling with "self-image" problems that have left them one of the most unorganized groups among their professional peers. (Chamot, 1974)

Experiencing unemployment heightened the antipathy of technical professionals toward vested organizational interests but it did not increase their consciousness of class—the critical prerequisite for collective action. The revolutionary potential of the technologist has long been of interest to the political left. Thorstein Veblen toyed with the notion that engineers might be the backbone of a revolutionary movement in America. He argued that their knowledge and skills made them indispensable to the industrial system. He knew they would witness enormous waste and inefficiency as ruling classes held back productivity for profit. This coupled with their feelings of powerlessness would, he hoped, arouse their anger, their class consciousness, and ultimately their political militancy (Veblen, 1933:133, 142). At times he hinted that this actually would happen (p. 71). But basically his analysis led him to doubt the real prospects of the radicalization process among technologists. Engineers, Veblen claimed, always the errand boys of the captains of industry, were unlikely to form a "soviet of technologists" (pp. 133–135). Yet Veblen could not close the consciousness door completely because an American socialist revolution was lost, in his view, without a technological elite at its helm.

Following Veblen, New Leftists in the late 1960s and early 1970s, such as Bogdan Denitch (1970:351–355) and Martin Oppenheimer (1970:27–32), viewed the increasing number of salaried professionals and their growing discontent as fertile sources of radicalism. If New Leftist notions have validity, then Route 128 technical professionals—frightened and under-utilized, unemployed and downwardly mobile—should have (1) become increasingly aware of the stratification system and their own position within it; (2) seen the need for new organizations and joined employment crisis groups; and (3) actively supported the unionization of scientists and engineers. Instead, in each of these areas where a radical thrust was possible, signs were always mixed and sometimes contradictory.

Social Class Identification

Seventies technical professionals were well aware of structure inequalities in American society. The differentiating factor was income and possessions according to 51 percent of the unemployed (53 percent of the retained), education and occupation according to 12 percent of the unemployed (10 percent of the retained), and status according to 16 percent of the unemployed (8 percent of the retained).[2] Even though education and career provided "historical *entree* for the New Class" (Bazelon, 1966:51), it was the economic parameters of position that were most frequently cited as fundamental. Yet experiencing unemployment did *not* heighten awareness of economic stratification. More of those who lost their jobs (28 percent) than of those who did not (18 percent) said that values, education, professionalism, and respect outweighed money alone in importance.

As distinct from the issue of inequality in general, consciousness of class became clouded when technical professionals considered their *own* position in the hierarchy of strata. Only 43 percent of each sample would indicate the class to which they thought they belonged.[3] Most professionals had trouble placing themselves in the societal scene they were able to recognize. Experiencing unemployment did not make matters clearer. In various ways, 57 percent of both samples said that class was not a salient concept for them.

> I don't know about classes. If you can get the job you want, are doing what you want to with your time, that's what counts.

> Haven't much thought about it. I think in terms of people with common interests—general outlook not classes.

Most of these unemployed professionals, first upwardly and then downwardly mobile, were confused and only vaguely aware of demarcation points in their class and status structures.[4] They did not want to think in terms of class, as we have seen. Previous patterns of identification with management and professionalism persisted. I asked them to select their most important self-designation, that.is, to choose the group with which they had most in common. There was no consensus, as Table 9-1 reveals.

---

[2] Twenty-two percent of the unemployed (29 percent of the retained) refused to mention criteria of differentiation.

[3] "Upper middle-class" was chosen by 21 percent of the unemployed (31 percent of the retained). "Middle-class" was selected by 22 percent of the unemployed (12 percent of the retained).

[4] There is an "inequality without stratification" school in contemporary sociology. Robert Nisbet (1959:11–17) noted that people who move up (or down) the social scale without encountering barriers other than occupational hurdles cannot feel boundaries of inherited class. Dennis Wrong (1972:76) wrote that the study of social stratification, in the sense of positioning "individuals possessing unequal amounts of income, prestige and power," should be abandoned.

Route 128 professionals lent some substance to these contentions. Yet there were no signs that inherited wealth was less important as a basis of upper-class power than it ever had been. Imposed class boundaries are no less real because mobile professionals and others may not be aware of them. It is clear, however, that in postindustrial society social groupings are increasingly complex and that traditional placement criteria of education, occupation, class, status, and power need reexamination.

TABLE 9–1
Most Salient Self-Designation

	Unemployed	Retained
Managers	14%	12%
Owners	2	4
Professionals in general	44	39
Technical people in general	20	33
All people who work for salaries	6	4
All people who work for wages	6	2
To some degree with each	8	6

Diffuse reference groups among the unemployed, added to shifting points of personal anchorage and the hangover of professionalism, all mitigated against the development of class identification.

New Groups

History tells us that without class consciousness effective organization to protect collective interests does not occur. Amid the general conditions of employment instability that gripped Route 128 in the early 1970s, there were some beginnings. Self-help groups emerged in many communities, interest in labor unions increased dramatically, and awareness of the need for organizational protection heightened. Yet status identification prevailed and radicalism was not a central tendency.

Several crisis groups formed spontaneously during the early days of massive layoffs. They varied widely—from management oriented professionals in Lincoln, to Needham engineers trying to help each other live it out, to the Lexington based Association of Technical Professionals, which sought a public forum for common interests, government grants, and political clout. Attendance at meetings was sporadic. The groups reached only a small fraction of the unemployed: 2 percent of the sample attended one of the groups regularly; 5 percent went to meetings a few times; 12 percent went to one meeting and never returned.

Perhaps it is significant that crisis groups sprang up at all in suburban communities. Such groups consisted of middle-class people accustomed to feeling self-sufficient; they sought protection and solace when they found they were not. But they remained essentially conservative in their orientation to society. They strongly supported business, private enterprise, and individual initiative and were generally anti-government, from which they nonetheless sought help. Members wanted organizations to protect their economic interests as professionals. The scope of their aims was narrow. New groups wanted only to insure their share of the federal fiscal pie and did not press for basic economic changes. They lasted only as long as layoffs hit the headlines[5] and never served to raise a collective conscience among technical professionals as the latter moved in and out of the labor force.

Unions

In times when jobs were plentiful, salaries high, and special skills scarce, scientists and technologists showed little interest in unionizing. Less than 1 percent of the nation's 1 million engineers belonged to affiliates of large labor unions and no more than 5 percent belonged to 24 small, independent professional unions (Brown, 1972:1). Changed conditions in the 1970s—layoffs, age discrimination, forced overtime without extra pay, termination prior to pension plan vestment—aroused an awareness of the need for organizational protection among the Route 128 unemployed and their retained but frightened colleagues as well.

Stiff opposition to unions for professionals was voiced by 38 percent of each sample: "Unions kill creativity"; "Unions destroy critical judgment"; "Unions prevent progress." Twenty-seven percent, previously opposed, were now unsure: "We need protection but not collective bargaining": "I want security against old age but we'd be giving up a lot": "In principle we need organizations but not traditional unions."

> I'm not sure about unions now. I don't think it would work due to individual aspects of people and jobs. Not possible for scientists to bargain collectively. Perhaps unions would be possible for engineers where the work is more standardized. We do need the protection though.

Thirty-four percent of the unemployed (37 percent of the retained) were solidly behind unionization—even though they knew that unions cannot create jobs and even though they felt colleagues would not join together. They wanted protection.

> Would be excellent but would be rejected by scientists and engineers. But unions aren't the answer either. A union organizer came to NASA. Many joined. The union never helped. They were all laid off anyway.

> Never had much use for unions in the past but being laid off twice made me realize that we need protection. We need unions but not like ordinary trade unions. Seniority should not be the only thing.

---

[5] New groups themselves made the news. Local reporters described their purpose, interviewed organizers, and sometimes publicized meetings (Keene, 1970:3, and 1971:16-17; Millman, 1971:6-9; Smith, 1971:54; Thomas, 1971:17).

An engineer is obsolete if he opposes unions now. It would be great if engineers could cooperate. They are slaves of companies, trained at dog-eat-dog.

Officials of the AFL-CIO Union for Scientific, Professional, and Cultural Employees sensed new receptivity in the seventies and launched membership drives (Shapley, 1972b:620). The Association of Technical Professionals invited Jack Golodner, executive secretary of the Council of AFL-CIO Unions for Professional Employees, to address a large public meeting in Lexington in December 1974. Dennis Chamot, Ph.D. chemist turned labor organizer, pitched to them instead. Chamot said in part:

> Working conditions and layoff decisions are made unilaterally by management. Professionals have problems that can't be solved through individual bargaining. . . .
> The professional in a technical organization has no consciousness that he is just another employee, but he is. The professional in an organization is ruled by company goals. The professional as an individual has no bargaining power. The professional comes to the job expecting autonomy; he expects to determine, control, have some influence on his work. Not so! . . .
> Scientists and engineers have no grievance procedures. They are "exempt employees," which means they can't work overtime for extra pay. To be an exempt employee means you get screwed. You give up overtime pay to be called a professional. . . .
> Unions can establish a formal grievance procedure. Unions can't prevent layoffs but they can *rationalize* and *objectify* procedures—severance pay, notice, health benefits.

The conservative looking, middle-aged audience of about a hundred scientists and engineers responded with interest. "How do we organize?" many asked. Chamot told them to work anonymously from within their companies until they enlisted enough support to hold an election for union recognition. Men stayed long after the meeting. Chamot was barraged with questions. People were excited but pessimistic. "It's coming," said an older engineer, "but unfortunately not within my lifetime."

Neither the unemployed nor the newly reemployed were in a position to sign up with a union. And retained, overworked professionals in a flooded labor market were fearful of undertaking organizational initiatives. The seventies modified attitudes along Route 128 and elsewhere but many obstacles to unionization remained. Each person felt he had to fight for himself, bargain as an individual, against the odds. A veil of professionalism blunted awakening class consciousness and shielded many from recognition of their downward mobility.

Downward Mobility

Tough times caused downwardly mobile professionals (64 percent of the unemloyed sample as measured by substantial or drastic income loss) to criticize institutions deemed culpable for their troubles. For instance, this group was less likely than those who were not downwardly mobile to give the defense industries high positive ratings (34 percent versus 44 percent). It was far more likely to describe a threatening military-industrial complex (47 percent versus 16 percent). At the same time, downwardly mobile professionals felt dependent on the system supports that funded possible jobs. Despite the inefficiency and waste they witnessed, for instance, the downwardly mobile were more likely than those who were not downwardly mobile to oppose all cuts in R&D appropriations (82 percent versus 54 percent). They were more likely, too, to justify all Defense Department expenditures (73 percent versus 47 percent). Downwardly mobile professionals protected the interests of firms from which they sought employment. They were therefore likely to favor full company ownership of individually earned patent rights (73 percent versus 55 percent). And despite their need for collective clout they were somewhat more likely than colleagues to oppose labor unions and collective bargaining (41 percent versus 37 percent).

While skidders showed signs of heightened social awareness and of anger at their powerlessness, they also exhibited "status defensiveness," characteristic of descendant groups (Bensman and Vidich, 1971:71), to a greater degree.[6] They felt alienated from a political system that did not assist them. Skidders were more likely than non-skidders to assert that the American political process did not represent their interests (68 pecent versus 45 percent). Yet far more skidders than non-skidders voiced disapproval of political protest demonstrations (45 percent versus 24 percent). Unemployed and downwardly mobile middle-class professionals blamed government policies and politicians for squandering the nation's technological manpower resources. But they also blamed themselves for their economic difficulties. Most important, these people were not about to join together and attack a system in which they still hoped to regain lost positions. What they came to understand about institutional failings had to be buried in their continued quest for economic security. Neither the trauma of job loss nor the financial floundering that followed could radicalize people who themselves once had proved that an individual achievement ethic is rewarded. They were disappointed and embittered but surely not the core of a new class conscious proletariat.

Missile Makers and Peaceniks

The US Maverick, a missile fired from planes against tanks, has a TV camera in its nose. When the camera is focused on the target, the missile is fired; and the missile tracks the picture in its nose until it hits the target. . . .

[6] Other studies of success oriented skidders found similar patterns (Lopreato and Chafetz, 1970:450; Wilensky and Edwards, 1959:17–18).

The ability to switch guidance systems is a key feature of many of today's smart weapons. The American Harpoon, a naval cruise missile that skims the surface of the ocean for use against ships, continually shifts radar frequencies to avoid jamming. . . .

Present generation long-range missiles that fly through the atmosphere, such as controversial cruise missiles, already have such guidance systems. By 1980, cruise missiles will have stored maps on board for TV comparison with the land below. By 1984, they will be guided by a Global Positioning System and able to find anything in the known position within 10 feet. (Hadley, 1977:A2)

The nuclear age and the knowledge explosion attendant upon it ushered in a new respect for science and technology. The arms race and the space race entrenched a scientific and technological establishment—the hallmark of postindustrializing society and the foundation upon which illusions of American superiority were built. Popular support for the enterprise of science was at its zenith. Six months after Sputnik, 94 percent of the American public believed that "science makes our lives healthier," 98 percent agreed that "science makes for rapid progress," 88 percent claimed "the world is better off with science" (Etzioni and Nunn, 1974:192). Few people pondered science's destructive potential. Scientists and technologists were not encouraged to assume social responsibility for negative consequences of their work, and most did not. Only the small group of physicists who discovered atomic energy directly confronted the devastation caused by the bombs they created. Those who felt guilt tried to transmit a sense of responsibility to their students and to others who would listen. But the atomic bomb won World War II. The other message of Hiroshima and Nagasaki went unheeded.

When I returned from the physical shock of Nagasaki . . . I tired to persuade my colleagues in government and in the United Nations that Nagasaki should preserved actually as it was then. I wanted all future conferences on disarmament and on other issues which weigh the fates of nations to be held in that ashy, clinical sea of rubble. . . . Alas, my official colleagues thought nothing of my schemes; on the contrary they pointed out to me that delegates would be uncomfortable in Nagasaki. (Bronowski, 1965:xiv)

Social responsibility did not surface as an issue for scientists and technologists until the 1970s. Historically, scientists' primary concern with the laws of nature insulated them from involvement with humanitarian issues raised by the application of their findings (Kornhauser and Hagstrom, 1962:206). Scientific and technological establishments abdicated social responsibility in favor of "prudential acquiescence" to the vested interests of the social institutions that funded their facilities (Haberer, 1972:715). They did not debate the difficult problems posed by their current research. Instead, according to Rene Dubos (1970:123), they occupied themselves with "safe intellectual titillation," with pseudoconcern for ethical problems that might emerge from future developments. Meanwhile, the mushrooming costs of advanced research and development became staggering in a contracting national economy. Congressional committees and some scientists called for social utility as a prime funding criterion (Weinberg, 1967:75–77). Opponents of the Vietnam war raised general awareness of the devastating consequences of military technology and automated decisionmaking. Ecologists documented the dangers of limitless development. Increased public realization that technological advancement might not always mean health, progress, and happiness brought a growing demand that research be relevant and scientists be responsible.

Scientists and technologists were accused of not warning the public about the dangerous herbicides used in Vietnam and about anti-personnel gases developed in the sixties and then used in Vietnam. They were criticized by the peace movement for working on napalm, on chemical agents, and on defoliants (Lapp, 1971:112). They were attacked by the ecology movement and others for not sufficiently investigating and warning the public about possible dangers from food additives, pharmaceuticals, pesticides, and nuclear radiation. Nowhere were pressures on scientists and technologists stronger than in suburban Boston.

Route 128 physicists, chemists, engineers, and data systems analysts ducked the responsibility issue, as did their colleagues elsewhere, for as long as they could. By the 1970s, however, there was undeniable negative fallout from rapid advances in many areas. Escalated R&D costs, the Vietnam war, inflation, and their own unemployment put them in a difficult position. To make matters worse, most of my sample knew they were working on the very technology that made continuation of the Vietnam war possible. Eighty-one percent of the people I interviewed (84 percent of the unemployed; 77 percent of the retained) spent all or some of their careers working under Defense Department or related contracts. With Vietnamization, the conflict in Southeast Asia became an automated, electronic air war on the American side. And the Route 128 companies that employed most of my respondents—Raytheon, General Electric, Itek, Polaroid Avco, Control Data, EG&G, Honeywell, Sanders, and RCA—were major contractors for the military. The electronics system division at Hanscom Field, a U.S. Air Force base right off Route 128, was the development and procurement center for the electronic air war. A system developed by Route 128 firms (code name Igloo White), entirely automated and air supported, directed much of the bombing over Laos and Cambodia after 1968 (Haseltine, 1971:15–16).

The Department of Defense remained the surest source of contract underwriting for technical professional jobs throughout the shaky seventies. At the same time, these people went home each night to communities such as Newton and Lexington, among the most dovish in the nation, where respect was based on social priorities as well as possessions. Cross-pressured by job supports and social position, they tried to justify, rationalize, and deny.

As we saw in Chapter 5, culture heroes of the fifties and sixties who had laid the cornerstone of the new industrial state came to doubt the worth of their work. Uneasiness about the military applications of projects they had worked on was one reason for this decline. Doubt that nuclear energy, advanced electronics, and colossal computers always bring efficiency, leisure, and progress was another. Their own employment insecurity was a subtle but important contributing factor, too. The effects of unemployment were always difficult to assess in this complicated context because the need for work clouded consideration of social utility.

Of all the questions in my study, those concerning social responsibility and guilt were, respondents told me, the most difficult for them to answer. I wanted to know how missile makers felt when they broke through lines of demonstrators calling them "murderers" as they entered the lab each morning. I wanted to know how they dealt with "peacenik" neighbors who scorned their work. First, in a general way, I asked, "Does the scientist or technologist bear any responsibility for the uses to which his work is put by others?" Twenty-seven percent answered yes; 30 percent thought technical professionals share responsibility for the applications of their work but added, "You have to eat"; and 43 percent felt that individuals are not accountable. Then I asked each directly whether he had moral or political reservations about projects he had worked on. Thirty-seven percent admitted deep personal reservations. They had difficulty coping with the frustrations and anxiety they experienced. Thirty-seven percent disclaimed personal responsibility but their responses clearly revealed ambivalence. Twenty-six percent said they experienced no guilt or reservations of any kind.

It was difficult to determine whether experiencing unemployment heightened feelings of personal guilt and social responsibility. More of the unemployed than of the retained were critical of the role of the defense industries and feared the power of a military-industrial complex. Fewer of the unemployed than of the retained, however, objected to the size of the Defense Department budget. Fewer of the unemployed than of the retained (20 percent versus 35 percent) thought that technical professionals should be held responsible for the ultimate uses of their work. And when it came to the question of personal guilt and moral or political reservations, there was very little difference between the samples (35 percent of the unemployed compared with 39 percent of the retained expressed such feelings). The open admission of personal responsibility was a luxury that unemployed professionals, despite increased social awareness, could ill afford.

A few unemployed defense technologists told me that their guilt about war work probably led to on-the-job inefficiency that might have contributed to layoff. However, most functioned well when they had jobs, regardless of ambivalence they felt. One-third of the sample actually volunteered the words "avoid," "rationalize," or "deny" to explain how they continued to do so. Responses to probing questions about guilt and responsibility were always lengthy, sometimes contradictory, and usually complex. The technical professionals I interviewed, unemployed and employed alike, used one or more of the following patterns of self-justification, avoidance, denial, or rationalization as they worked on weapons of war.

1. Basic research is benign. Science itself is neutral. It is the responsibility of the technical man to give the best, most accurate advice he can to all who ask. Intense involvement in scientific work prevents the scientist from evaluating potential uses.
2. The projects I work on aren't destructive; things others do are worse. I just work on the delivery systems but never on the bombs themselves. I was only involved in the design of the bombs; I never actually dropped them. MIRV disintegrating laser rays are okay, but I wouldn't work on those new anti-personnel bombs. I only worked on ABMs, but I'd never work on germ warfare projects.
3. Defense is necessary. The deterrent keeps the peace. My work is important to national security.
4. There is positive fallout, social benefits, from projects I work on. My work on missile guidance systems can be used to improve airport traffic control.
5. The work is mostly busywork. Most of the complicated electronics devices could never actually function.
6. If you want to continue working, you must close your eyes and walk away.
7. It's necessary to develop a split personality to believe in peace and work on weapons of destruction.
8. I'm too removed from any possible uses of my work to feel guilt or responsibility. I work on a tiny piece of a complex project; this insulates against responsibility for its use.
9. My responsibility to support my family comes first. If I walked off the job, someone else would take it and the work would be done anyway. But I would be out of a job.
10. The responsibility is with political leaders who make ultimate decisions, so I work in politics. The most I can do is help select political leaders who will make better use decisions of my work.

A guy has to make a living. I never felt guilty about anything because I never worked on a high enough level. We have to do these kinds of things to keep up with military technology. We get lots of positive fallout from these projects. There are certain things we should never do like build ovens to kill people, for example.

The question of social responsibility is a very difficult one. Missile system projects are ciritical for national defense. Germ warfare projects, however, should be discountinued.

I did work on military stuff but it was so far removed from anything I could actually envision—and I couldn't have stopped the work even if I had wanted to. A man has a responsibility to his family; it's too hard for him to quit.

When I worked on nuclear tests in the Pacific, I was so involved with my calculations and the intrigue and excitement of the science that I really didn't consider the fallout problem. Involvement in the work itself prevents you from feeling the guilt you might otherwise feel. I probably should have been more concerned than I was.

The scientist does bear significant responsibility. More and more of us are coming around to this way of thinking. You must ask first "Is what you are doing allowable morally?"

I have gone through a change of thinking about working on defense projects. In the early days I was really hawkish. I produced only one useful military device—all others were a total waste of time and money. My best work from both a scientific and military point of view was canceled. I worked on the development of strategic missile programs. I spent $50 million: only $12 million of this had any use—the rest was waste. I didn't like doing useless things.

The engineer only has the responsibility to take political action to see that his work is used wisely. I do have slight moral reservations. I do feel a certain sense of rightness about what I am doing—probably it's compensation. I tell myself that I'm working in the interests of national security. I don't know how much of this is self-justification.

I don't strongly feel that engineers should feel responsible for the uses of their work. I would never actually have the guts to walk off the job for moral reasons. I don't think that many would. There are always rationalizations: must do what the other side is doing; if I didn't do the job someone else would and I would be out of a job.

Recently I worked on a camera to shoot down yellow men on bicycles but I didn't feel guilty about it. I was for the war in Vietnam at the time. The thing didn't work anyway. Most of those things don't work so you really have nothing to feel guilty about.

The engineer is not responsible because he is not involved in the use decision. I don't see the result of my work so I don't feel responsible—and I hope I never do. It would be fantastically horrible if I ever did see the result of my work. I never worked on the bomb itself—just on getting it there—so I didn't feel that what I did was morally wrong.

———————

Worked on missiles in the sixties and was afraid of facing it—felt guilty. But once you're caught up in a job you can't get out. I was a prostitute—wanted the money. I knew what I was doing and kept doing it. Hard to change.

———————

As a pacifist it was really a problem for me. I had lots of reservations about working on radar systems data from missile tests but I didn't see what I could do about it. Perhaps this was the reason I wasn't effective at my job and got laid off. The question of responsibility is a tricky one. I felt it but didn't see what I could do.

———————

The engineer is an innocent pawn. I didn't make warheads themselves, only worked on how to get them there. I guess there was some sense of guilt. I should have campaigned against some of those kinds of things harder from within the company.

———————

Those who directly work on weapons of war should certainly face up to their responsibility. Not a problem for me. None of my contributions were unique so I have nothing to feel guilty about. My work can be used constructively as well as destructively. It can be used for surveillance from satellites to uphold test ban treaties and even the H-bomb has kept the peace. On the other hand it is part of the war machine. Look, you do your job and then have the responsibility to face the political consequences later.

———————

Nothing I've worked on has been put to use, fortunately. You can't see the whole picture from one small part. No sense of guilt but no sense of satisfaction either. I have some moral reservations about my work but I also have four children and can't be unemployed.

———————

I guess the scientist can't completely wash his hands of all responsibility. I wouldn't work on germ warfare projects but nuclear weapons projects have peacetime uses, too. The nuclear arsenal has an important deterrent effect.

———————

Einstein was not a murderer because he worked on the bomb. In that sense none of us is responsible either.

———————

It's strange to work on something you hope will never be used. I work on the ABM safeguard missile program and I hope Congress cancels it. It's a tremendous waste of money.

   If you decided to be an engineer, the only money is in working for the military. We all kid ourselves and tell ourselves that we are just working on scientific or technical problems and dissociate ourselves from military applications. It really doesn't wash though—you're only kidding yourself.

These attitudes persisted throughout the seventies. Most reemployed technologists accepted whatever work they could find: they were trapped in an institutional web that some could understand but none could control. Even if troubled by war work in 1972, they spoke of salary not social responsibility in 1975. Yet there was evidence that guilt took its toll. I encountered one long unemployed electronics specialist in the summer of 1975. He systematically studied the flow of defense contracts to various Route 128 firms with the serious intention of finding a job. He had impressive credentials and frequently made it beyond personnel men to interviews with managers. Once inside, he lost control. Each time, he "told them off," he said. Despite his desperate need for work, it was as though he sought opportunities to damn them for producing terrible devices of destruction.

Politics of Peace, Reform, and Rationality

The country must recognize that it now appears imprudent to move forward with a rapidly expanding nuclear power plant construction program. The risks of doing so are altogether too great. We, therefore, urge a drastic reduction in new nuclear power plant construction starts before major progress is achieved in the required research and in resolving present controversies about safety, waste disposal, and plutonium safeguards. (Union of Concerned Scientists, 1975)

One of the major mysteries of the recession has been the lack of visible anger with which it has been endured by the American people. There has been no violent protest and even orderly, peaceful demonstrations have been few and not very large.

   What the available statistics show is that the calm in the nation in the face of high unemployment cannot be explained on the ground that most of the unemployed are not suffering any serious deprivations. Compared to their former standards of living, most of the unemployed certainly are suffering even if they are not hungry or out in the street.

   No one knows how long tolerance for unemployment will last or if it would continue on the same scale in another recession. (Shanahan, 1975:E4)

The politics of Route 128 professionals, even more than their employment problems, first aroused my interest. A drive along the Golden Horseshoe was part of my introduction to the greater Boston area in the summer of 1968. Here in the defense electronics capital of America "Stop the Bombing," "McCarthy, for President," and "War Is Not Healthy for Children and Other Living Things" bumper stickers abounded. It was surprising to see missile makers display such outward support for the peace movement.

A national movement to end the Vietnam war was well under way by 1968. Its nerve centers were Massachusetts suburban communities. Eugene McCarthy had just won the state's Democratic presidential primary. Scientists, engineers, and data systems analysts who worked in Defense Department supported labs went home to be lobbied by wives and children, friends and neighbors. They were forced to question the uses of their work. Political activity on behalf of peace candidates was one way they assuaged feelings of guilt. Half of my Route 128 sample retrospectively recalled support for McCarthy. Others opposed the Vietnam war because funds were diverted from pet projects—bigger and better long-range advanced systems. The peace movement made it possible for technical professionals to share community values and simultaneously absolve *themselves* of social responsibility.

These patterns did not end with the Vietnam war; only the focus changed. Peaceniks became activists in energy conservation and antinuclear power plant politics. The Cambridge based Union of Concerned Scientists found widespread support in Route 128 communities. Technical professionals, funded now more than ever by Defense contracts, needed politics as a social responsibility trade-off. They entered the eighties with "No Nukes" bumper stickers on small foreign cars. ·

As unemployment struck and continued throughout the seventies and inflation dented the income of the reemployed, the politics of technical professionals produced other seemingly paradoxical patterns. These people were angered by unemployment and tortured by thoughts of downward mobility. I expected signs of political protest: there were none. I anticipated right-wing or left-wing polarization, possibly both; yet I found neither. The unemployed and the insecure were disappointed and embittered. They were distrustful of inefficient government and self-serving politicians. But they lacked class consciousness and militant politics was not an outlet for their feelings. They were not radicalized by their experiences. Status needs prevailed instead. They continued to reflect political patterns they thought characteristic of salaried professional colleagues. Even among the most disgruntled, it was politics as usual for the most part.

The Politics of Knowledge Workers: General Trends

Route 128 scientists and engineers shared the politics of other salaried professionals, the "knowledge workers" (a term first used by Dutton

[1971:151–152]) in postindustrializing society. As a new group groping for status and social identity, they sought "appropriate" ways to participate politically. Even though their political patterns often were unclear, there were some apparent trends.

In sociopolitical terms, salaried professionals are cross-pressured people. They hesitate to affiliate with any political party. All studies show that the Democratic party traditionally has been the party of working people, the poor, and racial and ethnic minorities. The Republican party, on the other hand, has attracted the support of big and small business and the very upwardly mobile (Lipset, 1960:285–309). Knowledge workers have high salaries relative to those of most Americans. Their need to reflect newly acquired status interests in political behavior is very strong. Caught between the parties, they want to be independent. Status insecurity makes them vulnerable to any candidate with style regardless of party (Bazelon, 1966:51).

Knowledge workers hold to a new political ideology manifest as a politics of rationality (Apter, 1967:30–40). As social class wanes in importance, professionalism emerges as the structural base of this ideology. It provides role identity and a sense of solidarity with colleagues. A major tendency of the politics of rationality is a "universal trend toward planning, calculation and rationalistic goals concerned with the future" (Apter, 1967:40). Knowledge workers believe that the findings of science, including social science, should provide the guidelines for social control and policy. They believe that tested theory and data should be applied to and incorporated in long-range planning to solve social problems. And for a variety of pseudointellectual and status reasons, candidates and movements that symbolize reform attract the support of this new middle class (Bensman and Vidich, 1971:40), which wants to separate itself from the partisan politics of working-class and immigrant parents.

The politics of seventies knowledge workers was marked by nonaffiliation, rationalistic ideology, and concern with the issues of peace and reform. Successful enough to be progressive, they advocated the needs of the poor, who were too far removed to pose a threat. They denigrated "narrow-minded hard hats" and the "misinformed." All of these trends were evident among Route 128 technical professionals—despite unemployment, which increased awareness but threatened position.

Route 128 People and Politics

Route 128 people shied away from political parties but they liked to be involved with the issues and the action. Rates of participation were high. Along Route 128, as elsewhere in Massachusetts, Democrats outnumbered Republicans more than two to one. In the spring of 1972, 15 percent of my sample (most of them Routinized engineers and Superstriver systems managers) defended Richard Nixon and the virtues of Republicanism. About one-third said they preferred the Democrats, at least on the national level. But half of the technical professionals I spoke with refused identification with any party: "It's the person, the issues," they said.[1] But when Route 128 people voted in national elections they tended to vote Democratic. In the 1968 presidential election only 27 percent recalled voting for Nixon; 61 percent went to Humphrey; 12 percent said they could not bring themselves to vote for either candidate. In the pre-Watergate 1972 presidential primary (the time of my initial interviews) 49 percent preferred McGovern; 22 percent chose regular Democrats (Humphrey, Jackson, or Muskie); only 18 percent favored Nixon.

Route 128 people were involved in the political life of their community and society. Participation provided tidbits for cocktail party conversation. They wanted to project an image of being with-it and in the know. Eighty-five percent of the sample systematically followed the daily news. Ninety-two percent had voted in the previous national election (compared with 55 percent of the national electorate). Eighty-one percent voted in local elections (compared with 50 to 60 percent in Massachusetts communities, where local voting is higher than national averages). Giving money always signifies political commitment. Forty-nine percent of my sample, compared with 5 percent of the population as a whole and 33 percent of a national sample of engineers (Perrucci and Gerstl, 1969b:158), contributed to causes or candidates. Forty-four percent of my sample signed petitions for or against some legislation, compared with 34 percent of engineers nationally (Perrucci and Gerstl, 1969b:158). Twenty-five percent of my Route 128 sample belonged to political groups of some kind and 22 percent actively worked for candidates, as compared with less than 5 percent of the general population. The good citizens of Route 128, cross-pressured and increasingly distrustful, still engaged in matters of governance.

On the issues, technical professionals were apt to favor reform, civil rights, civil liberties, peace, and curtailment of defense budgets. They were liberals with regard to federal spending in social welfare areas. Eighty-five percent, for instance, favored increased federal assistance for blacks; only 2 percent were opposed. Sixty-one percent favored increased construction of federally funded low cost housing. Eighty-two percent wanted nationalized health care. Eighty-seven percent wanted increased federal funding of mass transportation. Ninety percent favored increased spending to protect the quality of the environment. Upper middle-class professionals were not threatened by gains of the civil rights movement in the sixties. And they were overwhelmingly civil libertarian. Asked "Of course, the fact that a person believes in social equality doesn't prove that he's a Communist, but

[1] Thirty-six percent of the population in the sampled communities and 32 percent of the U.S. electorate as a whole were nonaffiliated at the time of the study.

it certainly makes you look twice, doesn't it?", 96 percent said "No." Almost half wanted fiscal cuts to come from the Defense Department budget even though it remained their lifeline. One-third of this sample saw a military-industrial complex as a threat to democracy in America, as the Defense budget increased nonetheless.

Some felt their interests were well represented by the American political party process but more were ambivalent or negative. Forty-two percent indicated approval or acceptance of the two-party system. But 50 percent give alienated responses: "Politicians are corrupt"; "Parties only pay lip service at election time—not real service."

What upset these people most was the lack of rationality they witnessed. Eighty-four percent of the people I interviewed wanted better long-range planning in political and social areas. Even when questioned at length, 76 percent could name *no* area in which they were opposed to this kind of planning. Technical professionals attributed employment instability to just such a failure of planning for the utilization of manpower resources. To people so committed to rationality, the American political party process epitomized chaos. But most technical professionals in the early seventies still hoped that the systems planning they had learned on Route 128 would influence economic decisionmaking through means that were politically efficient and effective.

Unemployment, Powerlessness, and Apathy

Experiencing unemployment had little effect on the political behavior of technical professionals. Ninety percent reported no change in kind or amount of political activity despite drastic changes in economic circumstances and life prospects. As scientists and engineers in a highly technical society they thought that knowledge brings power—at least the power to control some dimensions of their personal lives. Then abruptly, irrationally, they were stopped short at mid-career. Rarely could any justify or accept their own layoff. Some protested to superiors; most—fearing reprisals—left positions meekly. Whether active or passive all knew they were powerless: if they could not even hold their jobs, how could they possibly fight the system? There were no collective outlets through which grievances could be expressed and, had there been, few would have felt free to use them.

Instead of increased activity and radicalism, alienation and apathy were the responses to unemployment among seventies professionals, much as they had been among unemployed workers four decades earlier. Neither the Right nor the Left nor the activist center found Route 128 fertile soil.

Right-wing politics is sometimes appealing to dispossessed masses—not so among these unemployed and downwardly mobile professionals.

George Wallace ran for president on an anti-government platform in 1972. Before attempted assassination caused his paralysis, only 1 percent of the entire Route 128 sample said they could even take his candidacy seriously. This populist's message of alienation was not germane to cosmopolitan salaried professionals. Despite their troubles they still wanted to think of themselves as part of the establishment Wallace attacked.

For much the same reason, leftist appeals went similarly unheeded. Science for the People, a Cambridge based group of leftist technical professionals, tried membership recruitment at two consecutive meetings of the Economic Action Group, the most proletarian of the Route 128 crisis groups. They were allowed to distribute leaflets. The unemployed were polite but unresponsive. The young radicals were disgusted: "We're wasting our time here," one of them told me. "These groups are only interested in learning how to sell themselves to management. That's what the self-help bullshit is really all about."

Even the effort to build an independent special interest group of their own was seen by many as somehow unbecoming. The Association of Technical Professionals, which claimed a constituency of a thousand in 1972, featured itself the umbrella political organization for all other groups in the area. It sought to build an organizational base from which to exercise political clout for all technical professionals. A few hundred people actually paid dues for a short time. Leaders lobbied politicians, issues were addressed at public forums, and an informative newsletter was distributed. It took two government contracts to help the group limp along. Core leadership ended by counseling small business ventures; membership ultimately disintegrated.

The vast number of unemployed, underemployed, and anxious scientists and engineers were silent. Seventies professionals did not want to change the political system: they expected the system that "led them on" to "help them out." Unemployment sometimes stimulated insight but the very process of politicization threatened the generalized status orientation of their total life situation. An atomized mass, they voted in elections and waited, just as their fathers had before them. They hoped that new decisionmakers would make things better.

The Special Appeal of George McGovern

The electronics experts of the automated war were under fire. "Cut the funding, end the war" was the community chant. But unemployed technologists needed the jobs that George McGovern promised to cut. So I was surprised as I interviewed Route 128 people in the fall and winter of 1971 by the amount of support they showed so early on for McGovern, who as yet received only 6 percent in the national polls. By the April primary a bandwagon was building. McGovern tested the aerospace turf on Route 128 before moving on to more conservative engineers in southern California. He accepted an Association of Technical Professionals' invitation to speak at Bentley College in Waltham on April 17, 1972. McGovern did his homework well. This was more than just an ordinary political speech. It was an event. McGovern precisely articulated the occupational anxieties and fundamental concerns of the hundreds of scientists and engineers he addressed.

McGovern began by recognizing the importance of rationality.

> ATP's membership claims expertise in many fields. But today each one of you has an extra specialty that is unrelated to your training.
>   You know a great deal about the nation's failure to plan for the transition from a war to a peace economy.

He did not duck the fact that jobs would be lost by the kind of defense cuts he proposed.

> And a two-year transition to the $54.8 billion alternative defense budget I have proposed—coupled with the immediate application of those funds to civilian needs—would produce a massive net increase in production line jobs. This major re-ordering of spending priorities would guarantee a bright future for the average aerospace worker. But we need a more detailed policy in the case of technical professionals.
>   The new money we spend for housing construction and rehabilitation, for schools and hospitals, for better mass transit systems and for other programs of that kind will produce far fewer scientific and engineering jobs than equal investments in defense. They are less R&D intensive.
>   Meanwhile our colleges and universities are continuing to turn out still more technical personnel to compete for limited jobs.
>   And those of you who have aerospace expertise find that the younger guys are coming out ahead in the competition. They're not tied as tightly to a specific locality or to a professional specialty. They usually cost less. And they don't suffer from the aerospace prejudice which holds that a defense or space expert is a bad risk for civilian work.
>   So a more sensitive program is needed.

But he told them how government could provide other jobs by reordering spending priorities, keeping R&D high, and planning for expanded welfare state services.

> What I am proposing is increased funding for real research—for laboratory and feasibility studies, for experimentation and design. And we should be doing that across a broad range of civilian needs—in health, in water pollution control, in waste recycling, in energy conversion, in air traffic control, in noise abatement, in mass transit systems, in population planning, in lab enforcement methods, in drug rehabilitation, and in a host of others.

McGovern emphasized other themes especially salient to salaried professionals: working within the system for peace, reform, liberalism, and rationality.

> America knows the economic wreckage of military waste.
>
> We know the frustration and the outrage of neglected human needs.
>
> We know the fear of nuclear war that can incinerate most of mankind.
>
> We know too well the terror of war.
>
> We cannot remove those quantities from a war oriented economy. They are built into it.
>
> But we can take the pain out of peace.
>
> We can make it a goal that no one need fear—a dream we can all welcome with confidence and hope.

Half of my sample chose McGovern over Muskie, Humphrey, Jackson, or Nixon. Support for George McGovern, as it had been for Eugene McCarthy four years earlier, was an effective way to rationalize war work. Of those who were *most* likely to vote for McGovern, 45 percent said they felt no personal responsibility, the "innocent pawns," (compared with 22 percent of those who felt responsibility and 33 percent of the conflicted).

Distrust and Alienation

Distrust of politicians and the political system was rampant along Route 128 even before the Watergate revelations. One of the forms distrust took in 1972 was support for McGovern among the employed (57 percent). Among the unemployed it took the form either of support for McGovern (41 percent) or of rejection of all candidates (22 percent). One-fifth of the unemployed were too alienated from the political process to make a 1972 presidential choice.

"What do you think of the American political party system in general? Are your interests represented" I asked my sample. Fifty-eight percent of the unemployed gave negative responses, as did 42 percent of the employed. Increasing alienation from the political process was apparent in the early seventies, most notably among the unemployed.

Route 128 professionals did not support seventies candidates who sought to gain votes by pandering to people's alienation and distrust. Candidates who gave simplistic answers to problems that professionals knew to be complex did not inspire their confidence. Distrust and alienation were the themes of Jimmy Carter's 1976 presidential campaign. Carter wanted to be trusted. He would never "let us down." Professionals disbelieved these promises. They wanted a president who understood how to make government rational and efficient; they feared the incompetence of a Washington outsider. Carter was not popular along Route 128. In the 1976 Democratic presidential primary, Massachusetts professionals chose *none of the above* or Morris Udall. The Udall campaign was carefully targeted to cosmopolitan salaried professionals, emphasizing integrity, reform, moderate progressivism, and rationality. So in spite of job uncertainty, anger, and feelings of alienation, the politics of reason and reform continued to characterize the Route 128 scene.

"Proposition 13 fever" and single issue politics were national trends in 1978 but not among salaried professionals. Alienation and distrust notwithstanding, professionals knew that government services depend on taxation. They feared that advocacy of single issues distorted the political system. In Massachusetts, conservatism surfaced in the race for governor. In the Democratic primary the tax cutting, anti-abortion, capital punishment advocate Edward J. King upset moderate-liberal, incumbent Michael Dukakis by a 9-percentage-point plurality. But Dukakis outpolled King by 22 percentage points in the Route 128 communities I sampled.

The politics of unreason increasingly intruded on the national mood in the closing months of a difficult decade. Generalized anger soared with long gasoline lines, unprecedented oil company profits, astounding inflation, and fears of recession. John Connolly launched his campaign for the Republican presidential nomination with a "get tough" image. In Massachusetts he called himself another Edward King. Ronald Reagan, at work for years, had comprehensive computer files of single issue constituencies collated and ready to run. Public opinion polls showed low confidence in government in all classes—41 percent of the highest income groupings, 44 percent of the lowest income groupings, 49 percent among blacks (Caplovitz, 1978:54). More Americans blamed inflation on government and politicians (54 percent) than on big business (15 percent) or organized labor (14 percent). Yet,

> so far, the populace has faced these economic crises with seeming equanimity—there have been no marches, no riots and few signs of radicalization. Whether this equanimity will continue is a question that must hang heavily over economic policy makers today. (Caplovitz, 1978:54)

Increased unemployment should stimulate social criticism and substantive rationality among all groups affected. James A. Geschwender predicted the same process among working-class blacks that I found among middle-class professionals. He also doubted that higher unemployment would bring militant action.

> Periods of depression also tend to bring an increase in critical evaluation of the economy and an increased receptivity to socialism. A recession may facilitate the program of recruitment and political education of a black Marxist-Leninist movement but it will not facilitate action. Blacks who are out of work are also removed from their source of potential power. One cannot stop the forces of production if one is isolated from them. (Geschwender, 1977:227)

Among professionals, it is not at all clear whether new waves of unemployment will cause them finally to join the conservative mood or to move to the left. At best, seventies professionals face the prospect of continued underemployment in the eighties. Marxists once again see a potential source of radicalism, now in the growing ranks of the articulate, educated underemployed, people plugged into the means of production but at levels inappropriate to their skills (O'Toole, 1977: 59–60). Route 128 findings, however, argue to the contrary. The pain of unemployment increased awareness about how social institutions function but did not arouse a collective response. Class consciousness, which must come first, was hidden among these people, both upwardly and downwardly mobile in the same generation, and obliterated among the grateful reemployed. Dislodged professionals, disgusted with government, did not organize in protest against a system in which they still felt relatively well regarded. Status needs continued to dwarf class interests.

If a new conservative mood does take root among professionals, the reemployed, if underemployed, are likely to be its pioneers. But the political behavior of professionals is hard to predict. Contradictions, inconsistencies, and cross-pressures, experienced by technical professionals, now promise to become virtually endemic to American society. Scientists and technologists will most likely continue to build missiles and also to support the Eugene McCarthys of the future. And they will continue to view public issues, such as unemployment, as personal problems to be dealt with through the resources of their own life situations. Ideological attachments are loosened and even dissolved by increasing institutional complexity. And this group, as others, will make segmented and specialized demands on political institutions, projections of their own social preoccupations and particular circumstances, without a sense of collective responsibility or broad understanding.

10

Experiencing
Unemployment:
Typical Reactions

As we have seen, to endure unemployment is always stressful. The job hunt is never easy. Yet as in all human experiences, individual responses to adversity are varied. Accordingly, some people I interviewed dealt with the difficulties of joblessness better than others. In Chapter 8 we noted how the capacity for introspection differentiated less anguished professionals from their colleagues. When I reviewed the case histories of Route 128 people who functioned at least fairly well throughout, compared with those who did not, *cumulative insight* seemed to be the distinguishing substantive factor. The people who coped best questioned themselves and asked questions of others—employers, political leaders, heads of institutions. Answers accumulated over the years constituted a store of knowledge that helped them adapt to life crises. Based, then, on the degree of self-awareness and social awareness, two *general* reaction patterns to joblessness, labeled Skeptic and Conformist, emerged from the data.

Skeptic is the type of professional who is self-conscious and aware of his social reality. He is among the 20 percent of Levinson's (1978) subjects whose mid-life transition is smooth.

[Such] men in their early forties [are] aware of going through important changes, and know that the character of their lives will be appreciably different. They attempt to understand the nature of these changes, to come to terms with the griefs

194

and losses, and to make use of the possibilities for growing and enriching their lives. For them, however, the process is not a highly painful one. They are in a manageable transition rather than in a crisis. (Levinson, 1978:199)

Skeptic tries to understand his own needs as well as those of his family. Route 128 Skeptic questions the relevance of bureaucratic role requirements for personal and professional fulfillment. He is apt to be Savvy in his mode of adaptation to working conditions in advance systems laboratories (63 percent were previously classified as Savvy; 25 percent were Trapped; 12 percent were Routinized; none was Superstriver). He has a sense of his own worth. He thinks about the relationship of his work to culture and society. He analyzes the economic and political foundations of technical professional employment. He has a perspective on labor market parameters. Skeptic is distraught when unemployment hits; initially he may appear as upset as others but he copes despite stressful times.

A second reaction pattern to job loss, more common than the first, is found among people who lack resources of personal security—who have neither marked self-awareness nor heightened social consciousness. This is Conformist. He is among the 80 percent of Levinson's subjects for whom mid-life transition is a crisis, worse if latent than expressed.

> Some men do very little questioning or searching during the Mid-life Transition. Their lives in this period show a good deal of stability and continuity. They are apparently untroubled by difficult questions regarding the meaning, value and direction of their lives. They may be working on such questions unconsciously, with results that will become evident in later periods. If not, they will pay the price in a later developmental crisis or in a progressive withering of the self and a life structure minimally connected to the self. (Levinson, 1978:198)

Conformist thinks little about psychic needs or family dynamics. Unquestioningly, Conformist accepts performance goals and professional standards dictated by employers and internalizes them as his own. He is apt to be Routinized in his mode of adaptation to operational procedures in bureaucratized systems labs (63 percent were previously classified as Routinized; 34 percent were Trapped; 3 percent were Superstriver; none was Savvy). He thinks about the use value of his work but mainly in terms of vested organizational interests. Conformist spends little time pondering the institutional ramifications of technological development. He has minimal understanding of labor market conditions. When he loses his job, he has little perspective upon which to draw and is devastated. Conformist has difficulty determining strategies of survival.

Skeptic and Conformist both represent a range of attitudes and behaviors rather than a narrow descriptive or explanatory category. Skeptic tends to handle trouble better than Conformist does, but not all Conformists are immobilized. And all Skeptics do not cope equally well. Sometimes probing brings disturbing insights that cause Skeptic to withdraw in heightened cynicism. Conformist, in contrast, superficially accepts images and ideologies that suit his scene and cannot adapt to loss of anchorage in bureaucracy and status community. But prolonged crisis may lead Conformist to question social arrangements, usually for the first time. He may display increased introspection and adjust to altered life circumstances at least for a while. The Route 128 people I interviewed combined aspects of each of these types. They tended, however, toward one or the other. Skeptic and Conformist give us a way to glean meaning from the variety of responses to unemployment actually found among the seventies professionals studied.

Skeptic

Frank Brody was 45 years old when I first interviewed him in May 1972. He was born in New York City in 1927, the son of a skilled factory worker with a ninth-grade education. Frank wanted to be a scientist as far back as he remembers. He chose physics, the "fundamental discipline," as his undergraduate major at CCNY, received his M.S. in physics and almost his Ph.D., but marriage and Route 128 intervened.

> I was working in industry while finishing my degree. I planned to use my research findings as the basis of my dissertation. I thought I would teach in a college. Then the company decided to move the whole division to Route 128. My thesis advisor went. I went, too. I had a family by then.
>
> They tore up the lab and reconstructed it. But you take a year out just to get set up again. By that time my advisor lost interest in the project. And he was no longer connected with the university anyway. I moved to Massachusetts to keep my job. I never finished my doctorate.

Brody, an electronics engineer on Route 128, was titled an engineering specialist. His Defense-supported work involved R&D on semiconductor devices. Brody was laid off in May 1970. After 15 years with the company he was given four hours' termination notice; yet he said he was prepared for it even then.

> I knew it could happen any time. You must take these things as facts of life in this society. Jobs are always unstable when funded by Defense.
>
> These kinds of layoffs are not preventable given a capitalist economy and a Republican political administration. There would have been some decline under Democrats but it wouldn't have happened as sharply. Their economic philosophy is more Keynesian. The Democrats are also under more pressure from labor. Republicans use high unemployment to control distribution of income in favor of the companies.
>
> I didn't take it personally. It was a top bureaucratic decision. It came from the top corporate structure in New York. They decided to phase out the semiconductor division. Ultimately the whole division went.

Brody did not hang around the house. At first his search for work was a full-time job. He contacted friends and professional associates. He carefully scanned advertisements in newspapers, trade magazines, and professional journals. He made the rounds of the private employment agencies and headhunters. He sought help from professional societies. He went to the Route 128 Professional Service Center. He personally sent out 50 copies of his frequently revised resume. He estimated that friends and agencies distributed 50 others.

This is a man who made sure he got around. Brody's established patterns of social and political activity persisted, even increased. He volunteered in a congressional campaign. He worked for George McGovern in the 1972 presidential primary. He went to meetings—a "new politics" group, an economic conversion group, an ecology group. And of course he checked in at employment crisis groups—EAG in Needham, ATP in Lexington.

He spent more time with his family. Relationships at home were unchanged, he said. His wife, involved in her own career, understood and did not complain. His teenage daughters, busy with their friends and school, were as helpful as kids can be. But even sustained family support and high levels of activity did not completely cushion the painful effects of prolonged unemployment.

> There is no escaping the ego blow. I feel a diffuse sense of anxiety without work. I never had much faith in the system—understood the instability—blamed the system and not myself—and yet there was always a nagging sense of uneasiness. And we weren't financially in trouble.

Brody collected almost $7,000 in severance pay when he left the firm. (Company policy was still one week's pay for each year of service. And they owed him back vacation pay.) He collected unemployment compensation, $86 a week for 39 weeks. His wife was a research librarian at Boston University. They had savings.

> We never had it that bad. We had to cut back on new clothes, on entertainment, on food to some extent. But we never lived beyond our means—no debts, no credit cards. I guess it's the Depression heritage in me. My wife makes $11,500. Between that, the severance pay, and unemployment checks we never felt that dire pinch.

Unemployment continued. No job possibilities were on the horizon. But Brody refused to be idle.

> Compensation checks ran out. I took a job *very* underemployed, not as an engineer but as a jack-of-all-trades in a small local company. I was an accountant-bookkeeper. At first I made $2.10 an hour, 20 hours a week. Then I was up to $3.00 an hour for a 40-hour week. I wasn't making that much more than unemployment compensation, even at the end. It was better than being unemployed.

Brody kept looking for a suitable job by keeping in touch with friends and by visiting the Route 128 center regularly.

> The center isn't set up for dealing with professionals. The people there try but they can't cope with people like me. They don't know how to match professionals and jobs. But then again you can't find jobs for scientists and engineers if the jobs aren't there.

Finally in March 1972 an engineering job came through.

> A friend, a man who used to work under me, called and asked if I still needed a job. His company received some substantial contract awards. Now I work for him. I'm a product engineer at $16,000—a $4,000 cut. I work on tailoring existing products for the specific customer rather than on new products as before. I suppose it's the same kind of work but the orientation is different.

This job lasted two and a half years. In 1974 Brody was laid off again. This time financial pressures intensified. College tuition payments were immediately due. Savings were low. Barbara Brody's salary couldn't sustain the family. After three months on unemployment checks, Brody found a job through the Route 128 Center: at $9,000 a year he taught basic electricity to unemployed young adults, mostly black. He liked the work but not the salary.

Frank Brody had chosen a career in science because he found the work interesting. Route 128 was not the kind of stimulating research scene he had dreamed of, yet he adjusted.

> Lack of communications about decisions concerning your work is the basic problem. You certainly can't take part in the making of these decisions in large organizations. But those that are made are not communicated to you.
>
> I came to function without a high level of tension. I didn't let things bother me. I figured I wouldn't find a better situation anyway. I had trouble with those managers who didn't know what was going on. But this wasn't always true. I had one hard-driving type—I liked him the best because he got the best out of me.

Despite very rocky times in the seventies, interest in electronics and physics persisted. If he could choose his dream job, it would be doing research in pollution control for public institutions. But a more realistic option was vocational school teaching. This may not be Princeton, he said, but it engages young people in technology nonetheless, an original Brody aspiration. For him, the glitter of science never really faded.

That the military paid his salary was the most troublesome part of Frank Brody's Route 128 career. He never felt that the defense industries made positive contributions to the economy, to the development of scientific talent, or even to defending the nation.

> I don't believe we have an enemy with the desire and capability of conquering the U.S. . . . . The arms race proceeds at the level the powers can sustain it,

regardless of defense needs. The U.S. leads the race for interests of the military-industrial complex.

He was opposed to the Vietnam war from its beginning: "I was always a dove. This is an immoral war. We had no business intervening. The military-industrial complex pushed us for their own benefit. We had no right to be there in the first place." Yet he worked on military applications for years. I asked him whether he felt personally responsible for the ultimate uses to which products he worked on were put. I asked him about the moral and political reservations he felt and how he coped.

> This is the roughest question. Society is so organized that you have no power to determine how your work will be used. The end product of what I do is not within the realm of my knowledge. The Air Force funds several of the projects I've worked on. I always feel a sense of frustration.
>
> Engineers have no responsibility as individuals. Theirs is a collective responsibility. If scientists and engineers would organize they could have power; they might influence the decisions about the uses of their work. Then they would have responsibility. So I work to help organize scientists and engineers to see that this comes about. I work for peace groups and political action groups to try to influence the political decisionmakers. But that's all I can do. Sometimes I wore a peace button to work (making transistors for missiles).

Frank Brody denied that he wanted to return to technology row. But—if the job were interesting and the salary high—one wonders whether he would not return.

The living room where I spoke with Joseph Felden was sparsely furnished. "We got rid of the extras," he apoligized as he showed me in. On this snowy January morning the room was a garden of houseplants. He cared for them. He also did the shopping, all the cooking, and some of the laundry. At 45 years of age this solid state physicist called himself a "househusband who needs 20 cups of coffee to make it through the day."

Joseph Felden agreed to be interviewed because he wanted to talk *and* to learn about the job market and about how others coped with unemployment. He talked willingly, nervously, pensively. He grew up in south Philadelphia, over the grocery store his father owned.

> I could do well in physics when others couldn't. I wanted the approval and praise that came from my father and teachers. And physics was really important—the path to progress and the future. I could be *someone*, instead of a boy in a grocery.

Feldon won scholarships all the way through to his Ph.D. in 1953. He became a specialist in solid state, optical, and high pressure physics.

The Golden Horseshoe beckoned. As a member of an expensively equipped laboratory staff he performed research on topical properties of semiconductors. But the stimulation he hoped for never quite materialized. He argued with management. He was fired in 1959. Then Felden chose a large Defense contract firm from among the many job offers he had. As a research scientist he directed a group concerned with semiconductor lasers. After six years he left for a management position with a federally funded space facility. Here he was the chief of a major laboratory until 1970, when the research center closed (it reopened as an applied systems facility without him). During the subsequent year and a half Felden was out of work.

For 17 years Joseph Felden had qualified as a Route 128 superprofessional. He wrote two technical books: a text and a research monograph with a major house. He wrote 40 articles for professional journals. He was awarded numerous patents. He was elected a fellow of the American Physical Society and a senior member of the Institute of Electrical and Electronics Engineers. He participated in at least a dozen other societies and associations. But none of these accomplishments helped him hold his job.

Termination notice did not immediately put Felden out in the cold. Government scientists receive good benefits.

> There is a standard government formula for people at my level. I was earning $30,000. This entitled me to $5,000—the equivalent of two months' pay. It didn't cut my anger.
>
> Engineers were kept on and pure scientists were fired. People were kept at an inverse ratio to their competence and the good they would do. Top and second to the top people were kept in any case. I was just below that. Personal influence within the organization was the major factor. They made the decision to do away with basic research. I'm very bitter about this aspect of it. For the two preceding years I tried to get my people to do more relevant things. I was resisted from above and below. My boss said that this was the place to do nothing but basic research. That was supposed to be the beauty of the thing. Then they made the decision to lay off precisely on that basis.

At first Felden made a careful search for work. He contacted amazed friends. He answered some ads. He applied at a few private agencies. He went to the local DES office: "Routine, bureaucratic. Pleasant, but nothing more. What else can you expect?" He went to the Route 128 Professional Service Center: "They tried to be helpful. They did what they could. But they are very limited." Within a short time Felden learned that there was nothing for 45-year-old physicists.

Felden had always felt underutilized. He had had trouble coping with tight organizational structures; he had had trouble with managers—and all because he was nor permitted to use his knowledge creatively: "I felt like my father, the grocer, during most of my career, moving cans around on the shelf but not really interested in what was inside the cans."

He wanted to try something new, something creative, after layoff.

I stayed home, did the housework, and tried to write novels. I wrote one. It was rejected. I wrote another—it was rejected. I'm looking for a new way. Maybe I should open a health food store.

We've become vegetarians. It started with my daughter, who likes animals and won't eat meat. I started cooking for her. Now we all like it. I've come to feel a strong identity with the youth culture. So much about success is skin-deep.

Financially the Felden family was under considerable strain. They wondered how long they could continue to meet basic expenses. Joan was a tenured high school teacher; the extra salary became the mainstay. Severance pay helped. Unemployment compensation paid weekly food bills. But after 18 months assistance checks were long gone and so was their savings account. The Feldens did not see how they could keep their home.

We feel the pinch on Joan's $12,000 salary. We cut out *all* entertaining. We spend much less for food. We spend nothing on clothes. The kids work for spending money. We even held a garage sale to get what we could from extra possessions. We applied to the music school for scholarships for the children because of unemployment. We're making it—but just about. And I don't know for how long. If the money doesn't start to come in soon, we're going to have to move out.

Emotional strains accompanied unemployment. Family relationships suffered.

Unemployment is a form of castration—by wife and friends. Unemployment is a form of rejection and in a society where the job is everything the man without a job is not a man. I don't find much understanding from my wife or my friends.

My wife is a pleasant lady who lives on the surface of things. She is happy to support me if I want to stay home and write—as long as I'm happy. She tries. But there's a level in me she can't reach. She doesn't meet my emotional needs. I now have all kinds of neurotic needs and maybe some other kind of woman could meet them. I need to be mothered and I need all kinds of emotional support.

I'm a compulsive eater even though I only weigh 155 pounds now. I'm a fat man even though I'm very thin. I ate a long time after a fight last night. I make demands she just can't meet.

Sure the children are involved. The older two try somehow to compensate me for my failure. I feel terrible. And I just don't know what to do about it. Perhaps a radical change in lifestyle would be the best thing. Another job with Defense isn't the thing for me anymore. I have to find some way to mobilize myself again.

Relationships between psychological factors and the social environment of R&D labs were targets for Felden's introspective tendencies. He offered, for instance, a Freudian interpretation of staff-line conflict.

In part all scientists are paranoid because we see things in terms of structure, order, rational systems. We want to reduce the chaos in the society in which we live to systems. Management makes arbitrary decisions like a father. Management assumes the position of the father, the authority figure. So scientists direct hostility toward management and management turns hostility back toward the scientists.

All of this was present when I was in management. I played out the authority role and was hated by the scientists under me and I turned it back on them. The process is inevitable.

These reflections, as well as his own career problems, nevertheless did not diminish Felden's estimation of the ultimate importance of science for society.

Science is an important national resource, but its real importance goes unrecognized. Unplanned spending is nonsense. Science should be supported on a modest but continuing basis. The leaders of the scientific community never tried to convince Congress of this.

Science justifies itself either in commercial profit terms or as the way of staying ahead of the Communists—never for its own sake as a national resource contributing to the needs of society.

Scientists should be addressing critical social questions. But they think about themselves. They don't really care about social applications. They aren't interested in doing what they can themselves. They look only to government and will do only what government will pay for.

Persistent depression did not prevent Felden from maintaining an active interest in economic and political issues. He sought representation for the interests of scientists and engineers, and he went to the Needham employment crisis group a few times.

I was attracted by the pathology. I can't understand why technical professionals show so little interest in political action or economic organization. I can't understand the apathy, even in these groups. Unions would be good; political action groups would be good; anything would be good. We need help. But there is no hope in that direction. The apathy is staggering.

Most of Felden's career had been supported by Defense Department contracts. He even described his space research as war work, at least potentially so. Always a dove on Vietnam, he favored immediate and complete withdrawal with full reparations. The war, he said, made him more aware of what he called the "pernicious influence of the defense industries." He envisioned a powerful military-industrial complex and frequently referred to Charles Reich's *Greening of America:* "This is Reich's Consciousness II. The military, the industrial and government bureaucracies are all intermeshed and control our lives." I asked him what contributions the defense industries make to the overall economy. His reply: "The problem is that scientists and engineers have all done war production. This bolsters all parts of the economy falsely." I then asked, "What role do these industries play in the development of creative talent?" Felden said, "The problem is that this is where scientists and engineers have to work. But no talent is developed. There is only a waste of talent here. These industries have a warped view of their role in every area, even defense itself."

Understanding, guilt, and rationalization merged as irritating aspects of Felden's work world. They were as disturbing to him as his lack of job satisfaction and were intensified during his many months of unemployment.

> I didn't like being associated with the Defense Department and with war aims. They call it defense but it is really war aims. I resented my work being classified as military when it was only basic research.
>
> You can never tell in advance how a particular project will be used. But the scientist has the responsibility to carry through and see how his work is being used. Then you can complain if you don't like it. Most scientists don't even think about doing this. Few scientists feel responsible for the implications of their work. Scientists want to play like children and be supported. Engineers just want to be told what to do. They don't want to think beyond that and they don't care.
>
> As for myself, I was concerned that I had to work for the Defense Department. But my work is basic research. I can't fully deny its military implication though. . . . I wanted to leave but the salary was too high and I couldn't.

Fear and demoralization finally coaxed Felden back to defense work. When a former colleague told him about a good position, he applied and got the job: he was a physicist again—at a military base in the Southwest. His work was direct hardware development, no longer basic research. I was not able to contact him for a 1975 interview. His job description came from his wife, who had stayed in Lexington with the children. She found the situation difficult and hoped they could "find a better resolution."

Skeptic (31 percent of the unemployed sample) is practiced in understanding who he is and how he functions. Frank Brody and Joseph Felden exemplify Skeptic's reaction to unemployment. Brody is middle-range Skeptic; his career experiences and response to joblessness show how understanding fosters adaptation. Felden is overly introspective as he explores the meaning of self, career, and society; he becomes increasingly cynical yet adjusts nonetheless.

Skeptic is critical of the funding that supports technical professional careers. He is disturbed by the lack of long-range government planning for the utilization of the scientific and technological manpower resource. Too many programs, he says, are introduced and withdrawn for short-run expediency or at the whim of politicians. In the hope of receiving contract awards, it is common practice, he explains, for firms to hire all sorts of experts they do not really need and then terminate them if the anticipated contracts go elsewhere. Skeptic is disturbed by the development of military hardware at the expense of domestic industry. "We have the lowest rate of patent applications of any industrialized country. Germany and Japan have most of the important consumer goods patents. We should have listened to Seymour Melman years ago." He is disturbed by the waste and duplication he sees in cost-plus funded defense industries. Government contracts keep people working, he says, but only in an unproductive way. Sometimes Skeptic has the knowledge and perspective to analyze labor market conditions for technical professionals in terms of economic cycles. If he does, he comes to appreciate the need for individual job flexibility.

Skeptic distrusts many of the productivity and profit policies of private industry. He tends to see large corporations as impersonal and as frequently unfair to professionals. Skeptic describes instances of companies' terminating people immediately prior to their becoming eligible for retirement benefits and of important patents, on which the firm stands to make large profits, coming through after the inventor had been fired. Interviewing for jobs is always risky, says Skeptic, because interviews are often "fishing expeditions to get your ideas when real jobs just aren't there." Skeptic tends to see technical professionals as "unorganizable company slaves" or "corporate nomads." Skeptic despairs at the typical engineer's lack of interest in protective organization. Skeptic is distressed by the power of companies to sacrifice scientific progress for profits and by their ability to control working conditions so that job satisfaction is denied to many.

Skeptic has a sense of his own ability and importance quite apart from the judgment of corporate superiors. He has a sense of personal and social values that sustains and supports him. He is confident about what he knows and how much he could contribute to society if only he had the opportunity to do so. Despite economic cycles, laboratory organization patterns, or shifting employment status, Skeptic has an appreciation of his problem-solving ability, scientific knowledge, or managerial skills that remains with him and carries him through. Skeptic is frequently frustrated by underutilization and consequently he becomes angry at the organization.

Skeptic, for instance, is Route 128's Humphrey Bogart, who as inertial components manager had to cut his department's budget. Sure of himself and always independent, he laid himself off instead of three others. "It's hard for a manager to let good people go," he says, "and collectively they contributed more to company goals than I did." But 1970 was no time for heroism: he never found another top level corporate position. Skeptic is Route 128's conscientious objector, a vice-president who became increasingly disturbed by his company's hard-nosed military posture. He wants to use his knowledge of physics to serve society and phases himself out of a position. He suffers several years of virtual unemployment.

Skeptic really loves his work. He respects science, technology, and himself. His self-confidence frees him to work actively for changes he sees as meaningful.

Although Skeptic is usually laid off abruptly, as are others, the blow is somehow less intense. There is no escape from the demoralizing psychological effects of joblessness but adjustment is easier for people who have thought about the social roots of their situation. Skeptic saw the contract flow shifting and thought he was vulnerable, but because he knows his worth he's "shocked at not being needed." Skeptic frequently disagreed with management policy and expected the "troublemakers" to get the axe. When it happens to *him*, the problem is difficult but manageable.

Introspective Skeptic understands his plight and finds ways of helping himself. "In this society you are what you do. When you don't have a position you lose track of who you are. You must not lose your self-esteem. Self-confidence is worth fighting for." And sometimes in Skeptic, but not in others, distress followed by a period of successful adjustments has positive social and psychological effects.

> I felt under a tremendous amount of tension from the time I was laid off until the time I knew that my new business was going to be a success. Even if you understand why you had to be laid off, rejection is very difficult to take. This introduced much tension into the family. Things are great now. Changing habits was the most difficult part of the adjustment. When you're used to a work schedule it's very difficult to make your own schedule. Habits are hard to change. But the change is made, and it's good.

> Not a terrible thing to be laid off. It was a time for reevaluation. It forces you to see where your life is going. It can be viewed as a jolt to make you reevaluate your career. Unemployment helped me gain a new sense of direction; got me into a more interesting job. It helped me to see that what I really wanted to do was work on computer applications for transportation systems—not tracking systems for ballistic missiles.

Skeptic uses selective methods in his search for reemployment. He surveys the scene and then diligently does only those things that make most sense. Skeptic does not send out hundreds of blind resumes. He finds leads through friends and professional contacts, newspaper advertisements, private employment agencies, and the Massachusetts Department of Employment Security. If he has access to specialized services such as the MIT Alumni Placement Bureau he goes there directly. He sends out a letter of inquiry followed by his resume only if he locates a real job prospect. He rewrites his resume to emphasize the particular focus of each potential position. Where possible, he asks friends to act as intermediaries and send out resumes in his behalf. Skeptic sometimes writes the equivalent of a proposal for each interview. This takes a lot of time and in a tight market nothing seems to pay off. Skeptic has more patience with the Route 128 Professional Service Center than with the "bastards" at the private agencies. But there are problems at the center. The personnel "can't intelligently evaluate jobs or your qualifications. Computers can't fit people in positions," he says.

Sometimes Skeptic determines that the job market is hopeless—"My field is played out"; "I'm just too old." Instead of making the regular rounds he puts his all into a retraining program or into building a small, independent enterprise. Skeptic may be out of work as long as Conformist but his job hunting approach is targeted and purposeful.

To professionals accustomed to leading productive lives, idleness can be the worst part of the unemployment experience. So Skeptic is rarely idle. He works hard looking for work. At first this effort consumes all of his time. But as the months pass it is clear that a 40-hour-a-week job search is fruitless. Skeptic consciously fights against lethargy should it begin. He tries not to stay around the house. He makes an appointment of some kind that gets him dressed, up, and out each day. Perhaps he becomes active in an unemployment crisis group. If he must stay at home to wait for calls he tries to find something constructive to do. He needs some feeling of accomplishment. He builds a deck onto the bedroom, paints the woodwork, or builds some cabinets. Even after a year of unemployment, Skeptic fills the days in meaningful ways.

> I wanted to do something useful so I volunteered to teach auto mechanics at Concord Reformatory. What a revelation! I learned how these young men feel about being institutionalized. They hate the social workers. Yet each time I walk in they give me a tremendous welcome. I can provide them with a *real* link in a productive way with the outside. I know I make a positive contribution to society through these young people at the point at which they have to make basic decisions. It has given me a different outlook—I mean on myself. I have a role to play and it's important even if I don't have a job.

Unemployment can activate Skeptic. He seeks out other jobless professionals. Fifty-three percent of Skeptics (compared with 11 percent of Conformists) went to meetings of Route 128 unemployment crisis groups at least once or twice; some attended regularly. Activated Skeptic soon learns that unemployed colleagues are a poor source of job leads. He may go to meetings anyway, mostly for companionship: "The Lincoln group gave me a fix for the sort of things that are happening"; "I need to talk. The Economic Action Group helps morale more than anything else"; "I've gotten some good information at the Association of Technical Professionals' programs. We surely need a political lobby." Skeptic is more likely to favor unionization of scientists and engineers (53 percent) than is Conformist (16 percent) or the sample as a whole (35 percent). Skeptic wants technical professionals to develop national clout but he doubts this will come about: "Exploitation of professionals occurs in many places but engineers are too stupid to organize," he says. And Skeptic, more than others, understands the risk of organization: "We need protection but most unions move out of the individual's control, some become corrupt, and then you're no better off than before."

Skeptic's ability to understand and adjust, his constructive use of time, and his activism lessen the likelihood of family disruption. An *absence* of severe tension in family relationships was described by 52 percent of the Skeptics, compared with 13 percent of the unemployed sample as a whole. Skeptic is genuinely supportive of his working wife, even of her career development. Of course, joblessness somewhat increases overall family tension but Skeptic talks more of "working out problems" than of conflict, separation, or divorce.

Skeptic is experienced at coping with disappointment. At the outset of his career he was highly motivated to plow the frontiers of discovery, but working conditions in bureaucratized laboratories militated against promised satisfaction. He sees organizational constraints as endemic but when working he found ways to live with restrictions: "Sometimes management is enlightened and adjustments can be made. Competent people can work things out," he says. Skeptic regards organizational hassles as *"typical* problems one must always face."

> It's often hard to communicate with managers or others who make allocation decisions. I've sometimes been prevented from looking where I wanted to. You always run into managers who are too long removed from the laboratory, but this is the pattern you come to expect.

When employed, he understood the basis of his job dissatisfaction and worked out ways to reduce its impact. If conflicts were intense, Skeptic sometimes moved to a smaller company that allowed him greater task diversification. Ultimately Skeptic lowers his expectations about potential career fulfillment, yet he retains an overriding dedication to science and technology.

Skeptic was a staunch opponent of the Vietnam war. Working on weapons of destruction in the early seventies was therefore one of his greatest career related problems. When coaxed, Skeptic painfully discusses his dilemma and then consciously retreats to one rationalization or another.

> The defense industries don't defend with all that crap they are building. Half of the stuff absolutely doesn't work. The amount of money we spend on the military is obscene. But the scientist is an innocent pawn. I only worked on getting the stuff there, the delivery systems. There's no other use to what I did. I didn't make the warheads themselves. At times I tried to campaign against some of the policies of the company from the inside.

> I've always been against the war and high defense spending. We don't need that kind of defense at all. But the responsibility issue is a difficult one. My work was

far removed enough to disguise any immediate use. I had very little feeling for the ends. None of the projects really ever worked. I got a reverse feeling of satisfaction. One Vietnam camera project actually was a total failure. Confidentially I was delighted. I did refuse to work on proximity fuses for Vietnam. In that case destruction of life could be seen.

Lacking options, Skeptic usually stayed with his Defense supported job as long as he could, as did Conformist. The difference, however, is that Skeptic understood the stakes and was sorely conflicted. During months of unemployment his guilt intensifies. Usually without much success, he sometimes tries to disguise his past involvement in military R&D from himself even more than from others. But when pressed, he is able to confront his pain. Comprehension helps him cope with his feelings.

Skeptic is better able than his colleagues to salvage more from less than optimal situations. Subsequently this sustains him as he struggles to maintain self-respect and secure employment. He is aided in this quest by a deeply rooted conception of human values that minimizes the importance of culturally imposed success goals.

There is so much hypocrisy in American society. Money is the only thing we think of and we forget to be human. Money and status things just shouldn't be that important. The only real success is to be satisfied with yourself.

A reverence for life, combined with a special respect for intellectual and moral values, is part of the meaning of success in Skeptic's scheme of things. He balances individual self-worth with a sense of responsibility to society. And he survives.

Conformist

Arthur Myers asked me to come by on Saturday morning rather than in the evening so that we could chat by the pool. He was eager to tell his story. I drove up to a beautiful English Tudor. He asked me to come in while he looked for a copy of his resume, but I knew he really wanted me to see the house. Every room was *Better Homes and Gardens.* His wife was an interior decorator, he explained. At first I thought she must have wanted a showroom. But no, they really liked it that way. These were people who had to prove they had moved up—from the pavements of the Bronx to the lawns of Lincoln.

Arthur Myers told me he had been out of work a year. He was struggling desperately to keep the lifestyle he had always envied but only just achieved. He was not sure he could do it, but he had not given up: he had fought too hard to get there.

Myers was born during the depths of the Depression. He grew up in a working-class neighborhood in the Bronx. His father was a paperhanger, and family income was erratic. He spent most of his childhood and youth with the kids on the block. His friends, he recalls, wanted only to make a lot of money. But he wanted to be important.

City College was free but even with living at home he had to work nights to meet expenses. He graduated in 1957 with a chemistry major and high expectations. He took his first job with a New York company. He was there for four years as a chemist, a metallurgist, and finally, a senior project engineer. At the same time he went to a well-respected technical institute at night. It took until 1961 for him to earn a master's in metallurgical engineering. Then he entered a management program, also at night. He was credentialed, he thought, and surely on his way. He wanted more experience. By now he had a wife and child to support and decided to remain in the New York area a few years more. His next job was with an upstate aerospace firm: he was the program manager of multimillion dollar programs for the Air Force.

Myers was all set for the big move to Route 128. In 1966, a major firm gave him the chance. He managed an $8 million program involving countermeasure defensive techniques. Then he managed the tactical penetration aid rocket program. He sailed right along expecting to move into upper management until June 1971, when he was fired.

Arthur Myers was in a quandary about the reasons for his termination. He felt the layoff was unfair and he was angry. Though Myers asserted that he had been a loyal company man, he reasoned that the firm really did not have work for him. And he knew there were subtle status requirements he could not meet however he might try.

> I was getting close to 40. My salary was high. But the basic reason was that the big contract they had hoped for hadn't come through. They kept me on, waiting, for one year. The VP wasn't comfortable with me around. This guy was in the tennis group—buddies always play tennis together. They didn't lay off anyone who was on their team. They also have their bridge group. It helps to be in one of these groups to hold on to your job. I was president of the Toastmasters Club, but that wasn't enough. I felt they should have kept me on. I made so much money for them.

The Myers family was in financial trouble as soon as the paychecks stopped. Lincoln living is expensive, and the bills piled up. The pool, the symbol of it all, was not paid for. The Myers had spent most of what they earned to prove that they belonged. In summer 1971, Arthur was given two months' notice and a $2,400 termination package. Unemployment compensation was $86 a week. His wife made some money; he was ashamed to say how much, but it must have been more than the $5,000 he admitted. What savings they had went quickly. And that was it. They owed money everywhere. And he had to take another loan so that his daughter could go to Northeastern University, not Smith or Mt. Holyoke as they had planned. They skimped wherever they could.

We spend as little as possible. It looks like the end of the rope but we'll never go back where we came from. Must keep this lifestyle. This shithead government is not going to put me out of this lifestyle.

Myers tried every way he could to hussle a job. He was determined, however, not to let the market "cut him down." His identity was too closely tied to his career. Even in desperation he equated underemployment with unemployment. He answered ads in newspapers and professional magazines with resumes. Nothing happened. He called friends, people he had worked with, people from professional societies: "All of my great friends weren't there." He tried private employment agencies, but they did not return his calls. He went to the DES office.

I stood in unemployment lines. People drive by and look at me like I was shit. The girls have no idea how to handle me. They told me to go to the 128 center. It was ridiculous. The whole matching and placement process is stupid. I went a few times. They couldn't find the right holes to punch. They only had me as manager. But what about my degrees in chemistry, metallurgy, engineering?

One day a girl called and said I would be hearing from some guys about an overseas project. When they didn't call I went to the center and asked where the guys were. The girl said they were in a Boston hotel and were leaving in a few hours. They decided they didn't want engineers for that job. I wanted to get in touch with them myself because I was dying to get that job. I knew I could handle it. It was perfect for one of my skills not punched in those damn cards. The girl wouldn't tell me where to find those guys before they left town. I was so burned I never went back to the center.

He followed up every possible lead in person—all dead ends.

Arthur's job loss was a trauma from which neither he nor his family could recover. The psychological impact on all of them was severe. Arthur wanted to get away from the house but had nowhere to go. He would not do household chores: "Women's work is demeaning," he said. "I feel belittled enough as it is." He could not cope with the repeated rejections of his job hunt. It would have been easier to stop looking but he could not do that either. He showed me a punching bag in the basement. It was impossible, he said, to contain his anger.

I feel like a piece of shit. Take it out on my wife and kids. Tremendous personal problems for us all. The kids don't ask me for money anymore. Shirley is taking over the role as breadwinner. I hear them whispering "don't tell Daddy." I feel like I'm out of the family unit. Everyone is angry around here. I guess they're all having a hard time with me. My 15-yeard-old son is having a hard time. So is my daughter. We go to the Jewish Family Service for help. We're seeing a psychiatrist. My daughter goes with my wife. My son and I go separately. It all seems to stem from my unemployment. I fly off the handle. My wife can't take it. The kids can't take it. The problems with my son are terrible. I guess it's that father-son rivalry stuff.

I'm very depressed. It hurts so deeply when you can't take care of your family.

Protection of status, regardless of psychological or ideological cost, was the leitmotif of Arthur Myers's career profile. His view of the institutional underpinnings of his occupational position was influenced above all by his need for employment. He did not talk easily about manager-professional tensions. He did not think about problems his staff might have had with him. Yet suggestions of conflict were evident. He talked of red tape, of the need to watch out for top managers "who only wanted to get credit for your ideas," and of the need to get around the "big shots" and talk to the generals directly. But he hesitated to meet these problems openly. It was as though he feared that even our conversation might hurt his reemployability.

Myers favored all-out spending for military R&D—his meal ticket. "Only a strong deterrent keeps the peace," he told me. He wanted to be for and against the Vietnam war at the same time. He felt pride in his work, not guilt. That defense industries did not function as they should was the only problem he identified.

> The system that I ran that didn't get funded would really have prevented the loss of our planes in Vietnam. Every time I hear about another plane getting shot down, I feel a tremendous sense of frustration.
>
> There is a great frustration in working for and waiting for Defense Department contracts. The contracts don't get awarded on the basis of their superior technical potential, even their potential for defense. Projects get funded on the basis of politics. The guys don't really know what to fund and what to cut from the point of view of defense.
>
> You put your best work into projects. Write it up into proposals that no one reads. Buried because it's all classified. You put all of what you have, all of your creativity, into a project and some stupid jerk in Washington to please some political cronies can screw up the works. One hell of a system.

Myers also favored economic conversion.

> There are plants and facilities that do nothing on 128. If the canceled contracts were put into transportation, pollution control, energy research in the same amounts we could work wonders here. We just need some experts to come in with reorientation programs.

A year of unemployment changed some of Myers's attitudes. He no longer thought that companies are always considerate of loyal employees. He thought they should be more humane, especially about layoffs. He did not go to employment crisis groups: "I'm tired of the kind of crap I would hear there. I need a job, not more bullshit." He opposed unionization: "They don't guarantee jobs anyway." He regretted, however, that he had given so much of himself to the companies he had worked for: "I would go back to Route 128 but only at a high salary plus bonuses. Or else I'd rather work for myself for $10,000 a year." For a long time Myers did neither.

The years that followed our first interview were rough. The best Myers could get was a consulting job for the length of a contract here and there, amid stretches of unemployment. But he was working when I talked with him in May 1975.

> In December 1974, I answered a straight ad for a plant manager, commercial company. They interviewed me. I went through the plant. I told them what I would question. I hit 90 percent of the areas they had trouble in. They wanted me to work for several thousand dollars less than I asked for. I told them what I could do for them in six months at the salary I asked. So I'm on a six-month review, which is coming up. I cut down payroll costs without cutting production. We do the same job now with less people.

I asked Myers how it felt laying off people after his own experiences: "There was feather bedding. There was nothing professional about their management. Inventory is computer controlled now."

Arthur Myers was a man protecting a precarious position. Job survival instincts blocked other feelings. Possibly, heightened awareness had to be repressed. Myers, reprieved for a time, had to guard his new turf well. So he joined in support of a system that allowed him to salvage some piece of the action after all.

Soft-spoken and very polite, Martin Stewart had been out of work 14 months but was now working again. He agreed to talk and wanted to hear about my study. The old Victorian house was well cared for. We spoke in the living room—Oriental rugs and Indian vases, a marble coffee table, comfortable Scandinavian furniture, a colonial chest in the corner. I could not help commenting. He said I should have come two years ago, before they hit hard times.

My first impression of Martin Stewart remains—a conservative in manner and appearance. At age 42 he was an engineer's engineer. He never thought about a career, he said. His father was an engineer. All the men in his family were engineers. "I don't know what else I could do." Martin Stewart was a man of few words. Communication was not easy: he answered my questions in a phrase or a sentence—rarely did he elaborate and only if pressed.

He grew up among Chicago's middle classes. He went to a first-rate technical institute straight through to a master's degree in electrical engineering. His wife, too, came from a family of professionals. Her father was a doctor. She went to a renowned school of design. "Class," they said, meant interesting friends and lifestyle, not money. Still, their identity was tied to position. "How do you gracefully move out of the middle class?" she asked me.

The Stewarts managed to "hang in there." Susan was forced by their circumstances into opening an art gallery. "Ironically this was good for me," she said. "It forced me out of the house and into an interesting life of my own." But this was not so good for Martin. He barely mentioned the gallery during our interviews and spoke as if family finances depended solely on his salary.

Martin Stewart took his first job in his father's company. Father died a few years later and the company went under with him. Stewart moved to Route 128—large electronics firms, plentiful government contracts. His field was instrumentation; he developed peripheral equipment. For 17 years his skills were in demand. Stewart had his pick of jobs with the best firms. He moved up to project manager, 1971 salary of $24,000, and expected to be a top level manager earning $30,000 by 1975. He did not expect layoff but justified it nonetheless.

Stewart showed me an award he had received from NASA. He was responsible for designing instrumentation critical for the astronaut's life support system. His design was used for a moon landing.

> I was laid off when things were going well. The vice-president asked to see me. I thought he was going to give me a raise. As I walked down the hall I tried to figure out how much it would be.
>
> It was three weeks' notice of layoff. He told me how much my severance package would be: $6,000. I hadn't been with them that long. They had no new contracts. I had to go ahead of some of the others. The supervisor had no real choice.

A 14-month nightmare followed. Stewart went through the motions of a job hunt in a daze. He sent copies of his resume to every company around. He answered every ad he saw: "I can't express myself in writing. I just told them exactly how I could do what the ad requested and nothing else. And then I requested a personal interview." There were no replies, month after month, and the Department of Employment Security did not help either. He likewise found the Route 128 center useless and was rebuffed by private agencies.

The Stewarts' financial situation was critical. A few large medical bills wiped out the severance pay.

> We lost all our credit. How do they know you're unemployed? We only paid interest on the mortgage. We bought nothing new—we took used clothes for the kids from people we knew. We spend much less for food. You find you can live on less. I don't know how we did it. I thought if it went on one month longer we couldn't make it. It did go on and on and yet we got through. You never know how little you can live on until you must. I tried to get food stamps. It was humiliating to ask. I couldn't even get surplus food.

Martin did not like to talk about his feelings. He intimated that he was depressed: "I was so out of it that I forgot my own fortieth birthday. I was angry at them for making a party. We didn't have anything to celebrate."

Stewart hung around the house a lot, he said. He drove the car pool. He tried to "keep household things going" when his wife was out, but he never did cleaning or dishes. As far as possible he avoided talking to anyone. He delivered phonebooks. He was a guard six nights a week for a time: "Loneliness. Despair. Nothing helped. I'm not back to normal yet. How long will it take?"

He tried to avoid family arguments.

> My wife never understood how badly I really felt. Susan was always too busy. We had nothing to say to each other. Every time she tried to cheer me up I got angry. The kids didn't like having me around either. They used to ask me for things. They learned to leave me alone.

A year in the life of Martin Stewart—quiet desperation, suppressed anger, withdrawal. He never thought about employment crisis groups or organizations of any sort or of sharing his troubles with others. He saw himself primarily as an engineer oriented to assigned tasks and the interest of employers. He favored the defense industries, favored a large Defense budget, favored the war in Vietnam. "We must supply them even if we pull out," he said. Stewart admitted to no feelings of social responsibility, moral reservation, or personal guilt. "I only worked on projects for NASA and advance warning systems are defensive," he said.

One *Boston Sunday Globe* carried an ad placed by a small electronics firm for a precision instrumentation specialist. Stewart got an interview and then the job. It was real engineering: his abilities were utilized. But the salary was 40 percent lower than before; "All they can afford," he said. Another layoff two years later. This time he was out only two months. Again the *Globe*—the new job involved building electrical instrumentation used in cardiovascular research. In 1975 Stewart earned 25 percent less than he had in 1971. He said he "loved" the company: "I feel well placed; fairly secure; glad to be doing what I can do so well. I'm sure this company will keep me on as long as they can."

Conformist (69 percent of the unemployed sample) hesitates to think beyond the demands of organizational expediency. Awareness might hinder performance, promotion, and mobility. When faced with sudden crisis, he does not have the resources of personal perspective to help him cope. Arthur Myers and Martin Stewart exemplify Conformist's reaction to unemployment. Myers is a verbal, ardent, even bombastic Conformist. Stewart seems dull and inarticulate. Neither questions the system.

Facility with technical tasks, rather than burning involvement in scientific discovery, brings Conformist to his Route 128 career. The promise of guaranteed, highly paid, "professional" employment is the practical lure. Once there, he makes the necessary moves to protect his position. He tries to do what he thinks superiors expect. He learns normative opinions and voices them unthinkingly. Conformist is more likely to be an engineer (75 percent) than either a scientist (21 percent) or a data systems analyst (4 percent); as compared with Skeptic, who is somewhat more likely to be a scientist (38 percent) than either an engineer (31 percent) or a data systems analyst (31 percent). Conformist is most distinguished from others, however, by a marked disposition to accept and comply.

Conformist embraces the profit and productivity goals of his employers. He seeks to contribute to these goals and to move into management himself if not already there. Often company objectives become his own. "Individual goals are a lot of crap," one Conformist told me. If Conformist has problems with superiors or trouble getting ideas through to people in authority, he makes every effort "not to buck the system," He justifies the high profits his employers make even when based on his own ideas. He strongly agrees that individually earned patent rights should revert directly to the company.

Conformist is not likely to find fault with his employers. He thinks himself well paid for his contributions. If he can place blame for the seventies employment crisis (and often he cannot), it is not with the companies. He blames a mysteriously shifting economy for federal cuts in R&D. Conformist expects to be rewarded for his years of loyal company service, but mid-career brings job termination instead, and he is caught off balance. Lacking inner strength, Conformist is out of work and terrified.

Disbelief is his first reaction. Company policies were fair, he thought. Judgments of organizational superiors were the gauge of professional self-esteem. He knows valuable workers are not easily let go. How could he, the loyal technical servant, be dismissed? And yet with a pink slip in the office mail or a few curt words about canceled contracts and tight budgets, there he is, really out of work. Conformist leaves without an argument; he blames himself and not the system—"We were running out of work; no new contracts. They had no choice. I'm a failure in engineering. I'm in bad shape. Something must be wrong with me."

Conformist is overcome by feelings of helplessness and hopelessness for as long as unemployment lasts. Typically Conformist is out of work for six months or longer, and usually more than once in the seventies. He feels worthless to the degree that he internalizes organizational evaluations of his performance.

The worst part of it is that there's nothing I can do, absolutely nothing.

It was an emotional crisis. I have a family to support—high mortgage payments. I was terrified. Frightening to be thrown out of work. Horrible not to be able to control your own situation.

He cannot pay the bills or find a job. He wonders at times why anyone would hire him anyway. In frustration and anger he lashes out at himself and his family. He loses self-control. This disturbs him but he does not know how to stop. Numbly he watches game shows on television or looks out the window—waiting.

> I was severely depressed—impossible to live with, my wife said. I'm still in bad shape. It's hard to work as a routine programmer but I couldn't hold out any longer.

> With a doctorate in physics I thought there would always be something out there for me. I went to school all those years, spent all that time developing a good knowledge of physics—probably lost permanently. I know big companies won't hire me at my age. Why should they?

Up against the wall, Conformist eventually vents his rage at former managers, slick personnel men, or impersonal company policy.

> I was really frightened. Just the thought of not receiving a salary blew my mind. They laid off others. They had no choice but I didn't think it would come to me. I was always loyal. But the general manager was stupid. He had to get his budget down. It was a bad situation. He could have fired a secretary and technician and kept me on.

More typically, though, Conformist continues to blame himself. He refuses to consider collective action. Eighty-nine percent did not attend unemployment crisis groups, even in their own communities; 90 percent disapproved of labor unions for technical professionals; 70 percent opposed any form of organizational protection for technical professionals. Conformist becomes depressed. He does not talk to old friends or former colleagues. Pathologies return or develop—alcoholism, obesity, stuttering. Socially and psychologically he withdraws as far as he can.

> After 10 years I only had one day to pack up and leave. And I had refused another job the week before. They should have told me. I never had to look for a job before. And now no one wants me. They said "overqualified," "too old." They didn't believe my resume. Constant putdowns. I try to control myself. Booze helps. Nothing else does.

Conformist out of work is edgy. He takes Valium to make it through the day and barbiturates to cope with night. The early morning hours are worst of all. He lies in bed and thinks of an empty day ahead and an endlessly frightening future.

Conformist becomes a problem for his family to deal with. He alternates unpredictably between explosiveness and withdrawal. His wife is anxious about money, about slipping status, about her husband's moodiness. Tensions like these are disruptive. There is a lack of mutual understanding. Troubles do not bring these people closer. Two-thirds experienced a great deal of increased daily tension. Twenty-two percent more contemplated separation or divorce. Family relationships among only 11 percent were *not* affected.

The initial blow never really recedes. Still in shock, Conformist campaigns for reemployment. He tries everything he can think of. He makes lists of all companies that might be able to use him and blankets the area with hundreds of resumes—the same version for each job—and wonders why no one replies. He reads the newspapers daily and answers all ads for any position that looks possible. Finally he calls his friends, admits his joblessness, and asks for leads. He goes to DES offices and hates the personnel. He resents standing in unemployment lines with blue-collar workers. Conformist wears a suit and tie to identify himself as a professional. The Route 128 Professional Service Center is unhelpful, too.

Networks of colleagues usually make the difference, just as they do for Skeptic. In a few instances blind resumes bring results. Conformist is uncomfortable with words. A brief letter saying he can do exactly what an ad specifies occasionally lands him an interview. Unwittingly he gives no deselectors to potential employers.

Most Conformists (78 percent) had working wives. A majority of these women sought employment primarily to pay bills. Yet unemployed Conformist resents his wife's new breadwinner role. Such resentment fuels underlying tensions. Conformist's wife often blames him for his joblessness. She thinks he is not trying hard enough and his lethargy proves her point.

Conformist is accustomed to following orders without questioning. For most of his life this pattern pays off. Then everything—job, self-esteem, family life, and status community—is threatened and Conformist cannot begin to trace the causes. Conformist must confront conflicting ideologies of work world, where defense concerns predominate, and status community, where peace concerns prevail. He wants to adhere to both sets of expectations and is cross-pressured. First he protects his occupational base.

> The defense industries are an integral part of the economy. They provide jobs. They support technology and talent.

> The term "military-industrial complex" is unfair. It implies something is wrong. It isn't. The Defense budget is justified—all of it. We should try to win the war in Vietnam.

> I'm proud of the work I do. I'm proud of my contribution to society. You can go to sleep at night without worrying about a Soviet attack.

> It felt great to see the first missile I worked on come out on the test site. I don't have any reservations. I think about national security.

Originally Conformist supported the Vietnam war. By 1970 he has succumbed to community pressure and has modified his hawkish tendencies.

He discusses the waste and duplication he witnesses but he wants defense spending kept high and R&D increased. He dismisses the dangers of a military-industrial complex. Justification and rationalization block outward expressions of guilt.

> I was never up high enough to feel responsible personally. And there was positive civilian fallout to much of what I did. I would never work on ovens to kill people.

> We're not responsible. It's difficult to talk about it. It's a boondoggle but we have to keep it up. We have no alternative.

> Scientists and engineers were originally sold a bill of goods so we're not responsible. I felt guilty about the biological warfare project I worked on but the project dealt with the handling of smoke, so there are ecological uses, too.

Eventually there are signs of awakening insight in Conformist. Periods of prolonged inactivity erode what little self-confidence Conformist may have left. Successive shocks of layoff, rejection, and family disruption force Conformist to reconsider his situation. He takes a new look at things in one area of his life or another. He still tries to justify vested interests of his former position but now does so inconsistently. He accepts the priority of corporate profits but questions the aims of the defense industries. He wants expanded R&D facilities but humane advanced systems labs as well. He begins to consider the need for labor unions: "Professionalism is bullshit. You start to wonder where professionalism got the engineer anyway. We need protection. But I don't want another bureaucracy over me."

He wants engineers to have political clout, yet he still defends the a priori rights of companies—to own individually issued patents, to fire engineers in order to trim budgets. Conformist thinks about many things for the first time. Perhaps Karl Marx was right: crisis increases insight.

> The government shouldn't have pulled the money out of the military so quickly. But when I think about it, the stupid way they pour money in is fantastic—these huge amounts of money even when the design stinks. Too much waste to tolerate.

> I thought I was highly valued for nine years. But the manager didn't care about me when layoffs came. We need an organization now. I walked out without complaining. What I learned in the year was that it is important to make yourself heard.

We cut military R&D but didn't put the money into other areas. We could cut Vietnam spending and convert to medical technology, transportation. We could fund retraining projects. But that's not what is happening. I never thought things through before. But our whole way of handling technology is stupid. We cut inflation with the unemployment of scientists and engineers. We're cutting space in the same way. These are the very people who could be stimulating the economy.

I never thought about my patents until recently. Two came through in the year since I was let go. I was treated well when I was there. I expected a gold watch and a testimonial dinner when I retired. I never thought I'd be out of work. The first patent isn't worth much to them or to me. But they stand to make at least a half million on the second. I'm thinking about taking them to court.

After a bout or two with unemployment a real engineering job looks marvelous. The nightmare is over, at least temporarily. New contracts flow to Route 128 mostly for military hardware development. But the Vietnam war is over. Without pictures of burning babies on television, community pressure subsides. Missile making does not seem as dreadful as it did in the early seventies. Now more than ever Conformist shows devotion to his employer. Recent insight quickly recedes. Those who once swore off Route 128 gladly return to advanced electronics if only they can.

Conformist lacks self-awareness and does not gain a lasting social perspective from being unemployed. Unable to deal with situational factors, he remains at the mercy of forces beyond his control. Conformist cannot cope with personal, family, or career problems. He is destroyed or survives, as the system allows.

Types and Diversity

Identifying characteristic responses to the experience of unemployment summarizes the ways in which crisis affects middle-class professionals. There are diversities, however, within each pattern. We saw earlier how religious heritage influenced the capacity for introspection and, therefore, psychological reactions to joblessness.

Protestant professionals were more likely to be classified as Skeptic (45 percent) than were Jews (24 percent) or Catholics (12 percent). Protestants were no more likely than Jews to have been introspective at the outset, but increased insight during unemployment influenced adaptation to skidding in the years that followed. Most Catholics (88 percent) were Conformist but with a fatalism not found among Jews. Unquestioningly they displayed stability and masked what symptoms of distress and family disruption they surely must have felt. Jewish professionals were more likely to be classified

Conformist (76 percent) than their traditions of philosophical skepticism would have led us to expect. The desperate need to "make it" was reflected in their rapid upward mobility. Many Jewish technologists forced themselves to conform for fear they would lose what they had gained, but they were cross-pressured by their political liberalism. For many the issue of war work posed special problems. Some tried to justify military R&D and the Vietnam war under the guise of arms for Israel but they were conflicted and just as concerned about the federal funding of their own security.

> If you support an offensive, preventive war—as in Israel—you can't be a dove everywhere else. I don't believe this is possible. I finally came to oppose the war because of the immorality of supporting regimes like Guatemala—dictatorships. Israel is a democracy so the situation is different. It's wrong for the U.S. to have a national policy of opposing change throughout the world. We are not the policeman of the world.

When Arab nations signed large munitions contracts with several Route 128 firms in the mid-seventies, Jewish Conformists buried their anguish. This was a subject they would not discuss. Catholic Conformists backed arms for everything. Jewish Skeptics and Protestant peaceniks stood firm.

The characteristic response patterns to unemployment were tied to broader institutional ramifications: general economic and political consciousness and feelings about war work. As such they subsequently helped to explain why people, broken and bitter (Conformist) or with-it and angry (Skeptic), responded to government and politics with subtlety and ambivalence.

11

Crises of Faith

For the first time since public opinion research began measuring such attitudes in 1959, Americans believe they have lost substantial ground in their standard of living, and there has been a significant decline in their own expectations of what the future will bring. . . .

. . . For a still small but increasing number of Americans, the assumed national birthright of rising expectations—some might call it the American Dream—has been replaced by a sense of falling expectations.

"America is not over the hill," . . . a 33 year old college art professor . . . commented during an interview. "But tomorrow is not going to get better in the way that people in 1955 would say that tomorrow would be better. That's gone." (Lindsey, 1975a:1, 48)

The 1970s was the decade of disillusionment in America. People were disillusioned with the economy, government, the traditional family, and organized religion. Alienation from government grew after Watergate. Public bureaucracies failed adequately to service human needs. Representatives were not responsive to public opinion. Consumerism, for instance, was of increasing concern. Public opinion polls showed that two-thirds of the people favored a federal level consumer protection agency. Yet in

February 1978 Congress voted by a substantial margin against enacting such legislation. Neither government officials nor economic experts could control inflation. The energy crisis proved that remote multinationals monopolized economic power; yet few people favored nationalization of the oil industry because they no longer trusted government to tackle complex problems.

Louis Harris public opinion polls ("Louis Harris Finds Rising Alienation," 1978:23) documented a rising tide of alienation. Agreement with the statement "People running the country don't really care what happens to you," was 26 percent in 1966, 50 percent in 1972, and 60 percent in 1977. Agreement with the statement "What you think doesn't count much anymore" was 37 percent in 1966, 53 percent in 1972, and 61 percent in 1977. Agreement with the statement "The rich get richer and the poor get poorer" was 45 percent in 1966, 68 percent in 1972, and 77 percent in 1977. People were disillusioned with the value of education and with the promise of job satisfaction based on proven ability. Among the major sources of seventies disillusionment was the closure of organizational hierarchies as the new frontier of occupational security. The career disappointments and bouts of unemployment suffered by Route 128 scientists and technologists epitomized problems found among all salaried professionals and symbolized national trends.

With more skepticism in the seventies than in the thirties, people still looked toward government as the only institution that could help them find jobs for which they qualified. Disillusionment was fueled by government's failure effectively to deal with seventies unemployment anywhere in American society—among professionals and managers, among white- and blue-collar workers, among minorities and the poor, and among women and veterans. S. M. Miller's (1975:3–4) call for a "WPA for Professionals" went unheeded in a society needing services but lacking funds and commitment.

There were some legislative initiatives in the seventies. Full employment legislation, proposed by Senator Hubert H. Humphrey and Representative Augustis P. Hawkins, entered the 1974 national economic debate. The bill's primary goal, the guaranteed right to a job, was abandoned in the fervor of 1976 presidential politics. The original legislation was revised to target a 3 percent unemployment goal in four years (Shanahan, 1976b:28), at which time jobs programs would become operational (Rosenbaum, 1976:E3). President Jimmy Carter, under fire from labor and minorities, reluctantly endorsed Humphrey-Hawkins but never worked for its passage.

> Nor did it help that the unemployed were remarkably passive, unions offered little real fight, more and more workers were pitted against one another for scarce jobs, and few Americans—even among those who would benefit most from it—had grasped the concept of full employment and the right to a job. (Ginsburg, 1977:140)

Yet the bill did "establish targets for economic activity and jobs involving a degree of specificity the nation has never known before" (Raskin, 1977:1). After Humphrey's death, the further revised Full Employment and Balanced Growth Act of 1978 was enacted; it sought to hold unemployment to a 4 percent ceiling within five years (U.S. Congress, 1978b:13). Whatever the symbolic value of this legislation, authorities agreed that it did nothing to decrease either structural unemployment, which affects the many, or professional unemployment, which hits the relatively few.

Perhaps the most controversial jobs legislation in the seventies was the Comprehensive Employment and Training Act, which provided federal funding for public service jobs in state and local government, as well as special training programs. CETA, as it was called, funded 200,000 jobs in 1973 and expanded to cover 700,000 in peak year 1978 (U.S. Congress, 1978a). Sunk from the beginning in the quagmire of local politics, CETA seemed doomed to failure. Eligibility was supposedly restricted to the chronically unemployed and the disadvantaged, yet localities favored those who were job-ready for civil service employment. There was an annual maximum salary of $10,000 in 1973 ($12,000 in 1978) and a defacto exclusion of professionals. In 1976, a few enterprising members of the Massachusetts Society for Professional Engineers tried to show how CETA funds could be used to assist on-the-job retraining of older engineers. A test case was located through the help of the Newton Department of Employment Security and a large Route 128 R&D firm agreed to cooperate. CETA paid $6,000 for the first six months of the engineer's salary. He retrained on-the-job from electro-optical surveillance to computer software. Subsequently, the company kept him on at a regular professional level salary. This is precisely what CETA was established to do. The architects of this successful pilot project wanted CETA regulations modified to include engineers, teachers, and other professionals, but Washington was not receptive. CETA fell under the budget cutting axe as its programs were plagued by charges of misappropriating federal funds and of playing political favoritism with job distribution.

Least recognized of the proposed employment laws was the Reemployment Services Act, initiated in large measure by my own Route 128 research. I approached my congressman, Robert F. Drinan, whose constituency included several Route 128 communities, and outlined the problems that professionals and others encountered during the job search. Drinan's legislative staff and I discovered that there had been no new employment service legislation since the Wagner-Peyser Act established the U.S. Employment Service (USES) in 1933. Instead, additional functions were heaped upon the overburdened and archaic USES. The purpose of the Reemployment Services Act was

> to provide structural improvements in the existing public employment service system to facilitate and coordinate the flow of useful information, provide for

more effective management practices, insure attention to the needs of special categories of job applicants, and provide for the more effective allocation of human and fiscal resources within the system. (U.S. Congress, 1977:2–3)

The bill provided for improved job placement services for all categories of workers and for the first time specifically included professionals. It provided for the initiation and evaluation of innovative programs and for the utilization of employment service personnel as job placement assistants rather than compensation check dispensers. The legislation has been introduced in each session of Congress since August 1976—most recently as the Employment Service Revitalization and Reform Act of 1979 (U.S. Congress, 1979).[1]

People turned away from a government that did not respond as their problems mounted. Yet effective measures were not enacted in the seventies partly because they lacked the active support of the unemployed, who were already disillusioned, segmented sectors vying with each other as individuals for a decreasing number of good jobs. Engineers on compensation lines envied the layoff benefits of unionized workers. Women and veterans fought over special treatment. The educated were disgusted with the irrationality of a society where knowledge and experience went unrewarded. Professionals and others best survived employment instability if they had the personal resources to separate self-conception from position in the system, that is, if they could separate who they were from the work they did. All knew that credentials on paper surely counted. But if highly technical society permitted qualified professionals neither satisfaction nor security, expectations for the future seemed futile—for this special population and much more so for others.

Disillusionment Deepened along Route 128

Disillusionment is a negative way of orienting self to society. This feeling was evident from my first contacts with key informants among the unemployed in 1971 through to the last interviews with securely placed vice-presidents in 1975. In order to gauge the ramifications of this feeling I constructed a Disillusionment Scale based on each individual's response to six critical items: (1) job satisfaction, (2) frustration with organizational structure, (3) description of his ideal job, (4) perceived degree to which companies recognize contributions of individuals, (5) attitudes toward the

---

[1] The bill had 36 co-sponsors. The call to revise Wagner-Peyser and reform USES was endorsed by the Government Accounting Office, the House Government Operations Committee, and the National Governors Council and was applauded by business as well as labor. But a cautious Congress was in no mood for new ideas; employment service reform remained in the House Education and Labor Subcommittee on Employment Opportunities for three years without receiving formal hearings.

military-industrial complex, and (6) felt degree of importance of work to society. Factor analysis indicated that these variables were substantively interrelated.[2] According to this scale, 68 percent of Route 128 technical professionals were disillusioned with career and society; 32 percent were not.[3]

General disillusionment, as measured in the early seventies, was pervasive among those professionals whose prelayoff achievements fell far short of their prior expectations (disillusioned were 97 percent of those who felt their careers had not been successful, 80 percent of those with annual prelayoff salaries of less than $20,000, and 82 percent of those at low levels of supervisory responsibility). Career disappointment was nurtured by working conditions in bureaucratized systems labs. Professionals who were personally caught in intense staff-line conflicts were especially affected (85 percent were rated as disillusioned). War work was a contributing factor (90 percent of those with negative attitudes toward the defense industries were classified as disillusioned, compared with 41 percent of those with positive attitudes).

Disaffection increased among people who experienced "unjustified" layoff, the anguish of joblessness, and the irrationalities of the job search (disillusioned were 91 percent of the unemployed and 75 percent of the reemployed, compared with 57 percent of the retained). Unemployed professionals tried every avenue of institutional assistance that seemed to make sense; none did. For example, 83 percent of those who tried the Professional Service Center said that it could not help. The downwardly mobile were disillusioned (83 percent). People who felt insecure about their jobs were disillusioned (79 percent). Measured disillusionment was greater among politically affiliated Democrats than among their Republican counterparts: many Democrats who expected that New Deal initiated reforms were still viable discovered that professionals were not protected and that public service bureaucracies were not responsive (79 percent of the sampled Democrats classified as disillusioned, compared with 53 percent of the Republicans and 64 percent of the independents). Economic instability, political impotence, and withered expectations formed a core that eventually led to the disillusionment found among technical professionals in the early seventies.

Three years after the initial interviews I called on Route 128 professionals again, both employed and unemployed. Many of the previously

[2] The Disillusionment Scale is one-dimensional because 59 percent of the variance was accounted for by the first factor of the principal components analysis.

[3] For each item of the scale a value of 1 was assigned to the non disillusioned, a value of 2 was assigned to the moderately disillusioned, and a value of 3 was assigned to the highly disillusioned. The lowest possible score was 6 and the highest possible score was 18. Thirty-two percent of the sample scored between 6 and 9 and were classified as non disillusioned. Forty-four percent scored between 10 and 12 and were classified as moderately disillusioned. Twenty-four percent scored between 13 and 18 and were classified as highly disillusioned.

employed were now jobless or underemployed. As we noted earlier, age increased layoff vulnerability significantly, and people in my sample were now three years older. Bitterness toward the companies among the newly dislodged was more openly expressed in 1975 than it had been three years before. Faith in the government had diminished. Salaried professionals still favored manpower planning, but rationalization of manpower resources was not contemplated by the government in Washington.

Fifty-seven percent of my original employed sample held the same position in 1975 that they had in 1972. Only 32 percent felt any degree of personal security and fewer still (14 percent) were optimistic about career prospects. There were Superstrivers who bent reality to suit the strong mobility thrust of their bureaucratic careers. Some were older generation vice-presidents, 55 to 58 years of age. They were self-assured. They spoke of contracts coming in and of expanding Defense Department appropriations permitting continued expansion. Conversation was pleasant and superficial: Route 128 had "trimmed the fat," the world was beautiful, and things were better than ever. And there were younger Superstrivers, now 33 or 35 years of age on the make and making it. One of them was an environmental research scientist (self-converted from mechanical engineering a few years earlier). His company had grown from 20 employees in 1972 to 400 in 1975—largely his doing, he claimed. The market for environmental scientists was "great," and he expressed no concern about the possibility of fluctuating funding.

But 18 percent of the retained were distressed about aspects of their work worlds: ruthless company policy, mindless managers, and the elimination of funding for fundamental research. These professionals were Routinized or Savvy in the early seventies. Now they were all upset.

People who are chosen to be managers and vice-presidents are not the best people. They have to trust you 100% to be their man. When someone is selected for a top position he wants *his* men in key positions—only to please him, only to be loyal to him.

There is a fantastic amount of self-deceit on the part of those on the make. And much conflict. Image they have of who they are—completely ruthless; inhumanity astounding. They deny the value of people who are very good and have made real contributions to the company. Their ideas are stolen and others take credit for their work or ignore their value.

I was assistant director of research in 1971, if you recall. Two years later I was promoted to product development manager. I worked on the product research phase. This is a big operation. Now that we're at the development stage I moved along into the development division with them. The work is with solid state vapors. It has an environmental impact. By coincidence it saves energy.

This is playing a part in some fantastic game. I have been able to make it. I guess it will continue for me. There is the thrill of the competition and the lure of success. But good people go if they are in the wrong place at the wrong time. Some people are *too good,* their salaries are high, and they are fired in a budget squeeze.

I was told I had to cut $100,000 off my research payroll. You have to make the cuts so I played the games—sometimes hire two at lower salaries and keep some at higher levels. Sometimes keep the technicians and fire the chemists. It depends on the particular need at the moment. I had to conduct hundreds of exit interviews personally. I felt terrible [this was difficult for him to discuss].

The company had been firing right and left—250 chemists, two general managers, even one vice-president. Research division was cut from 85 at the time of our first interview down to 48. Everything tightened through the industry. My boss was fired last month. All of the three who put me in my present position (two above me and one below me) are now *gone*. We are doing without the think tank—it's happening all over. We're going with products that have been developed. We've totally abandoned our long-range research programs. No basic theoretical work is done here anymore.

I hired only two chemists in the last few years—older men on a short-term basis for specific specialties. I haven't been able to hire a single young chemist. The man whose name is on the basic patent worked with us on it for five years and on a related product for eight years before that. The news release I sent to 20 companies about this project just last week bears his name. The company hopes to make millions on this product. He was laid off one year ago: we fired him to save money. He was smart, capable, and personable. It doesn't make you feel good about industrial corporations. There is no such thing as loyalty.

Twenty-seven percent of the employed sample felt very insecure despite continued employment. Companies were reorganizing to maximize assets and people wondered what would happen to them in the shuffle.

The company is going to tighten across the board—not obvious from the outside because the total number of employees is up. This is only true because they diversified and acquired many commercial operations. But the signs inside are clear. We sell missile systems all over the world—living off that, that's why profits are high now. R&D tightening; things will be worse in five years. The company is going to become a conglomerate. Electronics is out. The company will grow and engineers will go out in the street. There is no security in . . . electronics engineering jobs. Maybe there is no security anywhere.

They were older, 48 or 53, and feared increasing vulnerability. Even Routinized started to ask questions.

I'm still a subdepartment head—feel much less security than three years ago. I'm 48 years of age now. . . This company shows a definite tendency to replace older with younger engineers on a regular basis—very depressing.

A friend of mine just called. He was pushed into early retirement—not very comforting. I heard that in California people are more mobile. You have to be in this field, especially as you get older. But your family is tied in and you can't move. Tough situation. Very fearful. It's about time engineers stopped subsidizing companies: engineers subsidizing companies is really ridiculous.

Whether Routinized, Trapped or Savvy, 29 percent of the employed in 1972 who could be located in 1975 were not working where they had been before. Some were in the process of relocating to California or New Mexico. A few were making mid-career changes; optometry school, a brokerage firm. And 11 percent were unemployed.

The most difficult question I asked in 1975 concerned success. Long silences disclosed their pain. Original dreams of success and satisfaction were gone. Uneasiness, sometimes defensiveness, showed how disillusionment had deepened, especially among professionals out of work once, twice, or more in the seventies.

People in my unemployed sample became increasingly distressed as the years passed. Forty-three percent managed to find jobs where their skills were utilized—sometimes after several layoffs, sometimes after years of unemployment. Most of the reemployed were Routinized and Trapped, a few were Savvy, and one was a Superstriver. All tried to be protective of industry and funding sources. But defensiveness did not disguise disillusionment about company and government, about security and the future.

> On third job since layoff. I don't look for security anymore. There is no security on this planet.

> Any idiot could do the work I do now. Simple data reduction. I should be doing engineering evaluation. Very fearful about the future. The whole system stinks. Hopeless.

Twenty-six percent of the early seventies jobless ultimately accepted underemployment in their desperate need to work.

> Out of work three years; almost hit bottom. Reemployed in 1974 at 25 percent less than before. I'm well pleased though. Glad to be doing what I can do well. There's no security in this country. I'm as secure in this company as anyone is anywhere else. Once you've gone through long unemployment you can never feel secure again. This company is a good place to work. They'll keep me if they can.

As the years passed, they settled into lowered expectations. But they forgot neither former position nor former lifestyle. Money was meager, satisfaction was scant, and resentment was deep. A few found satisfaction—teaching physics in a junior college, teaching basic electricity to unemployed young adults. But inflation diminished income and children entered college.

> I'm a nuclear physicist programming simple data systems for the state—underpaid, skills as physicist not used. Just hope the job continues. Political appointments bring unpredictable changes. No real security for anyone these days.

I don't enjoy my work. Feel very insecure. Just trying to hold a job until early retirement. My wife is working now, too. Never thought it would come to this.

I live in the present only. I couldn't make it back to any job after another layoff at my age. It's been five years now and the bitterness doesn't go away. You can't help thinking of the past and the way things should have been for you. Had several jobs since first layoff in 1970. I guess you might say I was settling into underemployment.

Still feel bad about our changed life situation. You try to cover. But I find myself talking about the setup I had. It's hard to work in this lousy, badly equipped lab after where I was before. I'm trying to adjust. I try to put up a good front. I don't really feel it yet. Perhaps I never will.

Eighteen percent of my early seventies unemployed sample was still without work (or virtually so) in 1975. A temporary job here and there, a small business venture that failed—but joblessness was the basic condition for these professionals after three long years. Success and security were not even discussed. Faith in the system was gone. A sense of powerlessness predominated. Symptoms of psychological and physical degeneration were obvious. Disillusionment was generalized.

Government won't do anything. Unions, organizations—nothing will help. Everyone is only out for themselves. I don't trust anything or anyone. Even family retreats when things get this rough.

Had no real work in mechanical engineering in the last four years. No reason for young people to go into the field. The schools are dishonest. They should stop recruiting with promises that aren't real. This society doesn't care about ability and creativity.

It was hard to leave these once productive people without sharing their sadness. Their talents were wasted; their creative impulses, eroded.

Too Much Education

Underemployment [is] increasing because of forces that predate the recession and promise to outlast it. Chief among them is the educational level of the work force. It has long been climbing at a dramatic rate that is expected to continue. But, sociologists say, there hasn't been a corresponding increase in the skills most jobs require or in the number of jobs that require well educated workers. As a result more and more Americans are overeducated for the work they do.

In the last 15 years, for example, . . . the proportion of college-educated men who had to settle for nonprofessional, nonmanagerial positions increased threefold, and the proportion for women went up fourfold.

"The golden age is over for higher education," says Richard Freeman, a Harvard University associate professor of economics. "A college degree no longer guarantees a good, high-paying white-collar job, so graduates are taking the best they can get." (Shaffer, 1976:1)

As it becomes clear that education will not pay off as promised, there is a very real possibility of a massive buildup of disillusionment and a sense of betrayal among those stuck with a "bad investment." Indeed, the selling of education solely as a passport to a good job could backfire, and an entire disappointed generation could withdraw its support for an important social institution. Then the important functions of education for self-development, leisure, family and citizenship will also be imperiled. The refusals of middle-class voters to approve school bonds, the cries of intellectuals to de-school society, and the general attack on the irrelevance of education may be the opening salvos of a general move to discredit an institution that has failed to meet the false economic expectations that have been created for it. . . .

Where Marx had forecast that mass unemployment would become the salient characteristic of labor markets in advanced economies, it is now clear that underemployment—working at less than one's full productive capacity—is more accurately the hallmark of work in industrial societies. (O'Toole, 1975:29–30, 26)

Equality of educational opportunity, spurred by an achievement ideology, gave substance to the American dream. In no other nation were institutions of higher learning for the masses established on a wider scale than in the United States. In 1956–1957, for instance, 27 percent of the 20 to 24 age cohort attended colleges and universities; compared with 4 percent in England and Wales and 11 percent in the Soviet Union (Lipset, 1967:296–298). The arms race, the space race, and the prosperity of the 1960s accelerated the trend toward advanced schooling. Ben Wattenberg estimated that during the sixties "America built a new junior college every 10 days" (O'Toole, 1975:27). By 1977, 80 percent of the population were high school graduates, compared with 33 percent 30 thirty years earlier. College enrollment increased 250 percent, from 2.6 million in 1952 to 8.4 million in 1972. The number of people who received first and second advanced degrees increased from 380,000 in 1955 to 1 million in 1970. The number of Ph.D.'s turned out annually increased from 8,000 in the mid-fifties, to 43,000 in the mid-seventies (O'Toole, 1977:38–39).

The 1970s witnessed a serious educational inflation at every level of the labor market. Job openings for the qualified did not increase to meet their growing numbers. Estimates based on scant statistics showed a relatively small growth in the percentage of professional and managerial level positions; professional jobs increased from 7 percent in 1950 to 9 percent in 1970, and management positions increased from 12.9 percent in 1948 to 13.6 percent in 1973. In 1973, 243,000 teachers competed for 111,000 jobs, most of which were replacement positions. Federal government employment expanded, from 10.5 percent of the work force in 1955 to 15.5 percent in 1975, but 60 to 70 percent of these new positions were aids, attendants, clerical workers, and custodians (O'Toole, 1977:46–50). Good jobs did not exist for most of the people who prepared for them.

In reality, there are precious few jobs that make much use of higher order skills, training, or intelligence. The Bureau of Labor Statistics estimates that only about 20 percent of all jobs will require a college education for successful performance in 1980. More depressing, the Office of Management and Budget finds that one-half of all current jobs do not even require a high school education. (O'Toole, 1975:32)

Meanwhile a surplus army of the trained and educated continues to emerge. In 1980, 2.5 college graduates competed for every interesting job (O'Toole, 1977:52). The National Planning Association projected an annual surplus of 700,000 college graduates by 1985 (O'Toole, 1975:33). The Bureau of Labor Statistics projected a 1985 Ph.D. surplus of 22.7 percent in the physical sciences, 26.2 percent in engineering, 36.9 percent in mathematics, 46.9 percent in the life sciences, and 43.3 percent in the social sciences. The National Science Foundation's estimates differed only in particulars but forecasted a similar 1985 oversupply. The NSF projected a 10.8 percent Ph.D. surplus in the physical sciences, a 28.9 percent Ph.D. surplus in engineering, a 25.9 percent Ph.D. surplus in mathematics, a 7.7 percent Ph.D. surplus in the life sciences, and a 37 percent Ph.D. surplus in the social sciences (Kolata, 1976:363). Underemployment, the only alternative to the compensation check, has become a national trend, as professors sell real estate, teachers work as receptionists and lawyers drive cabs.

Underemployment entails job displacement all the way down the line.

One consequence is a job-bumping process that ripples through the occupational spectrum. As Ralph Lewis, associate director of the University of Florida's placement office, explains, "We've overproduced Ph.D.'s so they're taking jobs that really require only a master's degree. So the M.A.'s have to take B.A. level work, and the B.A.'s displace junior college grads, who end up with jobs that used to go to high-school grads."

At the end of the process, the workers with the least education are left with no jobs at all. (Shaffer, 1976:21)

Ultimately, Ph.D.'s find work: Route 128 physicists, for instance, took jobs as computer programmers that necessitated, they estimated, a bachelor's degree at most. Employers emphasized *credentials* that usually had little to do with the performance requirements of a particular job (Berg, 1970:72–83). Forced underutilization resulted in widespread job dissatisfaction, and stagnation eroded skills (Berg, Freedman, and Freedman, 1978:98–109). And as World War II boom babies entered the labor force, the situation promised to get worse. Census Bureau statistics showed 58 million workers in the prime 25 to 44 age bracket in 1978; this was projected to increase to 78 million by 1990 (Flint, 1978:34). Labor market analysts predicted bitter competition for "worthwhile" jobs throughout the work force, as the underemployed, better educated than their superiors, tried to jockey for position and promotion. Economist Richard B. Freeman feared "substantial career disappointment for many and the possibility that persons in the 25–44 cohort of 1980 will receive low relative income for their entire lives" (Flint, 1978:35).

The 1970s taught Americans that education and demonstrated merit do not guarantee upward mobility. Disappointment with the time-honored rungs on the ladder of equal opportunity became critical to a new sense of betrayal. And incipient conflict between the 20 percent who had good jobs and the 80 percent who did not was muted by generalized disillusionment.

Varieties of Professional Unemployment

A Generation of "Lost" Scholars
    Motivated by a dedication to learning and encouraged by universities to pursue graduate degrees, the majority of young Ph.D.'s in the humanities now find they are a glut on the academic market. Today less than a third can find college jobs. (O'Brien, 1979:35)

Job Future Clouded for Teachers
    While the drop in students and the shutdown of school buildings has not yet cut deeply into tenured teaching staff, school officials in a number of communities predict that permanent teachers, once guaranteed job security, will have to be laid off within the next year. (Cohen, 1978:33)

Clergy Find Jobs Scarce in Churches
    While the shortage of in-church jobs affects ministers in virtually every Protestant denomination, it is particularly acute in the Episcopal Church. In the Massachusetts diocese alone, more than 100 of the 400 canonically resident priests are in secular occupations. (Longcope, 1976:14)

Scientists and technologists were not the only professionals out of work in the 1970s. The "educational-industrial complex" produced many kinds of experts in the sixties whom a cautious economy a generation later could not absorb. Federal, state, and local governments tried to cut the number of service professionals on public payrolls. People planned smaller families and school enrollment declined. Local school boards eyed high salaries of educational administrators as expendable items. Private colleges coped with financial crisis; some of them closed. At the same time education factories turned out new experts who accepted any job. There were too many teachers and librarians (Chamberlain, 1978:20), too many translators (Tinsley, 1973:3–4), too many artists (Chamberlain, 1976:14), and too many ministers (Longcope, 1976:38).

Teachers in all academic disciplines feared negative tenure decisions. New Ph.D.'s, academics with the best chance of finding university employment, could expect low salaries, heavy teaching loads, and contract termination before tenure, whether they published or not.

Graduating with highest honors from the University of Kansas in 1966, Fred Whitehead won a Fulbright scholarship and studied for a year in London. Then he earned a doctorate in English at Columbia University on a Danforth fellowship and landed a college teaching post.

"Everyone said I had it made," he recalls. But everyone was wrong. In 1974, during a severe budget cuback at Southern Illinois University, where he was an assistant professor, Fred was furloughed, along with 103 other faculty members. He spent months searching for another position, but the resumes he sent to universities across the country produced only two telephone interviews and no offers. To support his wife and two children, he worked in a cannery and on construction. Then, last year, he gave up hope of ever getting back into teaching and enrolled in vocational school. Today, Fred Whitehead, Ph.D., is a welder. (Shaffer, 1976:1)

Professors, supposedly more insightful than engineers and scientists, reacted to unemployment with the same hopelessness and fear. Many slipped into underemployment whether they were stopped six years down the tenure track or jobless fresh from graduate school.

Young Ph.D.'s who find the doors of the academy suddenly closed to them feel helpless. . . . These are middle-class people, almost all of them, who have been meeting every standard set for them since they entered school. Feeling defeated, often bewildered by the sudden devaluation of their greatest pride, their intelligence, many drift into unchallenging, monotonous jobs. (O'Brien, 1979:58)

Protestant clergy without parishes were among the displaced professionals of the seventies. Baptists, Methodists, and Lutherans felt the crunch; Episcopals, most of all. There were 11,000 ordained Episcopal clergy in 1976 for 5,000 parish positions (Longcope, 1976:38). Church membership and revenues declined, yet increased numbers of men and women prepared for positions that did not exist. Said one Episcopal minister who worked for the state:

Increasingly the clergy, especially the younger ones, are recognizing that this is the way a lot of us will have to live. . . . Some are bitter and feel short-changed. They're angry and upset that the parish ministry for which they have been training may be denied them. (Longcope, 1976:38)

No reliable figures detailed the percentages of the nation's teachers, professors, administrators, librarians, social workers, engineers, lawyers, clergy, scientists, architects, and middle managers out of work and actively seeking employment. Being a "consultant" or "working at home" became euphemisms for joblessness. Many collected compensation checks. Others struggled alone, ashamed to admit their plight and unrecorded in federal statistics. Employment legislation was targeted toward ghetto youths and blue-collar workers. People forgot professionals.

Three cases of salaried professionals terminated in 1977 illustrate the continuing dimensions of this problem. In February 1978, I interviewed

Andrew Kaplan, Norman Chandler, and Donald Fisher, unemployed professionals from three important social sectors. Kaplan, a media executive, was laid off at age 40. Chandler, a maverick lawyer, was a security management expert without work at age 55. Donald Fisher, a political scientist whose message was meaningful governance, was denied tenure at age 36. Kaplan, Chandler, and Fisher were nonrandomly selected. They were highly competent, self-assured, knowledgeable, and questioning. All were Savvy when working, and each was Skeptic as he reacted to layoff and unemployment.

Media Executive

First impressions of Andrew Kaplan—articulate, personable. Second impressions—imaginative, analytical. He was a communications expert in journalism and television. This is a rare blend; the printed word and the video image often compete. He combined the local and the cosmopolitan in his orientation to what he thought important. "How could *you* be out of work?" I asked, although I already knew the answer. "I've been *screwed*," he said.

Kaplan's beginnings were middle-class. His father was a successful small businessman in Springfield, Pennsylvania. But his mother, he said, always had upper middle-class status aspirations. Andrew went to the University of Pennsylvania. He majored in English, minored in music, and was interested in drama. He took some journalism courses. Always A's. Time for career choice came with commencement in 1958. He applied to only one graduate school, the best: Columbia School of Journalism. He was accepted, of course. Kaplan made good contacts at Columbia but he knew he had to start at the bottom for seasoning experiences. His first job—a New Jersey daily at $70 a week. There he uncovered a salve labor camp. Then he went to Georgia. He covered school integration, which became a continuing interest. Kaplan omitted incidents of racial conflict to keep his job in Georgia but simultaneously free-lanced more detailed stories for *Newsweek*.

By this time Andrew Kaplan was a married man with a child. He sought his first "good" job. His search was highly rational.

> I made a list of cities with dailies. Thirty cities were interesting. I sent them each $1 for a short subscription. I wanted a paper with commitment to local news, a state desk, and a D.C. desk. Twelve cities were possibilities. I zeroed in on Houston, Texas, an open town. Three papers filled the bill. I was offered jobs by all three. Took the *Houston Post* and loved it.

Upward mobility to education editor was rapid. Kaplan fought for a travel budget, which allowed him to cover innovations in education and school integration throughout the country.

Andrew Kaplan got around in the early 1960s. Keeping the *Houston Post* job, he free-lanced for the *Chronicle of Higher Education,* the *Southern Education Reporter,* and the *Harvard Education Review.* He consulted for the Corporation for Public Broadcasting and evaluated projects for the National Endowment for the Humanities. Harvard's prestigious Nieman Fellowship was his 1965 achievement. He described this as a "superheady year." Kaplan worked with people at Harvard in the School of Education and in the social sciences. He became involved with a Ford Foundation grant to study integration in a northern city—where he knew the action was. The Nieman Fellow was offered jobs by the *New York Times,* the *Washington Star,* and the *Boston Globe.* For reasons unrelated to his own ability, each fell through.

Education and Ivy League contacts brought Kaplan into the media intelligentsia. He needed his contacts and they did not disappoint him. Friends encouraged him to move into the television industry. Sensing the excitement of his scene, he took a job with a Boston television station. He was first hired as a news reporter and producer at $10,000 in 1966. He had moved up to $15,000 by 1968. He covered innovative developments in education and school integration in Boston. But there were personality conflicts with the program director. So Kaplan took a position as program developer and administrator in a major television organization. These were years of accomplishment; his salary doubled; he felt secure.

Then a health problem intervened. Kaplan needed a minor eye operation in June 1977. Recovery took longer than anticipated. He returned to find six weeks of mail dumped on his desk. There had been no support work during his illness, not even a secretary to open routine mail. He was called in to see his immediate superior on that first day back.

We had such a good year. Some exciting new plans were in the works. For the company, it was the best year in terms of profits. I was feeling great. So I was shocked when he said, "We're not going to make it on a long-term basis. My expectations for you are not fulfilled." I had no prior communication that anything was wrong. Never had any indication that there were problems. I asked for an explanation.

First he pointed to silly things: "I didn't like your proposals at a business meeting last December." Then he complained about things I hadn't done while I was in the hospital. Some were minor, others were more important, but all were impossible to be done at the time. And there was nothing of substance we couldn't have worked out.

I had to go home on the evening of my fortieth birthday and tell my family that I'd lost my job.

Savvy, self-assured Kaplan was thrown by notice of termination. He was depressed. For the first time in his life he even doubted his own abilities: "There was a sequence in how I reacted."

Deep depression for several days, followed by a general pattern of downness. This lasted for several months. Then anger. Anger brought detachment. In anger I could aggressively look for another job. But it took five months to get to this point.

The company gave him six months' notice—full pay while working half-time. He had begun "important projects." They wanted to "milk my talents under the guise of giving me time. Half-time was almost full-time. But next Friday is the end of my rope here." Kaplan planned to collect unemployment compensation. With four dependents he was entitled to $114 a week in 1978. The company owed him back vacation pay.

I asked him about his job search. Real help came from an inside lead to a private employment counseling service. "Usually these places take your money and do nothing. But I was assured this one would be different for me," he said. Andrew Kaplan, through a friend, had indeed found a special kind of assistance.

He began by spending an hour a week with a psychologist who did an ability and interest profile and provided supportive therapy.

Then lots of interviews with the psychologist. My wife went with me many times. We verbalized hostilities, worked our self-feelings. My family was supportive but there were conflicts. We worked things out in the psychologist's office. Then we came to strategies of job finding. Self-knowledge helped. I learned that I do better in situations where there is positive personal feedback. Negative feedback is the norm in the television industry.

The employment counseling service suggested new career alternatives—foundations, management consulting, affiliation with a university in communications.

The counseling service helped Kaplan put together a resume with pizazz. By February 1978 he was set on a course of superrational job hunting.

I listed all the people I thought I could rely on—friends and professional contacts. I started with 50 people, deleted some, added others; now up to 150.

First round: I send a letter and resume to 60 well-placed people. I have 25 primary contacts located in good professional networks. They are working in my behalf. I keep in touch with them, under one pretext or another, every 10 days.

It took months before I was ready to be this aggressive. I didn't tell people I was fired at first. It took months to get over feeling bashful about the situation.

I follow up leads on my own—from the *Boston Globe, Wall Street Journal,* professional magazines. I still see the psychologist but only once a month now.

At the moment Kaplan felt optimistic. He had two good employment possibilities. Kaplan realized that he had to hook into an organization for a $30,000 to $40,000 job, the salary he wanted. His children's needs and family finances pushed him in this direction. But he talked of a future, after the kids left the nest, in northern New England with his wife. He would be

able to free-lance and consult. He wanted professional freedom and independence from organizational restraints. Meanwhile he had no job.

Maverick Lawyer

Norman Chandler passed the bar exam wherever he lived—Missouri,
New York, Massachusetts—without any cram courses. He authored three
books with a major publisher and had earned an international reputation in
corporate management and industrial security. But at age 55 instead of a
high salary and a guaranteed retirement plan, he had no job.

A polite, conservative looking man, Chandler is a maverick in many
ways. He went to law school as a step to an "important" career. He did not
want to be chained to the service of a local clientele and he was not interested in becoming rich. He sought a career as a salaried professional in
government service and then in various institutional settings. His emphasis
remains systems control in risk management. His orientation is prevention,
not detection. Chandler demonstrated expertise in security management
but he fit no standard job description.

Chandler's career began in Washington, D.C., in the early 1950s. He
was a criminal investigations caseworker and later an administrator in a
federal agency. He received five letters of commendation for his work, but
Washington bureaucracy brought frustration: "If you do well on a job,
you're pigeonholed. If you do a job too well, you're passed over for promotion."

In search of independence, Chandler moved to Boston and combined a
variety of jobs into a career. He had a general law practice. He was a
security management consultant for public and private organizations. In
addition, he was the protective security administrator for a major university in the Boston area. But he was doing three jobs instead of one: he felt
fragmented. He looked for a solid position. The first day he found an ad in
the *New York Times* for a corporate director of security with a hotel operation in Boston. Previously he had met the company president at a con-
ference and called him directly. His call was subsequently put through to
the director of placement. The job was his with the single phone call. It
lasted two years. Then, after a lifetime of success, Chandler was fired.

> There was always a personality conflict between me and the director of security
> for the multinational that owns the hotel chain. He knew nothing about the hotel
> business and would make demands that were harmful to the company. I fought
> him. He waited for the president and the chairman of the board to leave the
> country and fired me. They were embarrassed when they returned. I had just
> published a book on the management of hotel security systems. My book is used
> as a text for a course offered by the trade association's educational institute. Peo-
> ple in the hotel industry still keep in touch.

It was hard to recover from the shock. The shock of layoff was one thing. I knew how much I was worth to the company, but the shock of income insecurity, at this time, at my age, was devastating. I had one month's notice and three months' severance pay. They let me use my secretary and their facilities to relocate during that month.

I started looking. Went to the Route 128 Professional Service Center—nothing but humiliation. I collected unemployment compensation for November and December 1974. You had to go every week then. It was painful each time I went. The line is an embarrassment. Then they talk to you. "Sit down, Norman." No respect. They rob you of any dignity. They treat you as if you're not entitled to common courtesy because you're unemployed. They make you wait while they chitchat and sit around drinking coffee.

Chandler found his next job himself, again through an open advertisement. A major financial institution wanted an executive to develop security and safety programs and policy.

The personnel officer thought I was overqualified but the vice-president insisted they interview me. It was a 12 percent salary cut but the situation seemed promising. It looked like a chance to be innovative.

Chandler thought he was doing a great job. He expected promotion. He had saved the institution from a very substantial loss because their internal security was so poorly organized. But from then on his responsibilities were not expanded; instead, they were curtailed. He had embarrassed his superiors and was a threat from that day on.

I was fired the last week in September 1977. One day's notice. I was told that they would pack up my things and send them. I packed my own belongings. They packed my books. The severance pay amounted to three months' salary and two months' vacation pay. So I had a five-month pad.

The Department of Employment Security was worse in 1977 than in 1974. You have to prove that you're looking for work with evidence of direct contact with potential employers. This is difficult for professionals to do. Advertised jobs usually have box numbers. It takes time to apply but that's difficult to prove.

I'm trying to develop a consulting business. They told me I could do that but only in the evenings and on weekends. They aren't interested in letting you make enough money so that you don't have to come.

I have two clients on retainer now—that plus employment compensation and we can make ends meet. If I pick up one more client, I'll stop collecting those damn checks.

Norman Chandler showed creative ability in a difficult field but he could not find an organizational slot. He liked independence but income was uncertain. His anxiety was apparent as he talked of "being on his own." College teaching remains high among Chandler's unfulfilled ambitions. "Law school faculties were small. There were just no openings when I was younger," he said. Guest lectures over the years whetted his appetite.

He was still trying. A 10-hour course at a local business school (a one-shot deal, pay insignificant) interested him. An important man in a critical field struggled to keep the pieces of a professional career intact.

Tenure Denied

"I'm still in a state of shock," he said when I called to request an interview. "It never occurred to me that tenure would be denied. I still can't believe it." A mutual friend had told me that Donald Fisher, the most popular political science professor on campus was put "out" in his "up or out year." I told him about *Professionals Out of Work;* he wanted to be a case study. He was calmer two weeks later when I met him but anger punctuated every sentence.

Fisher had an areawide reputation as a gifted teacher. His classes filled almost before they opened. He felt a special kinship with the young adults he taught.

> They are groping to find a way through this stinking mess we call a political system. I give them some analytical tools. And I care that they learn to use them.
>
> I never thought in terms of tenure. Obviously I should have figured out a formula—teaching and respectable professional credentials aren't enough. I thought I had it made.

So did everyone who knew him. Fisher was a success from the start. He fulfilled his working-class parents' aspirations for upward mobility. Professors at City College socialized him along the doctorate path from his first campus courses in political science. He went to "finishing school" at Yale on fellowships. American government and comparative politics were his fields of specialization. He picked up statistical tools and behaviorism along the way. Fisher liked fieldwork and community studies. He "sweated" his Ph.D. exams. He was more radical than his mentors. He respected C. Wright Mills, whom they accused of ignoring the field of political science. Power and manipulation were themes in his dissertation. Despite ideological obstacles, brains and determination got him through. It would be easy after that, or so he thought.

Job opportunities were numerous for a new Ivy League, Ph.D. in spring 1971. Fisher was a "safe-looking, with-it, hippie type" with Yale polish. He interviewed well. He had some options. A college 40 minutes from Harvard Square came through with a contract. He wanted to be removed from the pressure chamber atmosphere of grad school but he wanted access to Cambridge.

His student following took five minutes to develop. It grew with the bombings in Southeast Asia, the McGovern campaign (Fisher was campus coordinator), Watergate, the Senate impeachment hearings (he took some students to Washington), and the resignation of Richard Nixon. Meanwhile Fisher was too well trained to neglect professionalism. He studied politics in surrounding communities and published articles in establishment journals. Tenure time was gradually upon him.

> I wasn't naive about the difficulties of getting tenure these days. I was preoccupied with teaching a new course and organizing another community research project. When the letter came in the morning mail I was enraged. It was a short, blunt, impersonal form letter from the president. "Negative tenure decision." Not even "thanks but no thanks." Not even "no thanks." Merely "no." There was no recognition that I'd done anything useful for the students, the department, the university, or the profession. And I knew I had high marks on all four dimensions. Cynicism about the system doesn't soften the ego blow.
>
> I went in to see the chairman. He couldn't spare me much time. I tried to control my anger: "Did the department support me? Was the problem with the administration?" No response. The chairman is neither unkind nor unfriendly, merely petty bureaucratic.

Fisher found out a few things in the following weeks. Some of his colleagues had taken cheap shots at his articles. The university president thought him too radical. Older colleagues resented his popularity. The students wanted to demonstrate; Fisher stopped them. "I'll have to spend the rest of my career explaining"—Fisher was getting used to the idea that he had better start looking for another job. He was bothered by the impersonality, the cruelty, the inhumanity. The college campus was not a Route 128 systems lab or a competitive business enterprise. Fisher's colleagues were not managers trying to steal his ideas; yet there were more similarities than differences between Fisher and other professionals I interviewed.

Bureaucracy Erodes Creativity

> The increasing intellectualization and rationalization do not . . . indicate an increased and general knowledge of the conditions under which one lives. . . .
>
> It means something else, namely, the knowledge or belief that if one but wished one *could* learn it at any time. Hence, it means that principally there are no mysterious incalculable forces that come into play, but rather that one can, in principle, master all things by calculation. This means that the world is disenchanted. One need no longer have recourse to magical means in order to master or implore the spirits, as did the savage, for whom such mysterious powers existed. Technical means and calculations perform the service. This above all is what intellectualism means. . . .
>
> Scientific pleading is meaningless in principle because the various value spheres of the world stand in irreconcilable conflict with each other. . . .
>
> The fate of our times is characterized by rationalization and intellectualism and, above all, by the "disenchantment of the world." (Weber, 1958:139, 148, 155)

Postindustrializing society created hordes of rationalized experts and intellectuals to fill functional slots. All were disappointed by the bureaucratic nonrecognition of substantive accomplishment. Unemployment, inflation, and lowered expectations taught many the message of the seventies, Max Weber's message, that impersonal processes increasingly determined life chances. People fought to preserve autonomy in systems labs and elsewhere, all the more as they saw their independence slipping away. Savvy was lost in the shuffle. The ability to develop critical self-knowledge, the only way integrity can survive, decreased in the face of irreversible social processes. Routinized, Trapped, and even Skeptic were replaced by Robot, entirely vulnerable to impersonal commands.

Disillusioned experts retained respect for data and intelligent systems planning. Salaried professionals sought signs of societal rationality amid evidence to the contrary. They saw, for instance, waste and inefficiency in the defense industries. Despite President Carter's 1976 campaign promises to cut military spending somewhat, the fiscal 1979 Defense budget was projected to increase 3.4 percent to $125.6 billion. Yet zero-based budgeting prevailed in research and development while scientists knew that fundametal research had to be the backbone of development needed to spur long-term economic growth. The politics of short-run expediency to influence public opinion polls prevailed over policy based on planning. Problems became more complex and solutions more elusive.

The failure of bureaucracy to adjust to people problems was evidenced by the crisis in higher education. University tuitions soared in the era of inflation. Middle- and working-class parents sacrificed much so children could go to college. They had to—since only credentials produce the *possibility* of upward mobility. But classes got larger and students learned less. Academic departments had no place for young professors with new ideas and disciplines stagnated. Good teaching was down on the list of university priorities: overhead producing grants, publications in a narrow area demonstrating fragmented expertise, and willing submission to administrative authority ranked higher. Boards of trustees and administrators gained power in the financial crunch as the trend toward rationality without substance accelerated. Economic problems of the seventies stifled what concern there once was about what really comes through in college classrooms.

Bureaucracy diffused social responsibility everywhere in postindustrializing society. Defense technologists gladly cited the separation of their work from its uses so they could dissipate what guilt they felt over war work. Missile makers had no monopoly over the social responsibility issue, which became decreasingly salient among social scientists. Policy oriented evaluation studies became the province of contract research houses, which paid good salaries to specialized teams for writing fund producing proposals. Research was often shoddy but preoccupied bureaucrats had neither the time nor the inclination to assess its worth. Social scientists, robbed of the opportunity to do quality research, abdicated responsibility for its policy implications. Rationalization increasingly removed most professionals from

> the people whose needs they supposedly serve. Thus, the professor, preoccupied with research and publications, becomes increasingly separated from the needs and interests of students. The practicing physician interested in advancements in medical research becomes increasingly removed from treating sick people. The artist aiming for technical proficiency becomes increasingly removed from the tastes and interests of his audience. (Leventman, 1976:83)

Professionals in varied contexts sacrificed the sense of occupational accomplishment that derives from knowing that work is useful to others and to society.

Bureaucracy eroded the creativity of professional roles. Trapped people craved autonomy. Technical professionals longed to escape the microdivision of labor and tight managerial control. Route 128 people dreamed of leaving systems labs (91 percent of the long-term unemployed, 78 percent of the reemployed, and 71 percent of the retained). They wanted to be doctors, lawyers, or academics—independent professionals who could express critical judgment. Few knew they had nowhere to go. Doctors wanted to work for institutions to be freed from patients' midnight calls. Ossified academics envied the action mode of policymakers. Government officials felt boxed in by ponderous regulations. Increasingly segmented, each from the other, professional groups tightly guarded the secret of their alienation. For the fortunate few who retained professional positions, to be superconformists betrayed the American dream.

Bibliography

Apter, David. 1967. *Ideology and Discontent*. New York: Free Press.

Association of Technical Professionals. 1973. *Newsletter* (April 1):4.

———. 1977. "The Coming of the Computer Age." *ATP Economic Resource* (April): 1–4.

Bain, Trevor. 1968. *Defense Manpower and Contract Termination*. Tucson: University of Arizona, College of Business and Public Administration, Division of Economic and Business Research.

Bakke, E. Wright. 1934. *The Unemployed Man*. New York: Dutton.

———. 1940a. *Citizens without Work*. New Haven: Yale University Press.

———. 1940b. *The Unemployed Worker: A Study of the Task of Making a Living without a Job*. New Haven: Yale University Press.

Bazelon, David T. 1966. "The New Class." *Commentary* 40 (August):48–53.

Becker, Howard S. 1970. *Sociological Work*. Chicago: Aldine.

Bednarzik, R. W., and S. M. St. Marie. 1977. "Employment and Unemployment in 1976." *Monthly Labor Review* 100 (February):3–13.

"Beginning of Wisdom about Black Unemployment." 1977. *Fortune* 96 (October): 175.

Bell, Daniel. 1973. *The Coming of Post-industrial Society*. New York: Basic Books.

Bensman, Joseph, and Arthur J. Vidich. 1971. *The New American Society: The Revolution of the Middle Class*. Chicago: Quadrangle.

Berg, Ivar. 1970. *Education and Jobs: The Great Training Robbery*. New York: Praeger.

———, Marcia Freedman, and Michael Freedman. 1978. *Managers and Work Reform: A Limited Engagement*. New York: Free Press.

"Biologists Need Work." 1973. *Science* (August 31):831.

Blake, Andrew. 1975. "Route 128 'Golden Tiara' Tranished, But Still There." *Boston Globe* (October 13).

Bluestone, Paul. 1976. "Unemployment amidst Prosperity: Why?" *Forbes* 118 (October 1):30–34.

BOTWRIGHT, KEN O. 1970. "150,000 Bay State Jobless Face Cheerless Yule." *Boston Globe* (December 1).

BRAGINSKY, D. D., AND B. M. BRAGINSKY. 1975. "Surplus People: Their Loss of Faith in Self and System." *Psychology Today* (August):68–72.

BRAVERMAN, HARRY. 1974. *Labor and Monopoly Capitalism: The Degradation of Work in the Twentieth Century.* New York: Monthly Review Press.

BRENNER, M. HARVEY. 1973. *Mental Illness and the Economy.* Cambridge:Harvard University Press.

"Bright Side of Bay State Business." 1974. *Bay State Business World* (December 3):4.

BROMERY, KEITH. 1971. "184 Aerospace Experts ADAPT Themselves to MIT Course to Work on Urban Needs." *Boston Sunday Globe* (August 23).

BRONOWSKI, J. 1965. *Science and Human Values.* New York: Harper.

BROWN, MARTIN (editor). 1971. *The Social Responsibility of the Scientist.* New York: Free Press.

BROWN, TERRY B. 1972. "Ired by Unemployment the Nation's Engineers Move toward Unionization." *Wall Street Journal* (February 22).

CAPLOVITZ, DAVID. 1978. "Making Ends Meet: How Families Cope with Inflation and Recession." *Public Opinion* (May/June):52–54.

CAPLOW, THEODORE, AND REECE J. McGEE. 1958. *The Academic Marketplace.* New York: Basic Books.

CARTER, ALLAN M. 1971. "Scientific Manpower for 1970–1985." *Science* (April 9): 132–140).

Center for International Studies, Cornell University. 1972. *The Air War in Indochina.* Washington, D.C.: Indochina Resource Center.

CHAMBERLAIN, BETTY. 1976. "Artist Unemployment Statistics." *American Artist* 40 (December):14.

CHAMBERLAIN, TONY. 1978. "Public Employees or Public Victims?" *Boston Globe* (December 20).

CHAMOT, DENNIS. 1974. "Scientists and Unions: The New Reality." *AFL-CIO American Federationist* (September).

CLARKSON, KENNETH, W., AND ROGER E. MEINERS. 1977. "Inflated Unemployment Statistics." *Intellect* 106(November):183–184.

CLINK, RALPH. 1973. "The Relationship between Grief and Change: A Comparison of the Experiences of a Select Group of Bereaved, Unemployed, and Employed in a New Position." *Dissertation Abstracts International* 34 6-B, (December): 2923.

COHEN, MURIEL, 1978. "Job Future Clouded for Teachers." *Boston Globe* (July 9).

COLLINS, LAWRENCE. 1972. "Job Center Great—When There Are Jobs." *Boston Sunday Globe* (April 2).

"Company Contracts." *Bay State Business World.* 1975. (March 11, March 19, May 7, July 9, September 17, November 5, December 31). 1976. (January 7, January 14, January 28). 1977. October 19, October 28, December 28). 1978. (March 24, September 27).

COTTLE, THOMAS J. 1978. "Fires of Eddie Harrington." *New Leader* 61 (January 16): 12–15.

COWAN, EDWARD. 1976a. "Jobless Rate Unchanged Despite Employment Rise." *New York Times* (May 8).

———. 1976b. "Jobless Rate up to 7.5% for June from May's 7.3%." *New York Times* (July 3).

———. 1976c. "Rate of Jobless up to 7.9% in October after a Slight Drop." *New York Times* (November 6).

CRITTENDEN, ANN. 1978. "Guns over Butter Equals Inflation." *New York Times* (November 19).

DALE, EDWIN L., JR. 1975a. "Jobless Rate up to 8.7% in March, Highest since '41." *New York Times* (April 5).

———. 1975b. "Recovery except for the Jobless." *New York Times* (October 26).

———. 1975c. "U.S. Jobless Rate up to 9.2% in May, Highest since '41." *New York Times* (June 7).

———. 1976. "Unemployment: The Legacy of the Recession." *New York Times* (April 11).

DALTON, GENE W., AND PAUL H. THOMPSON. 1971. "Accelerating Obsolescence of Older Engineers." *Harvard Business Review* (September/October):57–67.

"Demise of Lincoln Job Opportunities Group." 1973. *Association of Technical Professionals Newsletter* (April 1):4.

DENITCH, BOGDAN. 1970. "Is There a New Working Class?" *Dissent* 17(July/August):351–355.

DUBOS, RENE. 1970. *Reason Awake: Science for Man.* New York: Columbia University Press.

DURKHEIM, EMILE. 1958. *Professional Ethics and Civic Morals.* New York: Free Press.

———. 1973. *Moral Education.* New York: Free Press.

DUTTON, FREDERICK C. 1971. *Changing Sources of Power: American Politics in the 1970s.* New York: McGraw-Hill.

EDWARDS, HARRY T. 1976. "Black and White Unemployment." *Intellect* 104(May): 555.

ELDER, GLEN H., JR. 1974. *Children of the Great Depression.* Chicago: University of Chicago Press.

"Employment Office Fails to Find People Work." 1974. *Boston Globe* (September 29).

ERIKSON, ERIK H. 1950. *Childhood and Society.* New York: Norton.

ESTES, RICHARD J. 1974. "The Unemployed Professional: The Social, Psychological, and Political Consequences of Job Displacement among Educated Workers." *Dissertation Abstracts International* 34 A (January):4403–4404.

ETZIONI, AMITAI. 1978. "Why We Chose to Have Stagflation." *Business Week* (February 27):18.

———, AND CLYDE NUNN. 1974. "The Public Appreciation of Science in Contemporary America." *Daedalus* (Summer): 191–205.

FARNSWORTH, CLYDE H. 1978a. "Private Economists Expect '79 Recession." *New York Times* (November 8).

———. 1978b. "Rate of Inflation Increases to 10%." *New York Times* (November 29).

FAUNCE, WILLIAM A., AND DONALD A. CLELLAND. 1967. "Professionalization and Stratification Patterns in an Industrial Community." *American Journal of Sociology* 70 (January):341–350.

FERMAN, LOUIS A. 1964. "Sociological Perspectives in Unemployment Research." In *Blue-collar Worlds,* edited by Arthur B. Shostak and William Gomberg. Englewood Cliffs: Prentice-Hall.

"Fired at 46: A Diary of Despair." 1977. *Boston Globe* (June 9).

FLAIM, PAUL O. 1974. "Employment and Unemployment during the First Half of 1974." *Monthly Labor Review* 97 (August):3–7.

FLINT, JERRY. 1978. "Oversupply of Young Workers Expected to Tighten Jobs Race." *New York Times* (June 25).

FOREMAN, JUDY. 1978. "Despite the Pay, They Pick Boston." *Boston Globe* (July 6).

FURSTENBERG, FRANK F., JR., AND CHARLES A. THRALL. 1975. "Counting the Jobless: The Impact of Job Rationing on the Measurement of Unemployment." *Annals of the American Academy of Political and Social Science* 418 (March):45–59.

GALBRAITH, JOHN KENNETH. 1967. *The New Industrial State.* Boston: Houghton Mifflin.

GARFINKLE, STUART H. 1977. "Outcome of a Spell of Unemployment." *Monthly Labor Review* 100(January):54–57.

GARSON, BARBARA. 1977. *All the Livelong Day: The Meaning and Demeaning of Routine Work.* Baltimore: Penguin.

GESCHWENDER, JAMES A. 1977. *Class, Race and Worker Insurgency.* New York: Cambridge University Press.

GILLETTE, ROBERT. 1972. "The American Chemical Society: Pepping Up Its Rescue Efforts." *Science* (April 21):260–263.

———. 1973. "Another Populist President Elect for ACS." *Science* (Januar 19):260.

GILROY, CURTIS L. 1974. "Black and White Unemployment: The Dynamics of the Difference." *Monthly Labor Review* 97(February):38–47.

———, AND THOMAS F. BRADSHAW. 1974. "Employment and Unemployment: A Report on 1973." *Monthly Labor Review* 97(February):3–14.

GINSBURG, HELEN. 1975. "Deliberate Unemployment: The Strategy of Misery." *Nation* 220(February):114–117.

———. 1976. "There's No Such Thing as Tolerable Unemployment." *America* 134 (February 7):91–93.

———. 1977. "Jobs for All: Congressional Will-o-the Wisp." *Nation* 224(February):138–143.

GLASER, BARNEY G. 1964. *Organizational Scientists: Their Professional Careers.* Indianapolis: Bobbs-Merrill.

——— (EDITOR). 1968. *Organizational Careers: A Sourcebook for Theory.* Chicago: Aldine.

GOLDFINGER, NATHANIEL. 1975. "About Unemployment." *Forbes* 116(October): 22–23.

GOODMAN, ELLEN. 1971. "What about the Jobless Man's Wife?" *Boston Sunday Globe* (August 8).

GOLDNER, FRED H., AND R. R. RITTI. 1967. "Professionalization as Career Immobility." *American Journal of Sociology* 72(March):489–502.

GORE, SUSAN. 1974. "The Influences of Social Support and Related Variables in Ameliorating the Consequences of Job Loss." *Dissertation Abstracts International* 34 8–A, PT2(February):5330–5331.

———. 1978. "The Adequacy of Research on the Impact of Work and Unemployment: Methodological Considerations." Paper presented at the annual meeting of the American Sociological Association, San Francisco, September 4.

GRANNOVETTER, MARK S. 1974. *Getting a Job: A Study of Contacts and Careers.* Cambridge: Harvard University Press.

GREENBERG, DANIEL S. 1973. "Science and Richard Nixon." *New York Times Magazine* (June 17).

"Growing Specter of Unemployment." 1975. *Time* 105(February 7):9–10.

HABERER, JOSEPH. 1969. *Politics and the Community of Science.* Princeton: Van Nostrand.

———. 1972. "Politicalization in Science." *Science* (November 17):713–723.

HADLEY, ARTHUR T. 1977. "A Revolutionary Change in Man's Ability to Kill." *Boston Globe* (April 3).

HALSTRON, WILLIAM. 1972. "Getting Jobless EEs Back to Work." *Electronics* (May): 107–109.

HASELTINE, WILLIAM. 1971. "The Automated Air War." *New Republic* (October 16):15–17.

HELMER, JOHN, AND THOMAS VIETORISZ. 1974. *Drug Use, the Labor Market, and Class Conflict.* Washington, D.C.: Drug Abuse Council.

HERSHEY, ROBERT D., JR. 1976. "Jobless Rate up to 7.8% in August, 3d Monthly Rise." *New York Times* (September 4).

HICKS, NANCY. 1976. "U.S. Study Links Rise in Jobless to Deaths, Murders, and Suicides." *New York Times* (October 31).

HUGHES, EVERETT C. 1958. *Men and Their Work.* New York: Free Press.

———. 1963. "Professions." *Daedalus* (Fall):655–668.

———. 1971a. "Of Sociology and the Interview." In *The Sociological Eye: Selected Papers,* by Everett C. Hughes. Chicago: Aldine-Atherton.

———. 1971b. "The Relation of Industrial to General Sociology." In *The Sociological Eye: Selected Papers,* by Everett C. Hughes. Chicago: Aldine-Atherton.

HUMPHREY, HUBERT H. 1976. "An American Paradox." *Saturday Review* 3(August): 6–7.

"Hundreds Vie for Chance at 550 Apprenticeships." 1978. *New York Times* (June 25).

HYMAN, MERTON M., ALICE R. HERLICE, AND GWEN BESSON. 1972. "Ascertaining

Police Bias in Arrests for Drunken Driving." *Quarterly Journal of Studies on Alcohol* 33(March):148–159.

"Is Unemployment on the Way Out?" 1978. *Forbes* 121(January 9): 221

JAHODA, MARIE, PAUL F. LAZARSFELD, AND HANS ZEISEL. 1971. *Marienthal: The Sociography of an Unemployed Community.* Chicago: Aldine-Atherton. First published in 1933 as *Die Arbeitslosen von Marienthal.*

"Jobless over 8% and Prices Are Going up Again." 1976. *New York Times* (December 5).

"Jobs: The Story That Figures Don't Tell." 1976. *U.S. News and World Report* 81(November 1):83–84.

JONES, ALFRED WINSLOW. 1964. *Life, Liberty, and Property.* New York: Octagon.

JUNG, C. G. 1939. *Modern Man in Search of a Soul.* New York: Harcourt Brace.

KAPLAN, ROY, AND CURT TAUSKY. 1972. "Working and the Welfare Cadillac: The Functions of and Commitment to Work among the Hard-core Unemployed." *Social Problems* 19(Spring):469–483.

KEENE, EVELYN. 1970. "From Pulpit, Jobless Engineer Tells What It's Like." *Boston Globe* (December 28).

———. 1971a. "Groups Spring Up to Console Jobless." *Boston Sunday Globe* (January 17).

———. 1971b. "The Recession along Rte. 128." *Boston Sunday Globe* (December 19).

KENNY, MICHAEL. 1978. "60's Poor People's Campaign Revived for Jobs Push in Boston." *Boston Globe* (July 21).

KILBORN, PETER T. 1975. "White-collar Unemployment: No Drop in Sight." *New York Times* (February 23).

KLAW, SPENCER. 1971. "The Faustian Bargain." In *The Social Responsibility of the Scientist,* edited by Martin Brown. New York: Free Press.

KLEIN, DEBORAH P. 1976. "Employment and Unemployment in the Frist Half of 1976." *Monthly Labor Review* 99(August):9–12.

KNAPP, R. H., AND H. B. GOODRICH. 1952. *Origins of American Scientists.* Chicago: University of Chicago Press.

KOLATA, GINA BARI. 1976. "Projecting the Ph.D. Labor Market: NSF and BLS Disagree." *Science* (January 30):363–365.

KOLKO, GABRIEL. 1962. *Wealth and Power in America.* New York: Praeger.

KOMAROVSKY, MIRA. 1940. *The Unemployed Man and His Family.* New York: Dryden.

KORNHAUSER, WILLIAM, AND WARREN O. HAGSTROM. 1962. *Scientists in Industry.* Berkeley and Los Angeles: University of California Press.

KRAMER, STEPHEN PHILIP, AND LEO FRIEDMANN. 1975. "Permanent Unemployment?" *Commonweal* 102(August 29):260–263.

LADD, EVERETT C. 1978. "The Nation's 'Most Important Problem.' " *Public Opinion* (May/June):30–32.

———, AND SEYMOUR MARTIN LIPSET. 1972. "The Politics of Academic Natural Scientists and Engineers." *Science* (June 9):1091–1100.

LAPP, MARC. 1971. "Biological Warfare." In *The Social Responsibility of the Scientist*, edited by Martin Brown. New York: Free Press.

LAUENSTEIN, MILTON. 1978. "Pitfalls along Route 128." *Bay State Business World* (March 22):1.

LAYTON, EDWIN. 1971. *The Revolt of the Engineers: Social Responsibility and the American Engineering Profession*. Cleveland Press of Case Western Reserve University.

LEGGETT, JOHN C., AND JERRY GIOGLIO. 1977. *Break Out the Double Digit: Mass Unemployment in the City of New Brunswick, New Jersey*. New Brunswick: John C. Leggett and Jerry Gioglio.

LEKACHMAN, ROBERT. 1975. "Managing Inflation in a Full Employment Society." *Annals of the American Academy of Political and Social Science* 418(March):85–93.

LENZNER, ROBERT. 1978. "Has Rte. 128 Met Its Match?" *Boston Globe* (February 19).

LEVENTMAN, PAULA GOLDMAN. 1971. Fieldnotes taken at meetings of the Lincoln Job Opportunities Group, the Economic Action Group, and the Association of Technical Professionals.

———. 1976. "Nonrational Foundations of Professional Rationality: Employment Instability among Scientists and Technologists." *Sociological Symposium* (Summer):83–112.

LEVINSON, DANIEL J. 1978. *The Seasons of A Man's Life*. New York: Knopf.

LEVISON, ANDREW. 1976. *Unemployment: The Problem We Can Solve*. New York: Public Affairs Pamphlets No. 534.

LINDSEY, ROBERT. 1975a. "Economy Mars Belief in the American Dream." *New York Times* (September 26).

———. 1975b. "Many Discouraged Job-Hunters Giving Up the Search." *New York Times* (May 3).

LIPSET, SEYMOUR MARTIN. 1960. *Political Man*. New York: Doubleday.

———. 1967. *The First New Nation*. New York: Doubleday.

———, AND MILDRED A. SCHWARTZ. 1966. "The Politics of Professionals." In *Professionalization*, edited by Howard M. Volmer and Donald Mills. Englewood Cliffs. Prentice-Hall.

LITTLE, CRAIG E. 1973. "Stress Responses among Unemployed Technical Professionals." *Dissertation Abstracts International* 34 1–A(July):429.

"The Lockheed Engineer Syndrome." 1972. *Human Behavior* 1(January/February):38.

LONGCOPE, KAY. 1976. "Clergy Find Jobs Scarce in Churches." *Boston Globe* (March 14).

LOOMBA, R. P. 1967. *A Study of the Reemployment Experiences of Scientists and Engineers Laid Off from 62 Aerospace and Electronics Firms in the San Francisco Bay Area during 1963–65*. San Jose: San Jose State College, Center for Interdisciplinary Studies, Manpower Research Group.

LOPREATO, JOSEPH, AND JANET SALTZMAN CHAFETZ. 1970. "The Political Orientation of Skidders: A Middle Range Theory." *American Sociological Review* 35(June):440–451.

"Louis Harris Finds Rising Alienation." 1978. *Public Opinion* (May/June):23.

Mannheim, Karl. 1940. *Man and Society in an Age of Reconstruction.* London: Routledge & Kegan Paul.

McCain, Nina. 1975. "Job Crunch in Academia: It's No Time for Tenure." *Boston Globe* (October 12).

McElheny, Victor K. 1976. "Forecast in Electronics Industry: Boston Area Cloudy, California Sunny." *New York Times* (November 12).

McGovern, George. 1972. "McGovern Sets New Science Policy." Address presented to the Association of Technical Professionals, Bentley College, April 17.

McLean, Deckle. 1972. "When Professionals Lose Their Jobs." *Boston Globe* (April 16).

Melman, Seymour. 1970. *Pentagon Capitalism: The Political Economy of War.* New York: McGraw-Hill.

———. 1974. *The Permanent War Economy.* New York: Simon and Schuster.

Merton, Robert K. 1957. "Science and the Social Order." In *Social Theory and Social Structure,* by Robert K. Merton. New York: Free Press.

———, and Patricia L. Kendall. 1957. "The Focused Interview." In *The Language of Social Research,* edited by Paul F. Lazarsfeld and Morris Rosenberg. New York: Free Press.

Miller, Herman P. 1963. *Trends in the Income of Families and Persons in the United States, 1947–1960.* Washington, D.C.: U.S. Government Printing Office.

Miller, S. M. 1975. "A WPA for Professionals?" *Social Policy* (September/October):3–4.

Millman, Joan. 1971. "Self-help for the Jobless." *Boston Herald Traveler Magazine* (September 5).

Mills, C. Wright, 1957. *The Power Elite.* New York: Oxford University Press.

———. 1958. *The Causes of World War Three.* New York: Simon & Schuster.

"Mondale Assesses Economy." 1978. *New York Times* (May 18).

Mooney, Joseph D. 1966. "An Analysis of Unemployment among Professional Engineers and Scientists" *Industrial and Labor Relations Review* 19 (July): 508–516.

———, Robert Brandwein, Walter E. Langway, and Leslie Fishman. 1966. *Stabilization of Engineering and Scientific Employment in Industry.* San Jose: State College, Center for Interdisciplinary Studies.

Muttur, Ellis R. 1971. *Conversion of Scientific and Technical Resources: Economic Challenge—Social Responsibility.* Washington, D.C.: George Washington University, Program of Policy Studies in Science and Technology.

"A New Layer of Structural Unemployment." 1977. *Business Week* (November 14):142–152.

Newman, Morton B., and Mary San Martino. 1972. "The Effects of Unemployment on the Middle-class Family." Paper presented at the annual meeting of the American Psychiatric Association, Atlantic city (May).

Nie, Norman, Dale H. Bent, and C. Hadlai Hull. 1970. *SPSS: Statistical Package for the Social Sciences.* New York: McGraw-Hill.

NISBET, ROBERT A. 1959. "The Decline and Fall of Social Classes." *Pacific Sociological Review* 2(Spring):11–17.

NOKES, GREGORY. 1978. "Prices Spiral Another 0.8%." *Boston Globe* (October 28).

O'BRIEN, DARCY. 1979. "A Generation of 'Lost' Scholars." *New York Times Magazine* (March 18).

"On Employment and Unemployment Compensation." 1974. *Society* 11 (January/February):11–12.

O'KELLEY, HAROLD E. 1978. "How to Motivate and Manage Engineers." *New York Times* (November 26).

" 'Okies' of the 70s: Mass Migration in Search of Jobs." 1975. *U.S. News and World Report* 78 (March 24):16–20.

OPPENHEIMER, MARTIN. 1970. "White Collar Revisited: The Making of a New Working Class." *Social Policy* (July/August):27–32.

O'TOOLE, JAMES. 1975. "The Reserve Army of the Underemployed." *Change* (May): 26–63.

———. 1977. *Work, Learning, and the American Future.* San Francisco: Jossey-Bass.

PATTERSON, RACHELLE. 1971. "Route 128 Employment Center Finds There Aren't Many Jobs Around." *Boston Sunday Globe* (May 16).

———. 1972. "D.E.S. Rated Poor in Industry Survey." *Boston Globe* (December 18).

PERRUCCI, CAROLYN CUMMINGS. 1969. "Engineering and the Class Structure." In *The Engineers and the Social System,* edited by Robert Perrucci and Joel E. Gerstl. New York: Wiley.

PERRUCCI, ROBERT, AND JOEL E. GERSTL. 1969a. *The Engineers and the Social System.* New York: Wiley.

———. 1969b. *Profession without Community: Engineers in American Society.* New York: Random House.

PERRUCCI, ROBERT, AND ROBERT A. ROTHMAN. 1969. "Obsolescense of Knowledge and the Professional Career." In *The Engineers and the Social System,* edited by Robert Perrucci and Joel E. Gerstl. New York: Wiley.

"Planned Unemployment." 1976. *National Review* 28(March 19):255–256.

POWELL, DOUGLASS H. 1973. "The Effects of Job Strategy Seminars upon Unemployed Engineers and Scientists." *Journal of Social Psychology* 91 (October):165–166.

———, AND PAUL F. DRISCOLL. 1973. "Middle-class Professionals Face Unemployment." *Society* 10(January/Februacy):18–26.

RAND, CHRISTOPHER. 1964. *Cambridge U.S.A.: Hub of a New World.* New York: Oxford University Press.

RASKIN, A. H. 1976a. "Long-term Jobless Are Hidden Suffering." *New York Times* (October 10).

———. 1976b. " 'The System' Keeps the Young Waiting." *New York Times* (December 5).

———. 1977. "A Tougher Approach to Jobs." *New York Times* (November 20).

"Recession: 55% Change by End of '78 or in '79." 1978. *Boston Globe* (June 30).

"Record Sales by Big Employers." 1972. *Bay State Business World* (January 26).

RICE, BERKELEY. 1970. "Down and Out along Route 128." *New York Times Magazine* (November 1).

RITTI, RICHARD R. 1971. *The Engineer in the Industrial Corporation.* New York: Columbia University Press.

ROBERTS, STEVEN V. 1978. "Social Mobility Found Key to U.S. Views on Class." *New York Times* (April 24).

RODGERS, WILFRID C. 1975. "Unemployment a U.S. Tradition." *Boston Globe* (July 3).

———. 1976. "Multinationals: Job Exporters?" *Boston Globe* (January 17).

ROSENBAUM, DAVID E. 1976. "The Job Bills Will Be Issues, Not Programs." *New York Times* (May 9).

ROSENBLUM, MARC. 1974. "Discouraged Workers and Unemployment." *Monthly Labor Review* 97 (September):28–30.

ROSS, ARTHUR M., AND JANE N. ROSS. 1968. "Employment Problems of Older Workers." In *Studies in Unemployment*, U.S. Senate, Special Committee on Unemployment Problems, 86th Cong. 2d Sess. Westport: Greenwood.

ROTHSCHILD, EMMA. 1975. "There's a Real Fear in Detroit That the Slump Is Permanent." *New York Times* (July 27).

"Rte. 128 Center to Get U.S. Aid." 1971. *Boston Sunday Globe* (May 12).

RUDOFF, ALVIN, AND DOROTHY LUCKEN. 1971. "The Engineer and His Work: A Sociological Perspective." *Science* (June 11):1103–1108.

SCHLESINGER, ARTHUR M., JR. 1959. *The Coming of the New Deal.* Boston: Houghton Mifflin.

"The Scientists." 1948. *Fortune* 38(October):106–176.

SELTIZ, CLAIRE, MARIE JAHODA, MORTON DEUTSCH, AND STUART W. COOK. 1959. *Research Methods in Social Relations.* New York: Holt.

SHABECOFF, PHILIP. 1978a. "Unemployment off to 5.7% for June." *New York Times* (July 8).

———. 1978b. "Unemployment: The Structural Variety Is the Toughest." *New York Times* (June 16).

SHAFFER, RICHARD A. 1976. "Down the Ladder." *Wall Street Journal* (January 16).

SHANAHAN, EILEEN. 1975. "The Mystery of the Great Calm of The Unemployed." *New York Times* (August 3).

———. 1976a. "Joblessness Cut to 17-Month Low: Record Employed." *New York Times* (June 5).

———. 1976b. "Jobs Bill Offered by Liberal Bloc." *New York Times* (March 14).

SHAPLEY, DEBORAH. 1971. "Defense Research: The Names Changed to Protect the Innocent." *Science* (February 26):866–868.

———. 1972a. "Professional Societies: Identity Crisis Threatens on Bread and Butter Issues." *Science* (May 19):777–779.

———. 1972b. "Unionization: Scientists, Engineers Mull Over One Alternative." *Science* (May 12):618–621.

SHAW, DAVID. 1976. "Unemployment Hurts More Than Just the Pocketbook." *Today's Health* 54(March):23–26.

SHEVITZ, JEFFREY M. 1971a. "Manipulation of Men for a War Economy." *Science for the People* (July):6–8.

——. 1971b. Review of *Profession without a Community: Engineers in American Society* and *The Engineers and the Social System* by Robert Perrucci and Joel E. Gerstl. *American Journal of Sociology* 76(January):774–776.

SHILLER, RAYMOND. "Too Trained to Be Hired." *New York Times* (June 27).

SHISKIN, J., AND R. L. STEIN. 1975. "Problems in Measuring Unemployment." *Monthly Labor Review* 98(August):3–10.

SLATER, PHILIP. 1970. *The Pursuit of Loneliness.* Boston: Beacon.

SILK, LEONARD. 1978. "Appraising Recession Risks." *New York Times* (November 12).

SLOANE, LEONARD. 1976. "Behind Every Jobless Figure, There's a Person." *New York Times* (January 4).

SLOTE, ALFRED. 1969. *Termination: The Closing at Baker Plant.* Indianapolis: Bobbs-Merrill.

SMITH, ANSON. 1978. "The GE Touch." *Boston Globe* (December 10).

SMITH, LUCINDA. 1971. "Group Helps Jobless Help Themselves." *Boston Sunday Globe* (June 13).

SOFER, CYRIL. 1970. *Men in Mid-career.* New York: Cambridge University Press.

SPEKKE, ANDREW A. 1976. "Work and America's Third Century." *Intellect* 105 (September):117.

SPIEGELMAN, ARTHUR. 1973. "How to Fire People and Win Friends." *Boston Globe* (February 28).

SPRING, WILLIAM J. 1972. "Underemployment: The Measure We Refuse to Take." In *The Political Economy of Public Service Employment*, edited by Harold L. Sheppard, Bennett Harison, and William J. Spring. Lexington: Lexington Books.

STANFORD, PHIL. 1975. "The Automated Battlefield." *New York Times Magazine* (February 23).

ST. MARIE, STEPHEN M. 1977. "Employment and Unemployment during the First Half of 1977." *Monthly Labor Review* 100(August):3–6.

——, and R. W. Bednarzik. 1976. "Employment and Unemployment during 1975." *Monthly Labor Review* 99(Febraury):11–20.

STEVENS, WILLIAM K. 1975. "The White-collar Worker Confronts Unemployment." *New York Times* (January 4).

STEWART, RICHARD H. 1975. "Job Placement Problem for N.E." *Boston Globe* (November 16).

STRAUSS, ANSELM L., AND LEE RAINWATER. 1962. *The Professional Scientist: A Study of American Chemists.* Chicago: Aldine.

"Technological Unemployment Again." 1975. *Bay State Business World* (January 22):1–2.

THOMAS, JOHN C. 1971. "Unemployed Scientists Plead for Help." *Boston Globe* (June 24).

THOMPSON, PAUL H. 1972. *"The Effects of Unemployment on Engineering Careers."* Draft report to the United States Department of Labor.

TIFFANY, DONALD W., JAMES R. COWAN, AND PHYLLIS M. TIFFANY. 1970. *The Unemployed: A Social-Psychological Portrait.* Englewood Cliffs: Prentice-Hall.

TINSLEY, ROYAL L., JR. 1973. "Too Many Translators." *A.T.A. Chronicle* 2(May/June):3–4.

TRIANDIS, HARRY C., JACK M. FELDMAN, DAVID E. WELDON, AND WILLIAM M. HARVEY. 1975. "Ecosystem Distrust and the Hard-to-Employ." *Journal of Applied Psychology* 60(February):44–56.

"Truth about Unemployment." 1977. *Forbes* 119(February 15):97.

"Unemployment Spreads and Worst Is Yet to Come." 1974. *U.S. News and World Report* 77(December 2):47–48.

Union of Concerned Scientists. 1975. "Scientists' Declaration on Nuclear Power." presented to the Congress and the President of the United States on the 30th anniversary of the atomic bombing of Hiroshima.

United States Arms Control and Disarmament Agency. 1966a. *Defense Industry Diversification.* Washington, D.C.: U.S. Government Printing Office.

———. 1966b. *The Post Layoff Experiences of the Former Republic Aviation Corporation Workers.* Washington, D.C.: U.S. Government Printing Office.

———. 1966c. *Reemployment Experiences of Martin Company Workers Released at Denver, Colo., 1963–65.* Washington, D.C.: U.S. Government Printing Office.

———. 1967. *The Transferability and Retraining of Defense Engineers,* by Carl H. Rittenhouse. Washington, D.C.: U.S. Government Printing Office.

———. 1968. *Reemployment Experiences of Defense Workers: A Statistical Analysis of the Boeing, Martin, and Republic Layoffs,* by Leslie·Fishman, Jay Allen, Byron Bunger, and Carl Eaton. Washington, D.C.: U.S. Government Printing Office.

———. 1969. *Pensions and Severance Pay for Displaced Defense Workers,* by Hugh Folk and Paul Hartman. Washington, D.C.: U.S. Government Printing Office.

United States Commission on Human Resources. 1973. *Doctoral Scientists and Engineers in the United States: 1973 Profile.* Washington, D.C.: National Academy of Sciences.

United States Congress, House of Representatives, Committee on Science and Astronautics. 1971. *The Conversion Research and Education Act of 1971: Hearings before the Subcommittee on Science, Research, and Development on H. R. 34.* 92d Cong., 1st sess.

———. 1977. H. R. 833: *Reemployment Services Act of 1977.* 95th Cong., 1st sess., January 4.

———. 1978a. H. R. 11086: *Comprehensive Employment and Training Act Reauthorization.* 95th Cong., 2d sess., February 22.

———. 1978b. H. R. 50: *Full Employment and Balanced Growth Act of 1978.* 95th Cong., 2d sess., February 6.

———. 1979. H. R. 270: *Employment Services Revitalization and Reform Act of 1979.* 96th Cong., 1st sess., January 15.

United States Department of Commerce. 1977. *Economic Report of the President.*

United States Department of Commerce, Bureau of the Census. 1976. *Current Population Reports, Consumer Income.*

United States Department of Commerce, National Technical Information Service. 1971. *A Survey of Aerospace Employees Affected by Reduction in NASA Contracts.* Columbus: Battelle Columbus Laboratories.

United States Department of Labor. 1972. *Manpower Report of the President.*

United States Department of Labor, Bureau of Labor Statistics. 1968. *Scientific and Technical Personnel in Industry, 1961–66.* Bulletin 1609.

———. 1970. *Scientific and Technical Personnel in Industry, 1967.* Bulletin 1674.

———. 1972. *National Survey of Professional, Administrative, Technical, and Clerical Pay, June 1971.* Bulletin 1742.

———. 1975. *Major Programs.* Report 441.

———. 1976a. *Handbook of Labor Statistics, 1975.* Bulletin 1865. Washington, D.C.: U.S. Government Printing Office.

———. 1976b. *News.* "The Employment Situation: May 1976." USLD 76-892.

———. 1977a. *Employment and Unemployment in 1976.* Special Labor Force Report 199.

———. 1977b. *News.* "Labor Force Developments: Second Quarter 1977." USLD 77-628.

———. 1978a. *Handbook of Labor Statistics, 1977.* Bulletin 1966. Washington, D.C.: U.S. Government Printing Office.

———. 1978b. *News.* "Labor Force Developments: First Quarter 1978." USLD 78-357.

———. 1978c. *News.* "Labor Force Developments: Third Quarter 1978." USLD 78-849.

———. 1978d. *News.* "Labor Force Developments: Fourth Quarter 1978." USLD 79-42.

———. 1978e. *News.* "State and Metropolitan Area Unemployment: August 1978." USLD 78-850.

———. 1978f. *News.* "The Employment Situation: August 1978." USLD 78-753.

United States National Research Council, Commission on Human Resources. 1978. *Science, Engineering, and Humanities Doctorates in the United States: 1977 Profile.* Washington, D.C.: National Academy of Science.

United States National Science Foundation. 1968. *Employment of Scientists and Engineers in the United States, 1950–1966.* NSF 68-30.

———. 1969. *American Science Manpower, 1968.* NSF 69-38.

———. 1971a. *American Science Manpower, 1970.* NFS 71-45.

———. 1971b. *Unemployment Rates for Engineers, June–July 1971.* NSF 71-33.

———. 1971c. *Unemployment Rates for Scientists, Spring 1971.* NSF 71-26.

———. 1975. *Characteristics of the National Sample of Scientists and Engineers, 1974: Part 1, Demographic and Education.* NSF 75-333.

———. 1976a. *Characteristics of the National Sample of Scientists and Engineers, 1974: Part 2, Employment* NSF 76-323.

————. 1976b. *Characteristics of the National Sample of Scientists and Engineers, 1974: Part 3, Geographic.* NSF 76–330

VEBLEN, THORSTEIN. 1933. *The Engineers and the Price System.* New York: Viking.

————. 1934. "The Intellectual Pre-eminence of Jews in Modern Europe." In *Essays in Our Changing Order,* by Thorstein Veblen. New York: Viking.

"Waltham Session to Aid Jobless Space Engineers." 1971. *Boston Globe* (December 17).

"Wanted: Electronics Engineers." 1966. *Electronics* (March): 165–166.

WEBER, MAX. 1958. "Science as a Vocation." In *Essays from Max Weber,* edited by Hans Gerth and C. Wright Mills. New York: Oxford University Press.

————. 1968. *Economy and Society* (3 volumes), edited by Guenther Roth and Claus Wittich. New York: Bedminster.

WEINBERG, ALVIN M. 1967. *Reflections on Big Science.* Cambridge: MIT Press.

"What It Takes to Create Jobs." 1977. *Fortune* 95(March):133.

"What the Unemployment Figures Really Mean." 1974. *Changing Times* 28(July): 13–15.

WHITE, DONALD. 1971. "128's Realistic View Gloomy." *Boston Globe* (January 3).

"Who Is Suffering Most from Unemployment." 1974. *U.S. News and World Report* 77(December 23):55–57.

"Why Unemployment Hangs So High." 1976. *Fortune* 94(November):24.

WICKER, TOM. 1975a. "Another Such Victory." *New York Times* (June 6).

————. 1975b. "How Jobs Could Fight Inflation." *New York Times* (November 16).

WILDSTROM, STEPHEN. 1977. "More Jobs Don't Mean Less Unemployment." *Business Week* (June 20):29

WILENSKY, HAROLD L. 1964. "The Professionalization of Everyone." *American Journal of Sociology* 70(September):137–158.

————, AND HUGH EDWARDS. 1959. "The Skidder," *American Sociological Review* 24(April):215–231.

WILHELM, SIDNEY M. 1971. *Who Needs the Negro?* Cambridge: Schenkman.

WRONG, DENNIS H. 1972. "Social Inequality without Social Stratification." In *Status Communities in Modern Society,* edited by Holger R. Stub. Hinsdale: Dryden.

"Young People without Jobs: How Real a Problem?" 1977. *U.S. News and World Report* 82(May 9):94–96.

ZAWADSKI, BOHAN, AND PAUL F. LAZARSFELD. 1935. "The Psychological Consequences of Unemployment." *Journal of Social Psychology* 6:224–251.

Index